"Honey, I've Shrunk the Bills!"

© Copyright 2000 by Jack Weber

Published by
Capital Books Inc.
22883 Quicksilver Drive
Sterling, Virginia 20166

Library of Congress Cataloging-in-Publication Data

Weber, Jack, 1957-
    "Honey I've shrunk the bills!" : how to save big money on
everything you buy / by Jack Weber.
        p.   cm.
    Includes bibliographical references and index.
    ISBN 1-892123-11-8 (alk. Paper)
    1. Consumer education.   I. Title.
TX336.W43   2000   99-32846
640'.73—dc21   CIP

NOTICE

This publication is designed to provide accurate and authoritative information in regard to
the subject matter covered. It is provided with the understanding that the author or pub-
lisher is not engaged in rendering legal, accounting or other professional
service. If legal advice or other expert assistance is required, the services
of a competent professional should be sought.

From a Declaration of Principles jointly adopted by a
Committee of the American Bar Association and a Committee of Publishers and Associations

"Honey, I've Shrunk the Bills!"

By
Jack Weber

CAPITAL
BOOKS, INC.
Sterling, Virginia

Dedication

I am my mother's son in more ways than I care to admit.

For more than twenty years – ever since I left college — she has mailed me envelopes stuffed with little scraps of paper torn from the stacks of magazines and newspapers that pile up in her den like cord wood.

For the longest time, I was never quite sure why she sent them. Little missives about how to remove a ketchup stain or how to keep a carton of yogurt from spoiling in the refrigerator. They are in my bottom desk drawer at this very moment. *Hints from Heloise*. Answers from the answer man. All the "how to's" and 10 ways." Laugh if you want, but I am probably the only person for a thousand miles that knows how to cure a cold with a clove of garlic or make my very own mozzarella cheese.

It's my mother's fault, of course. She is the one that turned me into a information junkie. Introducing me to the habit and then watching as I became hopelessly hooked. Now, we send envelopes back and forth to each other. My scraps for her scraps. Useful things. Helpful things. Things you might actually need to know some day.

Neither one of us has ever been very good at "warm" and "loving." So we've developed our own shorthand. My "Dear Abby" begets her "Reader's Digest" and in our own way love is exchanged.

Here, Mom ... some tips to help your joints from getting so stiff in the morning.

Here, Son ... five things you should know to avoid an IRS audit.

"I love you, Mom."

"I love you too, Son."

My mother made me do it. She's the one that encouraged me to keep a record of the things I learned. To organize so I could find what I needed, *when* I needed it. A lifetime's compilation of trivia, every bit as impressive as a museum archive, and I dare say a whole lot more useful.

She was my inspiration for this book. It's a tribute of sorts. Something to read and learn from. The kind of book my mother would write, if she wasn't so busy clipping newspapers.

Use it to improve your life and pass it on to those *you* love.

Introduction

The Most Important Book You'll Ever Read

Years ago, before I even considered writing a book, I attended a backyard cookout in our neighborhood. It was a typical gathering. Lots of kids. Plenty of small talk about schools, lawns, the weather, etc. In between bites of a hamburger, I mentioned to one of my neighbors that I was thinking about replacing the carpet in my home. My house is almost 3,000 square feet, so I figured the whole job was going to set me back close to $10,000 and I wasn't happy about it.

"Maybe I can help you," my neighbor said.

"Are you in the carpet business?" I asked.

"No ... but I ought to be," he chuckled as he reached for his pen. "Here's my phone number at the office. Call me in the morning."

I put the slip of paper in my pocket and went back to the grill for another hamburger.

That night, as I was getting ready for bed, I was half-tempted to throw the piece of paper in the trash, but then curiosity got the better of me. What was it that my neighbor knew about carpet that I didn't know?

The next morning, I called to find out.

It turns out my neighbor is a real estate developer who buys a lot of carpet. He also buys tons of furniture, but that's another story. Anyway, he proceeds to tell me that if I want a good deal on carpeting, I can forget about local carpet stores.

"I don't even bother with them anymore," he said. "I go straight to the carpet mills and buy direct from the factory."

"But I can't do that," I objected.

"Why not?" he said. "Call my friend 'Bill' at Blue Circle Carpets in Dalton, Georgia and tell him I sent you."

I've got to admit I was skeptical. How could some guy 1,000 miles away save me money on carpet? Even so, I promised to follow through.

When I called "Bill" two days later, he couldn't have been more friendly. He remembered my neighbor and said I was smart to call. He said that virtually all the wall-to-wall carpet in the United States is manufactured within 90 miles of Dalton and that for years, savvy buyers have been calling distributors like him for the best prices.

I asked him how the process works.

"Just go to any carpet store in your area and decide what kind of carpet you want," he said. "Make a note of the manufacturer, the color and style number, as well as the price including pad and installation. Then call me back."

I had already been to a carpet store for ideas, but I must admit that I hadn't paid any attention to things like style numbers and manufacturers. Following Bill's advice, I went back again, this time with pad and paper. The salesman had no problem with me taking notes. In fact, he encouraged me. I told him I liked an off-white Berber style by CabinCraft which he priced at $32 per sq. yd., including pad and installation.

When I called Bill back, he chuckled when I told him the price I had been quoted. He said he could get the exact same carpet for $17 per sq. yd and that he could ship it to me by UPS in less than a week! Even after allowing for shipping charges, padding and the expense of hiring a local installer, my total cost would be $21 per square yard — $11 per yard cheaper than the price quote from my local carpet store.

I took out my calculator and did some math. I needed 330 square yards to redo my entire house. Buying from Blue Circle would cost me $6,993 — a lot of money, to be sure — but a lot less than the $10,600 the local store had quoted me. There was even another bonus. Since I live in Virginia and I would be buying my carpet over the phone from a supplier in Georgia, I would not have to pay local sales tax which would save me an extra $279. That meant my total savings through **Blue Circle** would be a whopping $3,886! I immediately faxed Bill my room dimensions and six days later, my carpet arrived. (By the way, it looks great in my house!)

Worth the Trip

A few weeks later, I was on a flight to Los Angeles. It always burns me up when I fly cross-country. Unless you book your flight weeks in advance and stay over a Saturday night, the fares are ridiculously high. Coach class tickets from Washington's Dulles Airport to Los Angeles with a mid-week return will usually set you back $1,400 to $1,600.

It takes a lot of nerve to charge that much money, especially since the airlines are always running full-page ads that promise $350 roundtrip fares anywhere in the country. Of course, that's before the fine print and restrictions. Tell the reservations agent you need to travel next week and that you aren't staying over a Saturday and suddenly the skies aren't so friendly.

Back on the plane, I found myself chatting with the person sitting next to me. She was a marketing manager for a computer software company. We were commiserating about the poor service and lousy food when I complained that on top of everything else, my ticket had cost me $1,493. The reason, of course, was that I booked my return without the required Saturday-night stay in L.A.

"Don't you know about the back-to-back trick?" she said?

"What's that?" I asked as they cleared the meal trays.

This very nice woman proceeded to explain that for years, she worked for a start-up computer company that had a hard time making ends meet. They had such a limited budget that paying full-fare for airline tickets was out of the question. At a meeting one day, the boss asked the office manager if she could look into ways the company might reduce travel expenses.

It turned out that the office manager had a nose for bargains and couldn't wait to get going on the project. She scoured every source of information she could find on airlines, fare trends and ticketing practices. Before long, she had compiled an impressive amount of data which she organized methodically and summarized in a two-page memo that listed specific suggestions for reducing the company's travel costs. (Sounds to me like the office manager should have been the CEO!)

As my new friend explained, the office manager's memo was mandatory reading for everyone in the office. And since she was always traveling on mid-week, coast-to-coast flights, my "seat mate" was particularly intrigued by the manager's explanation of back-to-back ticketing.

According to the memo, rather than buy one roundtrip ticket for a mid-week itinerary at full-price, you buy two roundtrip tickets that are discounted because they require a Saturday night stay at your destination. You arrange the flights so that the outbound portion of each ticket corresponds to your desired itinerary and you simply discard the returns.

Had I used the back-to-back strategy, I would have purchased a discounted ticket departing D.C. on Monday, but instead of returning Friday (my desired date), I would have requested a return after Saturday night in order to qualify for the cheaper ticket. Then I would have purchased a second roundtrip ticket traveling in the opposite direction. This ticket would depart L.A. on Friday. Again, I would have scheduled the return long enough in advance to qualify for the Saturday night discount. On

my travel days, I would have simply used the outbound portion of ticket #1 when I departed D.C. on Monday and the outbound portion of ticket #2 when I returned from L.A. on Friday.

Of course I hadn't used the back-to-back strategy on this trip, which is why I had paid $1,493 for my full-fare, mid-week ticket!

It was at this point that my seat companion pulled out her own tickets to show me how much my "mistake" had cost me. My friend had indeed used back-to-back tickets. In fact, her schedule was nearly identical to mine, except that she was returning on Thursday. Do you know what the back-to-back tickets cost her? Are you ready? Only $900 for both tickets! In other words, $593 less than I paid.

I rang the flight attendant call button to order a double bourbon and soda.

"Why didn't anybody tell me about this?" I asked my traveling companion.

"Well, you don't think the airlines are going to advertise it, do you?" she said.

Of course she was right about that. What airline is going to give you step-by-step instructions on how to outsmart them?

I learned a valuable lesson on that flight. First, that the airlines will always take advantage of you if you let them. And second, that there are ways to fight back.

Inspiration

I might never have made a connection between my conversation on the airplane and the advice I got from my neighbor about buying carpet until I got my charge card statement for the month. There it was — my bill from **Blue Circle**, the company that saved me nearly $4,000 compared to what I had been prepared to pay my friendly, neighborhood carpet salesman. And there, too, was my airline charge – all $1,493 of it — exactly $593 more than I should have paid.

It felt great to get a good deal on carpet, and it felt just as rotten that I had been overcharged by the airline. I was both amazed and angry. How much money had I wasted over the years just because I hadn't bothered to do a little research? Most of the time I just walked into the store, grabbed what I needed, and left. I had no strategy or inside information. I simply pulled out my credit card and said, "Charge it."

What to do?

I knew that I didn't want to keep repeating the same old mistakes. I liked the feeling of power and control I got when I discovered the smart way to buy carpet. I wanted the same thing to happen every time I bought something. Of course, I couldn't walk up and down the street in my neighborhood hoping to run into an ex-car dealer when I needed a new car, or a former **Circuit City** salesman the next time I was in the market for a new stereo. I would need a more systematic approach.

My first thought was the library. There are lots of books and magazines in a library. Surely, there must be some resource that could tell me what I needed to know. I visited six libraries in my area including one at a major university. I searched under the general subject of "buying" and found nothing. When I tried specific categories, I did much better. There were plenty of books about real estate, furniture, clothing and all the other topics you might imagine. But there were several problems. First, a lot of the material was hopelessly out of date. There were lots of references to 12% mortgage rates and almost no mention of new technologies and the internet. I also found that most of the books were dull and boring. None of them contained golden nuggets of information like my neighbor had passed on to me. Instead of straightforward suggestions like — if you want a great deal on carpet, call Bill in Dalton, Georgia — I kept reading page after page of generalities.Where was the *good* stuff, I wondered?

I just couldn't understand why the facts I wanted most – the "who", "what" "where" and "how" of saving money – were usually the questions left unanswered.

Next, I tried the local bookstore. There I found books that were certainly more up-to-date. I also found titles that focused more on the "how-to" problem I was trying to solve. Yet even though there were current sources of information and more of them, I still could not find one source that had all that I wanted. I would have needed a wheelbarrow to carry all of the specialized books in the categories I sought, and even then I would have been just scratching the surface.

Over in the magazine section, I glanced at the current editions of several consumer journals. That month, there was advice about buying toaster ovens and a six-page article about choosing the best spaghetti sauce. (Unfortunately, I already have a toaster and my whole family is allergic to tomatoes.)

I left the bookstore as disappointed as I had been at the library. Not only was I frustrated, but I was becoming even more determined that I was not going to give up until I found what I was looking for.

Go "online"?

The internet was certainly less stressful to use. No traffic jams or parking problems, and my neck didn't get sore looking sideways at overstocked bookshelves. I could sit comfortably at my desk, let my computer do the heavy lifting and wait for the information to come to me! At least, that's the way it is supposed to work, but anyone who has spent any time cruising the "net" knows otherwise. Ask for something simple, like buying wallpaper, and back come the results showing that there are 17,000 sites that match your search criteria. Seventeen thousand! Then you discover that each search engine, like the ones maintained by **America Online, Yahoo!** or **Excite!**, try to steer you to sites that have paid them a fee to be part of their particular database. They are listed first, not because they are the best source for wallpaper or even the lowest-priced, but because they paid.

Even when I did find sites that looked interesting, most of them ended up delivering far less than promised. Instead of finding what I wanted quickly and easily, I wound up spending hour upon hour sifting through useless data. In other words, instead of saving me money, the internet was costing me something just as valuable — time.

No Single Source

I came to the conclusion that I was never going to find what I was looking for, at least not in the form I had envisioned. I wanted an integrated resource that could tell me where and how to buy everything I could ever possibly want in the smartest, cheapest and easiest way possible. Instead, I found that while there were valuable secrets to be discovered, they were hidden in a thousand places. Finding them, sorting through the false promises or hype and then discarding the stuff that wasn't specific was the *real* challenge.

And since no one else had done it, if I was really serious about the need to compile all the information, I had no choice but to do it myself. Thus, an idea for a book was born.

I started what became a 5-year research project. I spoke with vendors and salesmen. I read every article I could find from every conceivable source including magazines, newsletters, newspapers and trade journals. I used the web and monitored internet chat sites. I even interviewed friends and neighbors.

The result was a file box more than two feet thick. Hundreds of scraps of paper and notecards. And through the course of my research, I was stunned to find how much of what passes for consumer advice is useless. In much the same way **Cosmopolitan** magazine repeats the same tired and overworked stories about improving one's sex life, financial advice magazines recycle the same stuff on saving money. Most books are no better. Even with the best sources, the really good information that can save readers serious money can usually be distilled into a handful of critical facts and resources.

I wanted my book to be chock full of these specific references so I carefully edited and refined all that I had found into a concise format that became the outline for *"Honey, I've Shrunk the Bills!"*

You'll notice that each chapter discusses a specific list of related products or services. Each begins with a short primer on essential facts presented through a format of questions and answers. Why Q & A? Because when we — any of us — wants to buy something, our minds are usually filled with questions. It is the answers we crave and the sooner we get them the better informed we will be.

It was also important that the information could be put to use immediately. It does no good, for instance, to learn that you can fly internationally for ridiculously low prices as a courier for a major freight company if you aren't also told how to contact these freight companies and what to say on the phone. Therefore, I made sure that each chapter included plenty of sources with phone numbers and Internet addresses — as well as explicit, easy-to-follow instructions on what to do with them. In many cases, I even produced a suggested script you can use on the phone so that you can't possibly make a mistake.

So often, the difference between wanting to save money and doing it is taking the all-important first step. By presenting the bargain process in the form of a step-by-step instructions, I felt that it would be easier for you to follow through on the advice in each chapter.

Finding the best deal requires knowing the right people to call, the right questions to ask and enough about the product or service to be dangerous.

If you want to buy a camera, for example, *"Honey, I've Shrunk the Bills!"* will tell you where the professionals shop for the lowest prices and the best service. You'll find all the toll-free numbers and web sites of the best mail-order sources, plus practical advice on which type of camera gives you the best value for your money.

You will save money. I guarantee it. But you will also enjoy a by-product of bargain shopping — the fun of feeling in control and beating the system. There is nothing better than walking into a store fully briefed and totally prepared, ready to run rings around the salesperson because you know more than he or she does!

That's how you win. There's a thrill to a bargain. It satisfies some primal urge we've probably had since prehistoric days — to venture out into the world, stalk our prey and return to our cave in triumph. Think of *"Honey, I've Shrunk the Bills!"* as a way to save money, to be sure, but also as a means to becoming King or Queen of the bargain jungle. If you follow my advice, you'll more than deserve the title.

A Critical Priority

In 1998, the savings rate for the average American family was a negative number. That means most Americans spent more money than they earned. An aberration, you say? Hardly. According to government statistics, the savings rate in the U.S. has been in steady decline since 1945.

The ramifications are ominous. At a time when the U.S. economy is operating at peak efficiency and baby boomers are in their most productive years, many individuals and families are actually losing ground.

It makes no sense to waste money, particularly when you can buy the same things for less money by making a few simple changes. The results add up faster than you might think. Fifty dollars a week in savings, accumulated over the course of a year, is $2,600. That same sum, invested consistently over a working lifetime of 30 years and compounded at a 10% rate of return, becomes nearly $500,000. Double the amount to $100 a week and the final total is more than $1,000,000!

You can cut your grocery bills 20-40% without any sacrifice in what you keep in the refrigerator. You can lower your utility bills, buy better clothes at lower prices, enjoy the best restaurants, take the most spectacular vacations — do it all for less money and actually get wealthier in the process.

"Honey, I've Shrunk the Bills!" can be your roadmap. Keep it next to your telephone or on your desk. Use it often and incorporate the lessons it teaches every time you shop. Over time, you will find that you are internalizing the principles of shopping smarter and cheaper without even referring to the book. Your curiosity will get the better of you, just as it did me. You will want to uncover new secrets – better inside tips – and you will find them because there are always new things to discover. Who knows? One day you could even wind up writing a sequel. Anyone for *"Honey, I've Shrunk Even More Bills?"*

About the Author

Jack Weber is an advocate, author and lecturer who has developed straightforward systems to help consumers shop smart and pay less on all sorts of products and services.

Based in the Washington, DC area, he has consulted with numerous consumer and trade groups, including the Grocery Manufacturers of America, the National Association of Broadcasters, the Home Insurance Federation of America, as well as several Fortune 500 companies such as Allstate Insurance.

His audio and workbook plan, *Secrets of the Supermarket*, has been featured on the QVC Shopping Network and is in its 5th printing.

In various capacities, Mr. Weber has appeared on Larry King Live, CNN, Good Morning America, CNBC, the Today Show and even the Japanese Television Network (NHK) and Australian Public Radio to discuss consumer issues.

For six years, from 1980-1986, he worked as an aide to President Ronald Reagan, both at the White House and at the nation's top consumer protection agency, the Federal Trade Commission.

Mr. Weber is a Phi Beta Kappa graduate and former valedictorian of the University of Southern California, where he earned degrees in journalism and political science. Weber also attended Trinity College at Cambridge University in England.

The Ten Commandments

All prices are negotiable.

"Sale" is the most overused word in the English language.

The internet is a tool, not an answer.

What you know is less important than what you know to *ask*.

A dollar saved is $1.35 (after taxes).

Quality and price are *not* synonymous.

If you spend money to save time, you often waste money.

What you spend is often a function of what the seller *thinks* you'll pay.

The most careful shoppers often have more money than you do.

Saving money is easier than *making* it.

Table of Contents

Chapter One

Furnish Your House for Half Price

Why are home furnishings so expensive and what can I do about it?

Furniture, carpet and home accessories cost so much because of middlemen. Local dealers typically double the wholesale cost of these items before selling to you. For major purchases, this markup adds hundreds if not thousands of dollars to your final bill. Some manufacturers will sell to you directly or through discount sources, but you must know how to find them. We've listed the names and phone numbers for many of these sources in our three-part, step-by-step instruction guide included with this chapter.

Even if you do not buy from these outlets, knowing the wholesale price will help you negotiate better deals at local stores. The step-by-step system shows you exactly what to say and do.

How else can I save if I don't buy from these out-of-town sources?

Buy used furniture advertised in the classified section of you local newspaper. You can find incredible bargains, particularly on high-priced living room or dining room pieces which originally

sold for thousands of dollars. The only drawback is the time it takes to shop. Ask for a complete description over the telephone before you drive to someone's home. Be prepared to spend several weeks or months on your search, but the savings will be worth the effort.

As an alternative, shop furniture consignment stores. Patterned after the used clothing stores that have become trend setters in the fashion industry, furniture consigners re-sell high-quality furniture and accessories at a discount. You are more likely to find these stores in larger communities, but the trend is growing.

Another option is to become your own interior decorator. Professional decorators buy wholesale from showrooms that are not open to the public. At these display centers, often known as furniture or design marts, major furniture manufacturers offer their products to decorators at discounts of up to 40 or 50% off retail prices.

Most design centers are not open to the public. To gain admittance, you will need proof that you are "in the business," but the truth is that just about anyone can call themselves an interior decorator. All you'll need is a business card (i.e., Jane Doe Interiors), a business license from City Hall indicating that you are now doing business as an interior designer (who cares if you're the only client), and a business checking account which you can open at your local bank. You'll also need to look and act the part of an interior designer, which shouldn't be a problem if you follow the suggestions included in this chapter.

Is it risky to buy over the telephone or via the internet?

No. The companies we've identified have been doing business for years and enjoy excellent reputations. If you have a problem with the item you've purchased, most of the firms will do everything possible to satisfy you. For added protection, use a credit card. That way, if you are unhappy with an item or it arrives damaged, you are protected under the Fair Credit Billing Act. The law allows you to dispute any credit card purchase if you have a valid reason for not paying. You can get a full refund from your credit card company even if the merchant refuses to cooperate. (See Chapter 9 for detailed instructions on how to dispute a credit charge.)

Doesn't shipping add to the cost of items I buy from distant sources?

Yes. However, even with these added costs, you should save 30-50%.

What's wrong with buying from discount furniture warehouses I see advertised in the newspaper?

Just because the ad says "discount," don't assume you're always getting a great deal. Many warehouses offer low prices because they sell poor quality merchandise.

How can I be certain that I am buying quality furniture?

You must learn to recognize differences in materials and craftsmanship. For furniture, you must judge the types of wood or fabric and the quality of construction. For carpets, you must know about yarn weight and weave. You will learn specific tests for quality in the Step-by-Step guide that follows.

Are brand names important when buying furniture?

No. The vast majority of furniture is manufactured by small companies under contract to nationally known retailers and distributors. It is not unusual for a distributor to market the products of dozens of these manufacturers under a single brand name. Since you can never really be sure of the source, forget brands and concentrate instead on your own judgment of materials and workmanship.

What about brand-name carpets?

Names like "Stainmaster", "Anso IV" or "Trevira" refer to brand-name fibers used by dozens of carpet mills. High-quality fibers are important, but they do not give you any insights into the company which actually made the final product.

Guide to FURNITURE

Step 1

Make note of these phone numbers and web sites. They connect you with furniture wholesalers who can get you the lowest price on quality, American-made furniture.

Step 2

Visit several local furniture stores or department stores to get an idea of the items you like. Look at floor samples, but also ask if there are manufacturers' catalogs that you can glance through. Your goal is to identify particular furniture pieces which you can later price at the wholesale outlets identified at right.

Step 3

When inspecting furniture, pay close attention to the quality of materials and workmanship. Good furniture lasts a lifetime, so buy something built to last. Use the six quality tests listed below to judge any items you are considering.

- **Wood Composition**—Oak, mahogany or cherry wood is more durable than pine. Solid woods are always superior to veneers. Labels must accurately describe the type of wood used in construction.

Best Furniture Outlets

Shaw Furniture Gallery
252-638-2121
www.shawfurniture.com

Carolina Interiors
704-933-1888
http://ncnet.com/ncnw/car-int.html

Fields Furniture
800-222-4809
www.fieldsfurniture.com

Jones Brothers Furniture
919-934-4162
www.jonesbros.co

Triad Furniture
800-222-4809
(no web site)

Holton Furniture
800-334-3183
www.holtonfurniture.com

Greenfront Furniture
804-392-3430
www.greenfront.com

Reflections Furniture (leather)
828-327-8485
www.hfnet.com/Reflections/

Blackwelders
800-438-0201
www.blackwelder.com

- **Frame Construction**—Wiggle furniture legs, armrests and seat backs. They should feel solid (no movement or squeaking). Inspect how the furniture is pieced together. Legs and corners should be connected with wood pegs, glue and screws. Avoid furniture assembled with nails or staples, or "boxed" furniture you put together at home.

- **Springs**—Bounce up and down on seat cushions or mattresses. You should never hear squeaks or feel the internal coils.

- **Padding**—Inspect the inside seat cushions and pillows. Insist on solid foam or synthetic down, never shredded foam. Armrests should be thick enough so that you cannot feel the wood frame underneath.

- **Fabric**—All upholstery should be tightly woven and stretched evenly. Patterns should be straight and perfectly aligned.

- **Drawers and Hardware**—Moving pieces should align properly and operate smoothly. Handles should be secured firmly.

Step 4

Make a list of the furniture items that appeal to you most. Be certain to write down as many specifics as you can, including manufacturer, style number, price, fabric options, color options and delivery charges.

Furniture Shopping Checklist

Gather this information for each piece of furnishing.

✔ **Manufacturer**
✔ **Style number**
✔ **Color or finish**
✔ **Fabric color/pattern number**
✔ **Projected delivery date**
✔ **Delivery charge (if any)**

Step 5

Now leave the store and contact several of the discount sources listed in Step 1. Ask if they carry the exact same item you've identified. If not, describe the piece and ask if they have something with comparable specifications. Request that a catalog or "tear" sheet describing the item be mailed, faxed or e-mailed to you. Also ask for the price of the item, how long from order to delivery, terms of sale and delivery/setup charges to your address.

Step 6

Compare the store price to the mail order price, including delivery.

Step 7

Return to the furniture store you previously visited. Tell them you got a better price for the same furniture from an out-of-town supplier, but would prefer to do business locally if they can match the price.

Sample Dialogue

Hello. You may remember I was here earlier to look at furniture. I've done some shopping and have located an out-of-town distributor who will sell me the same item that I found in your store for $_____, including delivery. I would prefer to do business locally, but only if you can match the price.

Step 8

Contact another store if you cannot negotiate a comparable price or order directly from the out-of-town source.

Step 9

If you can't find what you're looking for from conventional sources or you want to act as your own interior designer, consider the following suggestions for gaining access to furniture marts and trade centers open only to professionals.

How to Shop at a Furniture Mart

Find the nearest furniture mart, which is likely to be located in a major metropolitan area. Furniture marts can be found in Dallas; Chicago; San Francisco; Omaha; Boston; Atlanta; Washington, DC; Los Angeles; Phoenix; Denver and Seattle, to name a few cities. You can also look in the Yellow Pages for furniture design centers designated as "wholesale" or "trade only."

Obtain business cards, a business license and a business checking account indicating you are a "home decorator."

Dress in a professional manner when you visit the furniture mart.

Register at the front desk with your business card and show your business license if necessary.

Sign the guest book of each showroom you visit in the mart.

A showroom will contain some, but not all, of a manufacturer's line. You may be shown catalogs containing information about various products that are not physically located in the showroom.

Do not volunteer that you are buying for yourself unless asked directly.

When you find an item that looks appealing, make note of the price. Chances are that the prices are coded in a way that only design professionals will understand. If you see a tag containing two numbers and a slash sign (i.e. 20/55), you are looking at what is known in the trade as a "5/10" price. To decipher the code, take $5.00 off the first number and 10 cents off the second. The code (20/55) thus becomes $15.45.

If prices in a design center are clearly marked, chances are that you are looking at the suggested retail price. (This is also true for catalog prices.) Discreetly ask for the trade discount, which is usually expressed as a percentage (i.e., 40%). If you are told that the trade discount is a "keystone," it means the designer discount is 50% off suggested retail.

If you find an item you wish to order, pay using a check from your newly established business checking account. Do not use a credit card, since this is a dead giveaway that you aren't really a designer.

If you think that it's a lot of trouble printing business cards and opening a business checking account, you're right! If you're just interested in buying a single piece of furniture, it probably isn't worth it. However, if you have several rooms to furnish and your budget is several thousand dollars, establishing yourself as an interior decorator is worth the time and trouble.

Guide to CARPETING

Step 1

Make note of these phone numbers and web sites. They connect you with mail-order carpet outlets in Dalton, Georgia, the carpet capital of America. These firms will quote you carpet prices by telephone and ship your order direct from the factory.

Step 2

Before shopping, precisely measure the area you need carpeted. Your calculations must be converted into square yards, the unit of measure used to purchase carpet. To determine square yardage, rooms must be measured in rectangles. Use the example below to help you visualize the process.

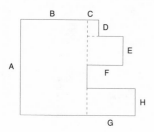

To measure the room, divide into rectangles. Multiply length x width and add the totals.

Best Wholesale Carpet Outlets

Beckler's Carpet Outlet
800-232-5537
www.carpetsales.com

Blue Circle Carpets
800-622-7561
www.carpetown.com

Michael's Carpets
800-634-9509
www.michaelscarpet.com

Access Carpets
800-652-2389
www.accesscarpets.com

Martin's Carpet
706-278-3209
www.martinscarpet.com

Worthington Carpets
888-883-5667
www.worthingtonmills.com

Quality Discount Carpet
800-233-0993

Carpets of Dalton
800-262-3132

Dalton Paradise Carpets
800-338-7811

How Much Carpet Will You Need?

A. Visually divide your room into measurable rectangles.

B. Measure the length and width of each rectangle in inches and multiply the two numbers together.

Example: <u>245</u> x <u>168</u> = <u>41,160 sq. inches</u>

Rectangle A   _____ x _____ = _____

Rectangle B   _____ x _____ = _____

Rectangle C   _____ x _____ = _____

Rectangle D   _____ x _____ = _____

Rectangle E   _____ x _____ = _____

Rectangle F   _____ x _____ = _____

Rectangle G   _____ x _____ = _____

Total sq. inches   _____

C. Divide the total in Step 2 by 1,296 to convert the measurement into square yards.

_____ ÷ 1,296 = _____

total square inches (step 2)   total square yards

**Approximate
Carpet Needed:** _____ Square yards

Step 3

Visit several local carpet or department stores to identify the styles and colors you like best. Forget brand names. Focus instead on fiber content, yarn patterns and weight.

Fiber Content

- **Wool** is best, but it is too expensive for most uses.

- **Nylon** is almost as good, plus it wears well. Look for new-generation nylons, such as **Antron, Anso, Ultron, Enkalon** or **Zeftron**. Since nylon is prone to staining, insist on stain-guard protection.

- **Polyester** feels softer and more luxurious than nylon, but it is not as durable and traps more dirt. It is not recommended for heavy-duty family use. Look for **Dacron** or **Trevira** brand fibers.

- **Olefin** is for indoor/outdoor or industrial uses. The best fibers are manufactured under the brand names Pentron, Herculon or Marquesa.

Yarn Pattern

- Different yarn patterns have distinct wear characteristics which should be

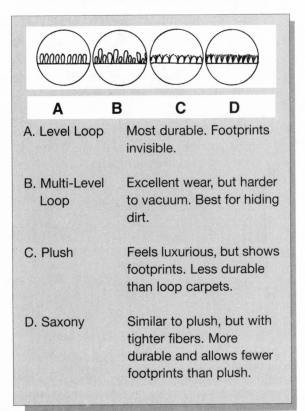

| | A | B | C | D |

A. Level Loop	Most durable. Footprints invisible.
B. Multi-Level Loop	Excellent wear, but harder to vacuum. Best for hiding dirt.
C. Plush	Feels luxurious, but shows footprints. Less durable than loop carpets.
D. Saxony	Similar to plush, but with tighter fibers. More durable and allows fewer footprints than plush.

factored into your buying decision. Choose the pattern that fits your taste and lifestyle, but be aware of the negatives.

Carpet Weight

- Choose the highest density carpet you can afford. At a minimum, nylon carpets should have a weight of 30 oz., while polyester styles should weigh at least 35 oz.

- You can test density by rubbing your fingers through the carpet. The heavier the carpet, the harder it will be for your fingers to touch the carpet backing.

Pad Weight

- All carpets are installed over a padding material which adds comfort and reduces wear. Pads are sold separately or as part of a package price including carpet.

- When buying padding, the most important consideration is pad weight, not the pad's thickness.

Recommended Pad Weight	
Pad Type	*Minimum Weight*
Natural Fiber (Jute)	40-48 oz./cubic ft.
Sponge Rubber	70-100 oz./cubic ft.
Prime Foam	2.5 lbs./cubic ft.
Bonded Foam	5 lbs./cubic ft.

Step 4

Take careful notes on any carpet samples that look appealing. If the salesperson asks you why you want the information, tell him it is for comparison purposes. Also inquire about pad prices, delivery and installation.

Step 5

Once you have answered the questions above, tell the salesperson you want to do some comparison shopping and exit the store. Return home and call several of the Dalton carpet outlets listed in Step 1. Ask them for the delivered price for the same carpet and pad you chose in the store. If they do not carry the same brand, ask for a comparable carpet with the same specifications and request that a sample be sent to your home.

Step 6

To accurately compare the mail-order price to the store quote, you must get a separate estimate for installation. Look in the Yellow Pages under "carpet installation." Call several sources and ask their price for installing carpet you buy elsewhere. Be sure the estimate includes the price for removing and hauling your old carpet, and any stair or trim work.

Questions to Ask an Installer

Will you remove my existing carpet for no charge?

Will you charge me a fixed price for the job?

Do you charge extra for stairs or moving furniture?

For how long do you guarantee your work?

Step 7

Compare the store price to the Dalton outlet price for delivered carpet, including installation.

Step 8

Return to the carpet store. Tell them you got a better price for the same carpet from an out-of-town wholesaler, but that you would prefer to do business locally if they can match the price.

Sample Dialogue

"*Hello. You may remember that I was here earlier and received a price quote for the carpet and padding, including delivery and installation. I've done some shopping around and have located an out-of-town source who will sell me the same carpet and pad, including delivery and installation, for only $_____. I would prefer to do business locally, but only if you can match the price.*"

Step 9

Contact another store if you cannot negotiate a comparable price, or order directly from Dalton source.

Carpet Shopping Checklist

Here is the information you'll need to shop competitively for carpet.

✔ Brand name
✔ Manufacturer
✔ Fiber content
✔ Color name or number
✔ Style number (if any)
✔ Fiber protection
✔ Warranty information
✔ Price per yard
✔ Insulation included?
✔ Pad included?
✔ Type of pad
✔ Pad weight

Guide to **Accessories**

Wallpaper

Step 1

Always shop discount wallpaper sources. You will generally save 40–70% off the retail price.

Step 2

Find the pattern you want in any retail store.

Step 3

Write down the style number and manufacturer.

Step 4

Call these mail-order wallpaper outlets listed at right.

China

China and crystal are never really a bargain. Less expensive tableware does the job for a lot less money and can still be very stylish. However, if you must buy the good stuff, try the sources listed in the next column.

Discount Sources for Wallpaper

Wallpaper & Blind Connection
800-288-9979
www.blinds.com

National Blind & Wallpaper Factory
800-777-2737

American Blind & Wallpaper Factory
800-735-5300
www.abf.com

Decorator's Edge
800-289-5589

Discount Sources for China & Crystal

Ross-Simons
800-521-7677
www.ross-simons.com

Michael C. Fina
800-289-3462

Michael Round
800-467-6863
www.mround.com

Replacements, Ltd.
800-737-5223
www.replacements.com

Almost Perfect
800-854-5746
www.almostandperfectchina.com

Vertical Blinds

Step 1

Always shop discount blind sources.

Step 2

Measure your window openings precisely, according to manufacturer's instructions.

Step 3

Select the color and style you want from any store.

Step 4

Write down the style number, color and manufacturer.

Step 5

Call the mail order sources in the next column for 50-70% savings:

Discount Sources for Blinds

National Decorators
800-288-9979
www.blinds.com

American Blind Factory
800-735-5300
www.abf.com

Blinds Galore
877-702-5463
www.blindsgalore.com

Blinds Network Corporation
888-425-4631
www.blinds.net

Window Blind Depot
800-944-7600
www.forblinds.com

Lighting

Light fixtures are always expensive, but you can sometimes get better prices by phone or online.

Lighting Deals

Lighting by Gregory
800-796-1965
www.lightingbygregory.com

Golden Valley Lighting
800-735-3377
www.gvlight.com

American Light Source
800-741-0571

Nationwide Lighting
800-525-4837

Blackwelders
800-438-0201
www.blackwelder.com

Fabrics

If you like making custom drapes, bedspreads or upholstery, price your fabric from any source. Then see if you can find it cheaper from these outlets:

Discount Sources for Fabrics

ABC Fabrics
800-548-3499

Fabric Center
508-343-4402

National Decorators
800-955-2559

Fabric Outlet
800-635-9715

Decorator's Edge
800-289-5589

FURNISHINGS

HERE'S THE PROOF

 Mail-order sources are an ideal way to save money on almost any type of home furnishings. To prove the point, we sampled prices at local retail stores in the Washington, D.C. area, and then searched for the exact same item through the mail-order sources we've listed in this chapter. As you can see from the examples below, you can save serious money following our suggestions.

Suggestion: Buy your furniture from a mail-order source in North Carolina instead of from your local furniture dealer.

Manufacturer Style No.	7-Drawer Solid Cherry Desk Hooker Furniture 04910-163
Price @ Local Furniture Store*	**Price from North Carolina Discounter***
$ 1,384.62 Mastercraft Interiors Merrifield, VA	**$ 1,046.00** Shaw Furniture Gallery 252-683-2121
Total Savings	**$ 338.62**

* prices include sales tax and delivery

Suggestion: Buy your carpet direct from the manufacturers in Dalton, Georgia. Then use a local source for the installation.

Brand of Carpet	Cabin Crafts "Unanimous II" (200 sq. yards)
Price @ Retail Store*	*Price @ Factory Direct Source**
$ 4,590 The Carpet Yard Fairfax, VA	**$ 3,518** Blue Circle Carpet 800 622-7561
Total Savings	**$ 1,072**

Brand of Carpet	Salem Carpet "Simply Irresistable" (200 sq. yards)
Price @ Retail Store*	*Price @ Factory Direct Source**
$ 5,250 Bill's Carpet Warehouse Fairfax, VA	**$ 3,854** Quality Discount Carpet 800-233-0993
Total Savings	**$ 1,396**

* Prices include carpet, pad, delivery and local installation.

Suggestion: Buy your window blinds by mail to save 50% or more!

Manufacturer	Hunter Douglas	
Style	Custom Pleated Blinds	
Color	White Shadow (#271)	

Window Size	Price @ Retail Store* Dannemann's Merrifield, VA	Price @ Mail-Order Source American Blind Factory 800 735-5300
36"x 72"	$ 275.00	$ 54.91
103"x 71"	102.00	137.40
71"x 73"	200.00	104.40
71"x 72"	200.00	98.71
77"x 82"	260.00	129.00
Total Price	$ 1,037.00	$ 524.42
Total Savings		$ 512.58

Chapter 2
Discount Guide to Travel

Which airlines have the lowest prices?

Ticket prices change constantly as airlines react to new competition or sudden shifts in passenger demand. At a given moment, any airline could have the best deal to your destination. Of course, certain airlines strive to be the low-cost leaders. These include **Southwest Airlines, Shuttle by United**, **Metrojet** and **AirTran**. If any of these airlines serve your local airport, it is a good idea to check their fares first. Pay particular note that **Southwest** and **AirTran** are excluded from some of the online and travel agent reservation systems. Unless you call these airlines directly, you will find it difficult to locate information on their fares and schedules.

How should I buy my ticket?

In the old days, you could either call the airline directly or contact a travel agent. Now you can take matters into your own hands by using the internet. Online travel services have helped to level the playing field by giving consumers direct access to information regarding fares and schedules. Even if you do not purchase your tickets over the web, the price comparison capabilities of the technology protect you against an airline reservation operator or travel agent that may not have your best interests at heart.

What the internet won't do is teach you the nuances of airline pricing and scheduling that can often make the difference between an O.K. fare and a real bargain. An experienced travel agent knows these secrets, but finding a good one is getting harder since airlines have cut back dramatically on travel agent commissions.

If you have access to the internet, by all means take advantage of it. Use the strategies outlined in this chapter to identify the best flights at the lowest price, then purchase your ticket from the source of your choice (airline, travel agent, web site).

Why don't the airlines charge the same fares for all passengers?

A single-fare pricing system would be a great benefit to the flying public, but the airlines make more money when they sell tickets on a sliding scale. Years of experience have taught them that on any given flight, some passengers are more desperate to fly than others. With the help of computers, the airlines closely monitor ticket demand, changing ticket prices and availability several times a day. For example, if the airline senses that demand for a flight is heavy among business travelers who, as a group, are less price sensitive than other customers, the airline will raise ticket prices or reduce the availability of discount fares.

Most travelers don't realize that the airline pricing system is rigged against them. They assume that if a lower fare is "sold out" or "unavailable", the reason is because lots of other passengers have already purchased the cheap seats. Not necessarily. It is just as likely that the lower fares were in very limited supply because the airline concluded they could fill the plane at higher prices.

You can either be a victim of this predatory pricing or use it to your advantage. By seeking out flights where demand is weak, you play the same game the airlines do, but in reverse. When passengers are scarce, the airlines have no choice but to entice customers with lower prices.

Can you give me some examples of how to exploit weak demand and the competition between airlines?

As a rule, airlines are packed during the most popular times for business travel — which include Sunday night, Monday morning and Friday evening. It is very difficult to find a discount fare during these periods, since airlines know enough business travelers will pay full fare. Turning the tables to your advantage, you want to fly when the free-spending business travelers are harder

to find, which therefore means concentrating your travel on Tuesdays, Wednesdays and Saturdays, if possible.

Another solution is to divide your trip into two separate flights which connect in a city where airline competition is stronger than where you live. For example, say you're flying from Dallas to Los Angeles. **American Airlines** has a virtual lock on the Dallas market so they charge hefty prices on their flights to California. The cheapest one-way fare we could find on a particular day was $552.

Southwest Airlines is far more competitive out of Albuquerque, New Mexico. Instead of flying **American Airlines** all the way to L.A., take them only as far as Albuquerque and then switch airlines. On the date we checked, the fare between Albuquerque and Dallas was $89, while the **Southwest** flight to L.A. was $98, for a combined fare of only $187. By using a "split" ticket, you would have saved $365!

Split Ticket Savings	
One Ticket	
Dallas to Los Angeles	$ 552
Two Tickets	
Dallas to Albuquerque	$ 89
Albuequerque to L.A.	98
TOTAL	$ 187
One Ticket	
Philadelphia to San Francisco	$ 635
Two Tickets	
Philadelphia to Las Vegas	$ 479
LasVegas to San Francisco	75
TOTAL	$ 554

An even neater trick is a "hidden city" fare. In this example, the goal is to find a cheap flight between two cities that makes an interim stop at your true destination. You book a ticket for the entire flight, but walk off the plane during the layover. For example, say you want to fly between New York and Chicago. On the day we surveyed, the lowest unrestricted coach fare was $429 on **United Airlines**. On that same day, **US Airways** offered a $99 fare from New York to Columbus, Ohio, with a layover at Chicago's O'Hare Airport. Had you taken the **USAir** flight and de-planed at Chicago, you would have saved $330.

How can I find "split ticket" or "hidden city" opportunities?

Certain routes have more potential than others, but the air wars change so fast that any example we publish will probably be out of date by the time you read it. You can find your own bargains by trial and error, or you can subscribe to a monthly magazine that publishes the routes for you. Details are included at the end of this chapter.

What about advance purchase fares?

You will always pay less when you book your reservations in advance. The airlines figure business travelers will pay more, so they put restrictions on the cheap seats most business people won't accept—7 or 21-day advance—purchase requirements and a mandatory Saturday night stay-over.

If you need to fly in a hurry, there isn't much you can do to beat the advance-purchase requirements. However, there is a great way around the Saturday night rule. Travel veterans call it "back-to-back" ticketing, and it allows you to fly Monday–Friday without paying the business fare. What you do is buy *two*

Hidden City Savings*

Direct Flight*	
New York to Chicago	$ 429
Hidden City Flight*	
New York to Columbus via **Chicago**	$ 99
Direct Flight*	
Dallas to Atlanta	$ 436
Hidden City Flight*	
Dallas to Toronto via **Atlanta**	$ 239
Direct Flight*	
Miami to NewYork	$ 511
Hidden City Flight*	
Miami to Hartford via **New York**	$ 99
* One-way unrestricted fare	

Back-to-Back Savings*

Business Fare *(without Saturday stay)*	
Detroit to Miami	**$ 725**
Advance-Purchase Fare *(with Saturday stay)*	
Detroit to Miami (ticket #1)	$ 242
Miami to Detroit (ticket #2)	242
TOTAL FARE (2 tickets)	**$ 484**
Business Fare *(without Saturday stay)*	
Boston to San Diego	**$ 950**
Advance-Purchase Fare *(with Saturday stay)*	
Boston to San Diego (ticket #1)	$ 392
San Diego to Boston (ticket #2)	392
TOTAL FARE (2 tickets)	**$ 784**
* Based on round-trip fares	

advance-purchase fares, scheduled in opposite directions. You then use only the first half of each ticket, which corresponds to your true travel plans.

For example, instead of buying an unrestricted weekday fare between Miami and Detroit, purchase two discount tickets that both require Saturday night stays. Ticket #1 leaves Detroit Monday and returns the following week. Ticket #2 departs Miami on Thursday and returns seven days later. You use only the outbound portion of each ticket. The back-to-back strategy saves $240 compared to the unrestricted fare. Airlines try to discourage back-to-back ticketing by threatening to cancel your reservations if they discover you using the strategy. However, legal experts differ about whether the airlines have the right to deny you the right to use tickets you have legitimately purchased. In fact, there are few if any reports of the airlines actually following through on their threats. You take a small risk using a back-to-back ticket, but the rewards are probably worth it. If you are discreet, you should have no problems.

What internet sites do you recommend for airline travel?

There are dozens of sites, some of which are much better than others. If you want a good overview of schedules and fares for all the airlines at a single web address, try *Travelocity* (www.travelocity.com), *Expedia* (www.expedia.com) or the *Internet Travel Network* (www.itn.net). For last-minute domestic travel, consider signing up for weekly e-mail directly from the major airlines. You will receive a message every Tuesday or Wednesday describing travel opportunities for the upcoming weekend. As this chapter is being written, for example, our e-mail has a message from USAir touting a last-minute one-way fare from Balitimore to Los Angeles for only $89. To sign up for these services, try:

US Airways (www.usairways.com)
American Airlines (www.amrcorp.com)
Southwest Airlines (www.southwest.com)
Continental (www.flycontinental.com)
TWA (www.twa.com).

Several internet sites promise low fares by allowing you to bid on the price of your airline ticket. At *Priceline* (www.priceline.com), you choose the day you wish to travel and the price you are willing to pay. Several hours later, you get an e-mail that tells you whether your bid has been accepted. So far, we have not been very impressed by the results. Getting your answer takes way too long. Even worse, you have no option regarding your airline or time of departure. We've heard lots of horror stories about midnight departures and three-hour layovers.

Remember that with any internet site, your results depend largely on whether you understand how to manipulate airline schedules and rules to your benefit. Follow the instructions at the end of the chapter to make certain you know all the tricks.

Do the same money-saving strategies work for international flights?

Overseas flights are governed by international tariff agreements that make it harder to use the same strategies that you might on a domestic trip. To find the real bargains on flights to Europe, Asia, Latin America and the Middle East, you should first consider ticket consolidators. These rarely publicized clearinghouses buy unused tickets from airlines flying overseas and then sell them quietly at deep discount. You fly with major airlines like **Air France**, **Alitalia** and **British Air**, as well as U.S. carriers with international routes including **American, Continental** and **United**. You will find detailed instructions for contacting consolidators in the step-by-step instructions at the end of this chapter.

Consolidator Savings

Ticket Purchased from AIRLINE		Ticket Purchased from CONSOLIDATOR
$ 1,198 (American Airlines)	Dallas to Frankfurt, Germany	$ 599 (Lufthansa)
$ 1,150 (China Airlines)	San Francisco to Hong Kong	$ 720 (China Airlines)
$ 1,222 (American Airlines)	New York to Buenos Aires	$ 698 (Aerolinas Argentinas)

Many carriers are starting to use the internet in the same way they have traditionally used consolidators to dispose of unsold seats. This is especially true during winter months on flights to Europe and Asia, and summer months for Mexico, the Caribbean and the rest of Latin America. On the **United Airlines** website (www.ual.com) for example, we found a mid-winter special

fare between Washington, DC and Amsterdam for just $274, roundtrip.

Can I save even **more on an international flight?**

If you're feeling adventurous, why not be a courier? There are several well-established companies that will sell you a deeply discounted ticket to major cities in Europe, Asia, the Middle East and Latin America. The catch is that you agree to pack all the clothes you will need for your trip in carry-on luggage. The courier company then uses your normal baggage allowance for their cargo shipment. Flights are on regularly scheduled airlines with all of the usual amenities. Other than checking in with a representative of the courier company upon your arrival at the airport, your trip is totally routine. For detailed information about flying as a courier, check out the instructions at the end of the chapter.

Do you have any other money-saving tips for airline tickets?

If you are buying tickets from any source other than a consolidator for domestic or international travel, make a preliminary reservation directly with the airline to assure availability, but then contact a ticketing service that refunds to you a portion of the airline's regular travel agent commission, which can be worth 5-8% of a ticket's value. You contact the service by phone or online, then they book a new reservation and send the tickets to you by mail, along with a rebate check. In exchange, you pay a processing fee which is generally between $10 and $20 per ticket.

Reliable travel agencies include *Travel Avenue* (800-333-3335), *All-American Travel Club* (800-451-8747/ www.travel-city.com) and *Traveler's Advantage* (800-255-0200 / www.travelersadvantage.com).

How do I save money on a hotel room?

Like airlines, hotels vary their prices according to demand. The same room that goes for $175 a night when a major convention comes to town is deeply discounted (50% or more) when every hotel in the city is begging for business.

Hotels try to be discreet about their pricing tactics. After all, customers would not be very happy if when they called and inquired about the price of a room, management responded by saying "It depends. What's it worth to you?"

Instead of being so blatant, hotels use "discounts" and "promotions" (or the lack thereof) as a way of manipulating the price of a room to encourage business. On a slow night, the front desk will be more than happy to tell you about their complementary breakfast special or 25% off on a two-night stay. In fact, in these situations, you can often *negotiate* your room rate. Other times, when the management knows you can't take your business across the street, they will act as though you should be grateful for a room at any price.

Clearly, you'll never know if you can get a lower price if you don't ask. So ask! We have a few suggestions on how to pose the questions, which we've out-lined for you at the end of the chapter. You'll learn the exact dialogue to use with a reservations agent as well as what to say when you want to negotiate at the front desk.

Am I out of luck if the hotel is not in the mood to negotiate a lower price?

Not entirely. There are a few tricks you can try. For instance, hotels are notorious for quoting different prices depending on whether you phone the national toll-free reservation line or contact the hotel directly. We've seen discrepancies as high as $95 in some cases. Sometimes, the local rate is lower. In other cases, the toll-free operator has the lower price. Always try both numbers to make sure you've been quoted the best rate.

Hotel Price Discrepancies
Toll-Free Operator vs. Front Desk

Hotel	Front Desk	Toll-Free Reservation Line
Holiday Inn Washington, D.C.	$ 145 / night	$ 67 / night
Best Western Motel Telluride, CO	$ 52 / night	$ 60 / night
Hotel Nikko San Francisco, CA	$ 145 / night	$ 89 / night

You can also use the internet. At www.hoteldiscount.com and www.hotelbook.com, you can search for special rates at hotels by city and price range. You can also log on to the home pages of the major hotel chains. *Hilton Hotels* (www.hilton.com) and *Holiday Inn* (www.holiday-inn.com)

are particularly well known for posting good deals on their sites. If you don't have access to a computer, try a hotel reservation broker. They can usually help you find a discounted room over the telephone. Some of the better services include *Central Reservation Service*, *Room Exchange* and *Quickbook*. For a complete catalogue of all the discounters, check out the lists in our step-by-step guide at the end of this chapter.

I hate to negotiate, and I don't own a computer. Do you have any other suggestions for lowering the cost of a hotel room?

Yes! If you don't like to shop or negotiate, you can still save up to 50% off standard room rates by purchasing one or more discount coupon books from *Entertainment Publications* (800-445-4137/www.entertainmentbooks.com). The coupon books usually offer 2-for-1 restaurant deals, as well as discounts on hotels, car rentals and tours. The bad news is that the hotel deals are generally not available when a hotel is more than 80% full.

Another option is to join one of several travel clubs. For an annual membership fee of $60-100/yr., these clubs give you a discount card which offers the same 50% discount at hotels around the world. Some of the better travel clubs include *Travelers Advantage* (800-255-0200), *Quest International* (800-325-2400/www.questbiz.com), *Encore Travel* (800-638-8976 /www.emitravel.com) and *European Travel Network* (www.etn.nl/twocards.htm).

What about booking hotels overseas?

Timing plays a major role in the price you will pay. Try to avoid peak tourist seasons. Off-season hotel rates are often 50% to 70% less than rates during prime season, particularly at resorts in Mexico, the Caribbean and Hawaii. If you want to pay less for your room,

Off-Season Rates Around the World

UNITED STATES		EUROPE		PACIFIC		CANADA	
Alaska	May, Sept	Austria	Oct, Nov	Australia	June-Sept		May-June,
Aspen, CO	April-Nov	Belgium	May, Sept, Oct	New Zealand	April-Nov		Sept-Oct
Cape Cod	May, Sept	England	Oct-March	Tahiti	Apr-July	MIDDLE EAST	
Hawaii	June, Sept-Nov	France	May, Sept			Egypt	Oct-Nov, Feb-Mar
Key West	May-Nov	Greece	May, Oct	CARIBBEAN		Israel	Mar-May, Oct-Nov
Las Vegas	May-Sept	Italy	Apr-June, Oct	Virgin Islands	Apr-Sept		
Miami	May-Sept	Spain	May, Oct	Bahamas	Apr-Sept	FAR EAST	
New Orleans	May-Sept	Switzerland	Apr, Sept	Barbados	Apr-Sept	HongKong	Apr-May, Sep-Nov
Palm Springs	June-Aug	Scandanavia	Apr, Sept			Tokyo	May-June, Nov-Dec
Wash., D.C.	Jan-March	Germany	Apr-May, Sept-Oct	BERMUDA	Sept, Apr	Bejing	May-June
Yosemite	May, June, Sept					India	Apr-May, Sept-Oct
Disneyworld	Sept-Nov			MEXICO	May-Sept		

travel during these off-season periods as indicated in the chart on page 34.

Also try the internet. At www.hotel-wiz.com, www.ase.net and www.hotel-guide.com, you can use powerful search engines to find hotels to match your budget in almost any city in the world. These sites put a tremendous amount of information at your fingertips, allowing you to shop for the best deal quickly and efficiently.

Should I buy a tour package or put a vacation together myself?

A tour package can be less expensive that purchasing airfare, ground transportation and hotel accommodations separately. Packages are especially popular to heavily traveled destinations such as the Caribbean, Mexico, Las Vegas, Orlando and the major snow resorts in Colorado and Utah. To be sure that you are getting a good price, always compare the package price with what it would cost if you purchased airfare, hotels and transportation from other sources.

Many travel agents and web sites advertise "last-minute" tour packages which they claim are deeply discounted. Sources you might try for these last-minute specials include www.travelocity.com, *Last Minute Travel* (617-267-9800/www.vacationoutlook.com) and www.travelhub.com.

When is the best time to buy a cruise?

For years, the best way to save money on a cruise was to buy at the last minute. Many passengers would actually show up at the docks, bags in hand, hoping for an extraordinary bargain. You can still find a good deal 2-4 weeks before a ship's scheduled departure (if cabins are available), but the trend in cruise discounting is moving in the opposite direction. Today, cruise companies offer the best deals to early birds, in part to discourage last-minute buyers. If you place your reservation 8–14 months in advance, you will probably save more than at any other time before departure. In fact, the deals are so good that many of the most popular ships are sold-out many months in advance.

The best place to buy your tickets is from a travel agency that specializes in sea vacations. Because they do a high volume of cruise business, these agencies can obtain extra discounts and free cabin upgrades not available to all-purpose travel agents. In most cases, you can save an additional $150–$200 per person if you book your trip through a cruise specialist. To find out which agencies to call, consult *Cruising for Less*, a buyer's worksheet included at the end of this chapter. The worksheet also summarizes all the major cruise lines worldwide, their ships and ports-of-call.

What about an even cheaper cruise?

Try booking on a freighter. Several shipping carriers offer limited accommodations to passengers. The quality of service and meals varies, so do some advance research to make certain the trip will match your expectations. Average costs are approximately $80 per day compared to $160 – $220 per day on a regular cruise.

How can I save money on car rentals?

The best way to cut costs is by methodically checking prices from several rental agencies at your destination. It will take you about 15 minutes to get prices from five or six companies over the telephone, or you can survey all the major rental firms in 60 seconds over the internet by logging on to www.expedia.com or www.travelocity.com. You will generally find lower rates from *Enterprise Car Rental, Dollar Rent-a-Car* and *Thrifty*, although occasional specials from *Hertz* or *Avis* are equally competitive.

Once you find the lowest daily rate, keep it low by declining supplementary insurance coverage which is overpriced and usually unnecessary. Chances are you are already covered for a rental car under your regular automobile insurance policy. Check with your insurance agent to be certain before you rent.

You will find details on how to contact all the major car rental companies in the Step-by-Step Guide to Rental Car Bargains on page 52.

Guide to
AIRLINE BARGAINS

Toll-Free Reservation Numbers and Web Sites

T
R
A
V
E
L

U.S. Carriers

Air Tran
800-825-8538
www.airtran.com

Alaska Airlines
800-426-0333
www.alaska-air.com

Aloha Airlines
800-367-5250
www.alohaair.com

American Airline
800-433-7300
www.aa.com

America West
800-235-9292
www.americawest.com

Continental
800-525-0280
www.flycontinental.com

Delta
800-221-1212
www.delta-air.com

Horizon
800-547-9308
www.horizonair.com

Kiwi International
800-538-5494
www.jet.kiwi.com

Midway Airlines
800-446-4392
www.midwayair.com

Midwest Express
800-452-2022
www.midwestexpress.com

Northwest Airlines
800-225-2525
www.nwa.com

Reno Air
800-736-6247
www.renoair.com

Southwest Airlines
800-435-9792
www.iflyswa.com

TWA
800-221-2000
www.twa.com

United
800-241-6522
www.ual.com

US Airways
800-428-4322
www.usair.com

International Airlines

Aerolinas Argentinas
800-333-0276
www.aerolinas.com

Aer Lingus Ireland
800-223-6537
www.aerlingus.ie

Aero (Mexico)
800-237-6638
www.wotw.com/
aeromexico/

Air Canada
800-776-3000
www.aircanada.ca

Air France
800-237-2747
www.airfrance.com

Air India
800-223-2420
www.airindia.com

continued on next page

Toll-Free Reservation Numbers and Web Sites

International Airlines

Air Jamaica
800-523-5585
www.montego-bay-jamaica.com

Alitalia Italy
800-223-5730
www.alitalia.it

ANA Japan
800-235-9252

Avianca
800-284-2622
www.flylatinamerica.com

British Airways
800-247-9297
www.british-airways.com

Cathay Pacific
800-233-2742
www.cathayusa.com

China Airlines
800-227-5118
www.china-airlines.com

El Al (Israel)
800-223-6700
www.elal.co.il

Finnair
800-950-5000
www.finnair.com

Iberia (Spain)
800-772-4642
www.iberia.com

Icelandair
800-223-5500
www.icelandair.com

Japan Airlines
800-525-3663
www.japanair.com

KLM Holland
800-374-774
www.klm.com

Korean Air
800-438-5000

Lufthansa (Germany)
800-645-3880
www.lufthansa-usa.com

Mexicana
800-531-7921
www.mexicana.com

Philippine Air
800-435-9725
www.philippineair.com

Quantas (Australia)
800-227-4500
www.quantas.com.au

Royal Jordanian
800-223-0470
www.sita.int/rj/info/rj.html

Sabena (Belgium)
800-955-2000
www.sabena-usa.com

SAS Sweeden
800-221-2350
www.flysas.com

Singapore Air
800-742-3333
www.singaporeair.com

Swissair
800-221-4750
www.swissair.com

Thai Air
800-426-5204
www.thaiair.com

Varig (Brazil)
800-468-2744
www.varig.com.br

Virgin Atlantic
800-862-8621
www.fly.virgin.com

Web Sites for Airline Schedules & Fares

Travelocity
www.travelocity.com

Expedia
www.expedia.com

Preview Travel
www.previewtravel.com

Internet Travel Network
www.itn.com

Travelbug
www.travelbug.com

AIRLINE BARGAINS WORKSHEET

Follow these steps to identify the lowest possible airfare to your destination. Complete each step thoroughly to guarantee maximum savings.

Part I (Domestic Flights Only)

Step 1

Answer these questions:

1. **What is your destination?**

Destination: _____

2. **What are your travel dates?**

From: _____ To: _____

3. **Are you flexible in your travel plans?** (i.e., can you fly during periods of low demand such as Tuesday, Wednesday, Thursday or Saturday?)

Step 2

Call any domestic carrier and ask for a complete list of airlines which fly to your destination.
Alternatively, if you have access to the internet, log on to *Travelocity* or another appropriate site to identify schedules and fares. Remember to contact *Southwest Airlines, AirTran* and *Midway Airlines* directly if they service your departure city, since these airlines may not be listed on the general web sites. If you cannot access a computer, you can also research airline schedules by visiting your local library and asking for the latest copy of the *OAG Pocket Flight Guide*. If you are a frequent traveler, you can subscribe to the guide by contacting 800-323-3537.

Airlines to your destination:

_____

_____

_____

AIRLINE BARGAINS WORKSHEET

Step 3

Call each airline identified in Step 4 and request the least expensive fare to your destination for the travel dates you have selected.

If you are using the web sites listed on page 27, this step should be done for you once you have entered your selected itinerary.

To be certain you have not missed a last-minute bargain, you may also wish to log-on to one of the airline sites that offers e-mail notices of special discount internet fares for weekend departures. Note that these internet fares will not be identified in your regular fare search using sites like **Travelocity** or **Expedia**. You can only find them when you log on to the airline's home page and request e-mail.

Airline	Flight Number	Travel Date(s)	Round-trip Fare	One-way Fare

Step 4

Determine whether it is cost effective to buy two tickets "back-to-back," if your trip does not include a Saturday night stay.

Example: Instead of buying an unrestricted ticket from NY to LA, departing on Monday and returning on Thursday, buy two restricted tickets which require a Saturday night stay. Arrange the first ticket to depart NY on Monday, with a return at least 7 days later. Schedule the second ticket to depart LA on Thursday also returning in 7 days or more. You use the outbound leg of each ticket to duplicate a Monday–Thursday itinerary.

Airline	Round-trip Ticket Outbound	Date of Departure	Date of Return	Fare
	Return			

Combined Fare (Ticket #1 + Ticket #2): _____ .

Step 5

Determine whether you can save money using a "split" ticket.

The easiest way to find "split" tickets is to subscribe to a travel newsletter called **Best Fares.** For $58 per year, it will provide you with a revised monthly listing of "split" ticket fares to dozens of destinations across the U.S. To subscribe, call 1-800-635-3033.

If you are an infrequent traveler, you can also find your own split-ticket bargains by checking fares to and from a number of competitive airports. Savings will vary depending on the route you select and current travel demand.

To arrange a "split" ticket, buy one round-trip fare from your point of departure to a city where airline competition is greater than average. Then buy a second ticket, distinct from the first, from the competitive city to your final destination.

Example:

Ticket #1: Dallas – Phoenix
(American Airlines)

Ticket #2: Phoenix –
Los Angeles
(Southwest Airlines)

Allow at least one hour to make connections at the competitive airport. Use carry-on luggage exclusively, since suitcases must be claimed and re-checked when you change airlines.

(A) Departure to Connection

Airline	Round-trip Fare	Departs	Arrives
_____	_____	_____	_____

(B) Connection to Destination

Airline	Round-trip Fare	Departs	Arrives
_____	_____	_____	_____

Combined Fare (Ticket A + Ticket B) _____

Competitive Airports

Columbus, OH
Austin, TX
Albuequerque, NW
Newark, NJ
Houston, TX
BWI) Baltimore/Wash., DC
Kansas City, MO
New Orleans, LA
Phoenix, AZ
Providence, RI
Salt Lake City, UT
Tampa, FL
Orlando, FL
San Antonio, TX
(Midway) Chicago, IL

T
R
A
V
E
L

AIRLINE BARGAINS WORKSHEET

Step 6

Can you save money with a "hidden city" ticket?

The easiest way to identify "hidden cities" is to subscribe to Best Fares. (See step 7)

If you prefer to find hidden city fares yourself, you must identify an airline flying to a competitive airport with an interim stop at your desired destination. You exit during the layover, but do not reboard.

Example:
NY – Chicago – Columbus, OH
       (exit @ Chicago)

To find hidden cities on your own, experiment with different schedule combinations on one of the internet sites previously identified. Alternatively, call the airlines and make the following inquiry using the sample dialogue.

Outbound Airline	Outbound	Connection	Final Stop	One-way Fare
_____	_____	_____	_____	_____

Return Airline	Outbound	Connection	Final Stop	One-way Fare
_____	_____	_____	_____	_____

Total Fare (Outbound + Return) _____

Sample Dialogue

❝ *Hello. I would like to fly to (competitive airport) with a layover in (true destination). Do you have such a flight, and if so, what is the one-way fare?* **❞**

Airlines will try to stop you from using a hidden city ticket by cancelling the rest of your trip if you fail to reboard at any leg of your scheduled itinerary. To circumvent this problem, use only one-way tickets. Also, since your departure is undisclosed, you must use carryon luggage only (no checked luggage).

AIRLINE BARGAINS WORKSHEET

Step 7

Compare the prices for each fare option you have identified.

* *Special Note to Seniors:* If you are 62 or older, you may do better by purchasing senior travel vouchers. You buy discount coupons in books of 4 or 8 and use them for one-way travel within 12 months of purchase. Coupon prices vary by airline, so check each carrier for details.

Direct Fare .... _____

Back-to-Back Fare (no weekend stay) ..... _____

Split Ticket Fare .... _____

Hidden City Fare .... _____

T
R
A
V
E
L

Step 8

Once you have identified the best travel option, contact the airline directly and make a *preliminary* reservation, but do not pay for your ticket. If you are using the internet, most sites make it difficult to reserve a seat without paying at the same time.

Therefore, we suggest that you call the airline by telephone once you have the information you need from the net. The one exception would be if you have identified an internet-exclusive last-minute bargain fare from an airline's e-mail service. These last-minute deals can only be purchased via the internet.

Step 9

Call Travel Avenue (800-333-3335) and ask them if they can sell you an identical ticket for the itinerary you have chosen and rebate the travel agent commission.

If the rebate, minus the processing fee, is substantial, purchase your ticket through Travel Avenue and allow the reservation you made directly with the airline to expire. Alternatively, if the Travel Avenue rebate is not worth the extra work, call back the airline and pay for the reservation you already made. You may also buy your ticket on the airlines' web sites. Some airlines offer special bonus incentives for booking online.

Travel Dates	Airline	Asking Price	Phone #
_____	_____	_____	_____
_____	_____	_____	_____
_____	_____	_____	_____

AIRLINE BARGAINS WORKSHEET

Part II (International Flights)

Step 1

Answer these questions:

1. **What is your destination?**

   Destination: _____

2. **What are your preferred dates for travel?**

   From: _____ To: _____

3. **Which airlines fly to your destination?**

   Airlines to your destination:

   _____

   _____

   _____

   _____

   Call an international airline. Ask them for a specific list of airlines which fly directly, or with connections, to your destination. Alternatively, if you have access to the internet, log on to *Travelocity* www.travelocity.com, *Expedia* www.expedia.com or other appropriate site to identify schedules and fares. If you do not have access to a computer, consult the *OAG International Pocket Flight Guide* available at most libraries.

Step 2

Call each airline listed in Step 3 and ask them to quote you the least expensive fare to your destination based on your desired itinerary.

Airline	Flight Number	Travel Date(s)	Lowest Fare
_____	_____	_____	_____
_____	_____	_____	_____
_____	_____	_____	_____
_____	_____	_____	_____

AIRLINE BARGAINS WORKSHEET

Step 3

If you are traveling to Europe, Africa or the Middle East, it may be cheaper to fly on a low-cost carrier to London (*Virgin Atlantic*) or Luxembourg (*Icelandair*) and then make connections to your final destination.

(A) Flight to Europe

Airline	Gateway City	Travel Date(s)	Lowest Fare
_____	_____	_____	_____

B) Flight from Gateway City to Destination

Airline	Gateway City	Travel Date(s)	Lowest Fare
_____	_____	_____	_____

Step 4

After you have identified the best prices in Steps 4 & 5, contact several ticket consolidators from the list below. Ask them if they can beat the airline prices on the days you wish to travel.

Consolidator	Airline	Travel Date(s)	Lowest Fare
_____	_____	_____	_____
_____	_____	_____	_____
_____	_____	_____	_____
_____	_____	_____	_____
_____	_____	_____	_____

Consolidatators

Gateway Express
800-334-1188

PCS
800-367-8833

STA Travel
800-825-3001

Solar
800-388-7652

Travnet
800-359-6388

Interworld Travel
305-443-4929

Consumer Wholesale Travel
800-223-6862

TFI
800-745-8000

Travel Avenue
800-333-3335

Travel Hub
www.travelhub.com
Searches offerings of 100+ consolidators

AIRLINE BARGAINS WORKSHEET

Step 5

Would you be willing to travel as an air courier to save more money?
If so, contact several of the couriers listed below to inquire about rates and specific rules. Alternatively, contact *Now Voyager*, a membership organization that serves as a travel clearinghouse for many courier companies. For $50 per year, they can provide an up-to-minute summary of courier travel opportunities.

Courier	Airline	Travel Date(s)	Lowest Fare
_____	_____	_____	_____
_____	_____	_____	_____
_____	_____	_____	_____
_____	_____	_____	_____

Air Couriers

International Association of Air Couriers
561-582-8320
www.courier.org

Air Courier Association
800-822-0888
www.aircourier.org

Now Voyager
212-431-1616

International Bonded Couriers
718-526-2300

Step 6

Compare your travel options to identify the best fare.

Direct Flight _____

Connector thru Icelandair or Virgin Air (optional) _____

Consolidator Fare _____

Courier Fare (optional) _____

Step 7

If the best choice is a direct flight from the airlines, contact a ticket rebate agency listed below. Ask them if they can purchase the tickets for you at the same fare or lower and rebate the travel agent commission. If the answer is "Yes," order your ticket from them for an extra 8–10% savings.

Travel Agencies Who Rebate International Airline Commissions	
Travel Avenue	800 333-3335
Smart Traveler	800 448-3338

If your best option is a courier or consolidator, you must buy your ticket directly from these sources.

T
R
A
V
E
L

Guide to
HOTEL BARGAINS

These steps will help you find the lowest-priced hotel room at your destination. Complete all steps to be assured the lowest rates.

HOTEL BARGAINS WORKSHEET

Step 1

Answer these questions.

1. **Where do you need a room?**

City: _____

2. **When?**

From: _____ *To:* _____

Step 2

If you have access to the internet, use one of the hotel search engines to research room rates and availability based on your itinerary.

If you do not have access to a computer, or even if you want to cross-check information you received on a web site, contact one of the last-minute hotel booking services.

Hotel Finders on the Internet

Domestic Destinations

www.hoteldiscount.com
www.hotelbook.com
www.hotelwiz.com
www.travelweb.com
www.1travel.com

Overseas Destinations

www.hotelwiz.com
www.asenet.com
www.hotelguide.com

Last-Minute Hotel Discounts

Utell's Hotel Book
800-207-6900

Room Exchange
800-846-7000

Accommodations Express
800-444-7666

Hotel Reservation Network
800-964-6835

Central Reservation Service
800-950-0232

Quickbook
800-789-9887

Express Reservations (NY/LA only)
800-356-1123

San Francisco Reservations
800-333-8996

Step 3

List the 5 hotel options that are most appealing to you based upon price, location and amentities.

Hotel	Location	Rate
		$
		$
		$
		$
		$

Step 4

If you are not happy with the options based on your research so far, consider contacting a hotel chain directly either by phone or on the internet.

Sample Dialogue

❝ *Hello. Do you have any hotels in _____? I need a room for ___ nights beginning on _____. If there is a room available, what is your least expensive room rate?*

Are you offering any "specials" or other bonus discounts? How about a corporate discount? Frequent Flyer discount? Auto Club?

What will my room cost with these or other discounts?

Thank you for your assistance. I need to do a little research before I make a reservation. By the way, in case I need to contact the hotel in _____ directly, could you please tell me the direct number? Thank You. ❞

HOTEL BARGAINS WORKSHEET

Toll-Free Reservation Numbers and Web Sites

Budget Hotels

Budget Host
800-238-4678
www.budgethost.com

Comfort Inns
800-228-5150
www.comfortinn.com

Econo Lodge
800-446-6900
www.econolodge.com

Fairfield Inns
800-228-2800
www.fairfieldinn.com

Hampton Inns
800-426-7866
www.hampton-inn.com

Ibis Hotels
800-221-4542
www.ibis.com

Knight's Inn
800-722-7220
www.knightsinn.com

La Quinta Hotels
800-531-5900
www.laquinta.com

Motel 6
800-437-7486
www.motel6.com

Red Roof Inns
800-843-7663
www.redroof.com

Red Carpet
800-251-1962
www.reservahost.com

Rodeway Inns
800-228-2000
www.rodeway.com

Scottish Inns
800-251-1692
www.reservahost.com

Super 8 Hotels
800-843-1991
www.super8.com

Moderately Priced Hotels

Best Western
800-528-1234
www.bestwestern.com

Courtyard
800-321-2211
www.marriott.com

Days Inn
800-329-7466
www.daysinn.com

Doubletree Hotels
800-426-6774
www.doubletreehotels.com

Embassy Suites
800-362-2779
www.embassy-suites.com

Four Points Hotels
800-325-3535
www.sheraton.com

Howard Johnsons
800-446-4656
www.hojo.com

Holiday Inn
800-228-5151
www.holidayinn.com

Quality Inn
800-228-5151
www.hotelchoice.com

Ramada Inn
800-228-2828
www.ramada.com

Residence Inn
800-331-3131
www.marriott.com

HOTEL BARGAINS WORKSHEET

Toll-Free Reservation Numbers and Web Sites

Luxury Hotels

Clarion Hotels
800-252-7466
www.hotelchoice.com

Crowne Plaza
800-465-4329
www.crowneplaza.com

Four Seasons
800-332-3442
www.fshr.com

Hyatt Hotels
800-228-9000
www.hyatt.com

Hilton Hotels
800-445-8667
www.hilton.com

Intercontinental Hotels
800-327-0200
www.interconti.com

Marriott
800-228-9290
www.marriott.com

Radisson Hotels
800-333-3333
www.radisson.com

Renaissance Hotels
800-228-9898
www.renaissanceho-tels.com

Ritz Carlton
800-241-3333
www.ritzcarlton.com

Sheraton Hotels
800-325-3535
www.sheraton.com

Westin Hotels
800-228-3000
www.westin.com

Wyndham Hotels
800-996-3426
www.wyndham.com

Step 5

After getting a rate quote from the toll-free operator or via the web, call the local number for the same hotel(s) and repeat step 4. Is there any price difference?

Hotel	Toll-Free Rate	Front Desk Rate
_____	$_____	$_____
_____	$_____	$_____
_____	$_____	$_____

Step 6

Make your reservation from the source that quotes you the best rate.

Step 7

If you have no reservation and arrive at a hotel in the evening, negotiate your room rate using the following suggestions:

The best time to negotiate is from 6 pm to midnight. Be pleasant but firm. You can usually expect at least a 30% discount unless the hotel is full. Be prepared to go to another hotel if you don't like the final rate you're quoted.

Sample Dialogue

" *Hello. Do you have any rooms available for this evening? I was planning to go to a less expensive hotel, but you were closer. What is the room rate? (_____) That's more than I really planned on paying. I would like to stay here, but it's a little overpriced for me. Would you consider $ _____. (40–50% less than the final rate they quote you)*

(If the clerk refuses) Well, can't you do better? How about some sort of discount? What is your best discounted rate? "

Step 8

If you travel frequently, you may want to consider joining a Travel Club. With most clubs, membership entitles you to a 50% discount on standard room rates or a second night free. Offerings vary, so check with several clubs to find one that matches your tastes and budget.

Travel Clubs

Travelers Advantage 800-255-0200 (www.travelersadvantage.com)	$59/yr. (first 3 months free)	50% off standard rates in 4,000 hotels world-wide.
Quest International 800-325-2400 (www.questbiz.com)	$49/yr. (30 days free)	50% discount off standard rates in 2,200 mid-priced hotels.
Encore Travel 800-638-8976 (www.emitravel.com)	$59/yr.	50% discount or second night free at 18,000 hotels worldwide.
European Travel Network	$69/yr.	50% discount on 10,000 hotels

Guide to
CRUISING FOR LESS

This worksheet will help you to save on the cruise of your choice. Generally, you save on cruises when you book far in advance (6–8 months) or 30–45 days before departures. Late buyers often get free upgrades to larger, more comfort-able rooms in addition to cash discounts. For the very best deals, we encourage you to be flexible, taking advantage of exceptional bargains on whatever ship is offering them.

CRUISE BARGAINS WORKSHEET

Step 1

Answer these questions:

1. **Where would you like to visit?**

2. **What are your preferred travel dates?** Remember that the best deals are available far in advance or just before departure.

3. **What length of cruise do you prefer?**

4. **Do you have a cruise line in mind?**

   See the listings in the Cruise Lines of the World chart on pages 45-46, con-sult a cruise directory at your local bookstore or library or use a web site such as www.travelpage.com.

PORTS OF CALL:

_____   _____
_____   _____
_____   _____

TRAVEL DATES: _____

                        _____

NUMBER OF DAYS: _____

SPECIFIC CRUISE LINES _____

                        _____

                        _____

CRUSE BARGAINS WORKSHEET

5. Do you have a preference for the location of your cabin?

- Inside cabins without a view are cheapest.

- Choose mid-ship or aft locations if you are prone to seasickness.

- Prices rise as you move higher in the ship.

- Don't agonize over your cabin; you won't spend much time there anyway.

PREFERRED CABIN LOCATION _____

Step 2

Contact several of the cruise discounters listed in this worksheet. Cruise discount specialists have access to lower prices than typical travel agencies because of their high volume. Contact more than one agency, since prices will vary even among discounters. Always ask for rate quotes "with" and "without" air transportation. In many cases, you will save money arranging your own air travel. In general, the best discounts are available between September and mid-December.

SEE "CRUISE COMPARISON WORKSHEET" ON NEXT PAGE

SEE "CRUISE COMPARISON WORKSHEET" ON NEXT PAGE

Cruise Discount Specialists

All Cruise Travel
800-227-8473
www.allcruise.com

Cruise Adventures
800-545-8118
www.cruiseadventures.com

Cruises Inc.
800-854-0500
www.cruisesinc.com

Odessa America
800-221-3254
www.odessamerica.com

Spur of the Moment
800-343-1991

The Cruise Line
800-777-0707
www.cruiseline.com

World Wide Cruises
800-882-9000
www.cruises.com

CRUISE BARGAINS WORKSHEET

	Cruise #1	Cruise #2	Cruise #3	Cruise #4
Discounter				
Cruise Line				
Ship				
Duration				
Where to				
Dates				
Cabin Type/Location				
Cruise Price				
Airfare Supplement				
Total Price				

Step 3

After you have identified your best deal, consider contacting *Cruise Club of America* (800-982-2276/ www.travelcity.com). Ask them to quote you a fare for the identical itinerary.

For a 1-year membership fee of $29 and a $35 fee per passenger, Cruise Club will rebate the travel agent commission for each ticket. If Cruise Club can't beat the deal you have already identified, make your purchase through your original source.

Step 4

Consider freighter travel, if you are looking for a more relaxed and less expensive way to cruise. Most **freighters cost $100/day or less and offer gourmet cuisine, large cabins and plenty of solitude.**

Information Sources for Freighter Travel

Freighter World Cruises
626-449-3106
www.freighterworld.com

Maris Freighter Cruises
800-996-2747
www.cruisemaris.com

Polynesian Freighter Co.
800-972-7268
www.aranui.com

Ivarian Lines
800-451-1639
www.ivarian.com

Bergen Line
800-323-7436

CRUSE BARGAINS WORKSHEET

Cruise Lines of the World

Admiral Cruises
www.admiralcruises.com
Casual atmosphere
Bahamas, Caribbean, Mexico

American Canadian Caribbean
www.accl-smallships.com
Informal, small ships
Caribbean, Canada

Carnival Cruise Lines
www.carnival.com
Mass market, big & loud
Caribbean, Europe

Clipper Cruise Line
www.clipper.com
Small ships,
historic programs
All-American crews
Canada, East Coast,
Pacific NW, Antarctic

Commodore Cruise Line
www.newatlantis.com
Short cruises, simple
and friendly
Caribbean

Costa Cruises
www.costacruises.com
Italian atmosphere,
European crowd
Caribbean, Greece,
Mediterranean
Europe, South America

Celebrity Cruises
www.celebrity-cruises.com
Upscale, mid-size ships
Bermuda, Alaska,
South America, Caribbean,
Europe

Disney Cruises
www.disney.com
Family-oriented,
Disneyworld packages
Caribbean

Crystal Cruise Lines
www.cruisecrystal.com
Very upscale
Worldwide

Cunard Lines
www.cunardline.com
Upscale. tradition reigns
Worldwide

Delta Queen Cruises
www.deltaqueen.com
Riverboat cruises
Mississippi River

Royal Olympic Cruises
www.royalolympiccruise.com
Greek crews adventurous
Greece, Baltic, Amazon,
Caribbean, South America,
Mediterranean

Holland America Cruise Line
www.hollandamerica.com
Good value, no tipping
Alaska, Caribbean, Europe,
Orient

Norwegian Cruise Line
www.ncl.com
Theme cruises, classic
experience, highly-rated
entertainment
Caribbean, Alaska,
Mediterranean, Mexico

Premier Cruise Line
www.premiercruises.com
Smaller ships, family-
Caribbean oriented, South
America

Princess Cruises
www. princesscruises.com
"The Love Boat"
Worldwide

Radisson Cruise Line
www.rssc.com
Formal, upscale
Worldwide

Renaissance Cruises
www.renaissancecruises.com
Ultra luxury, small yachts
Worldwide

continued on next page

TRAVEL

CRUISE BARGAINS WORKSHEET

Cruise Lines of the World

Royal Caribbean
www.royalcaribbean.com
All ages and tastes, big ships
Caribbean, Europe, Alaska
Mexico, South America

Seabourne Cruises
www.seabourne.com
Ultra luxury, all suites,
Worldwide

Silver Sea Cruises
800-722-995
Ultra luxury, all suites
private verandas
Worldwide

Windstar Sail Cruises
www.windstarcruises.com
Excellent cuisine, big sails,
water sports
Caribbean, Tahiti,
Mediterranean

Windjammer Cruises
www.windjamer.com
Very informal, older
sailing boats
Caribbean

Guide to DISCOUNT TOURS & LAST-MINUTE TRAVEL

Last-Minute Travel Sources Airfares (E-Mail Notices)

US Airways
www.usairways.com

American Airlines
www.amrcorp.com

Southwest Airlines
www.southwest.com

Continental
www.flycontinental.com

TWA
www.twa.com

One Travel Place
800-621-5505
www.1travel.com

Tour Packages

All-American Travel Club*
800-451-8747
www.travel.city.com

Frommers Travel
www.frommers.com

Last-Minute Travel
617-267-9800
www.vacationoutlet.com

One Travel Place
800-621-5505
www.1travel.com

 * Free 30-day membership
 ** $49/yr.

Travelers' Advantage**
800-548-1116
www.travelersadvantage.com

Vacation Hotline
800-325-2485
www.caribbeanmagic.com

This worksheet will help you to locate last-minute travel bargains and tour packages, and help you to determine just how good these deals really are.

Because last-minute deals become available on short notice, using the internet is the best source for information. The airlines listed above, for example, will send you weekly e-mail messages highlighting weekend specials which are only available via the internet.

For travel which includes airfare and hotel accomodations, try one of the tour package specialists listed on page 47 by phone or via the internet.

When you have identified one or more travel opportunities which appeal to you, review the terms and conditions for answers to the following questions.

TRAVEL & TOURS BARGAINS WORKSHEET

Step 1

Answer these questions	Package #1	Package #2	Package #3
1. What is the tour itinerary?	_____ _____ _____	_____ _____ _____	_____ _____ _____
2. What are the travel dates and departure times?	_____	_____	_____
3. How many nights will you actually spend at your destination?	# of nights _____	# of nights _____	# of nights _____
4. What is included in the package?	__ Airfare __ Hotel __ Ground Trans. __ Meals __ Tours __ Rental Car __ Other	__ Airfare __ Hotel __ Ground Trans. __ Meals __ Tours __ Rental Car __ Other	__ Airfare __ Hotel __ Ground Trans. __ Meals __ Tours __ Rental Car __ Other
5. How much does the package cost?	$ _____	$ _____	$ _____
6. What is the cost per night? (cost ÷ number of nights)	$ _____ /night	$ _____ /night	$ _____ /night

TRAVEL & TOURS BARGAINS WORKSHEET

	Package #1	Package #2	Package #3
7. Is the package price per person, based on double occupancy, or is the price the same if you travel alone?	__ Double Occupancy?	__ Double Occupancy?	__ Double Occupancy?
8. If airfare is included, is it from your home town or must you pay extra for a connection?	$_____ Air Surcharge *(if any)*	$_____ Air Surcharge *(if any)*	$_____ Air Surcharge *(if any)*
9. What is the cheapest airfare you could find if you arranged the trip yourself? (For step-by-step instructions, see **Guide to Airline Bargains.**)	$_____	$_____	$_____
10. What is the name of the hotel where you will be staying?	_____	_____	_____
11. Do you know anything about the location or the quality of the room?	_____	_____	_____
12. Are there any terms in the tour package indicating where your room is located? (*ocean view, lower floors, etc.*)	_____	_____	_____
13. Are any recreational activities you are looking forward to, such as golf or tennis, included in the package, or do they cost extra?	$_____ Additional Charge	$_____ Additional Charge	$_____ Additional Charge
14. If you make your own hotel reservation(s), what would your stay cost per night? (For step-by-step instructions, see **Guide to Airline Bargains.**)	_____	_____	_____

T
R
A
V
E
L

TRAVEL & TOURS BARGAINS WORKSHEET

	Package #1	Package #2	Package #3
15. Is the price the same for one or two people?	Yes / No	Yes / No	Yes / No
16. Are any meals included in the tour package? 17. At what hour is each meal served?	*Hour served* ❏ brkfst: _____ ❏ lunch: _____ ❏ dinner: _____	*Hour served* ❏ brkfst: _____ ❏ lunch: _____ ❏ dinner: _____	*Hour served* ❏ brkfst:_____ ❏ lunch:_____ ❏ dinner:_____
18. Can you get a credit if you do not eat all of your meals at the hotel?	_____ Meal Credits?	_____ Meal Credits?	_____ Meal Credits?
19. What do you estimate you would spend at restaurants, if you arranged your own meals?	$_____	$_____	$_____
20. Are guided tours or other activities included in the package price?	_____ Tours?	_____ Tours?	_____ Tours?
21. Would you buy these tours separately, if they were not included in the package?	Yes / No	Yes / No	Yes / No
22. Is ground transportation to and from the airport included in the package?	Yes / No	Yes / No	Yes / No
23. What would it cost to travel from the airport if you arranged your own transportation?	$_____	$_____	$_____
24. Are there any other activities included in the package?	_____ _____ _____	_____ _____ _____	_____ _____ _____
25. Would you choose to pay for any of these activities separately, if they were not included in the package?	Yes / No	Yes / No	Yes / No

TRAVEL & TOURS BARGAINS WORKSHEET

	Package #1	Package #2	Package #3
26. Is the package price guaranteed, or is it subject to change without notice?	__ Fixed __ Subject to Change	__ Fixed __ Subject to Change	__ Fixed __ Subject to Change
27. Is there a cancellation penalty if you do not make the trip?	Cancellation Penalty	Cancellation Penalty	Cancellation Penalty

Step 2

Compare the price of the tour package to the cost of arranging a similar trip yourself.

When making comparisons, do not attempt to duplicate the package exactly. Put your own vacation together based on your own tastes and budget, omitting any package extras you would not purchase yourself.

	Package #1	Package #2	Package #3
a) Airfare (see #9).................................	$	$	$
b) Hotel (see #14)..................................	$	$	$
c) Meals, if any (see # 19).....................	$	$	$
d) Transportation, if any (see #23).........	$	$	$
e) Tours, if any	$	$	$
f) Other...	$	$	$
g) Total expenses on your own..............	$	$	$
h) Cost per night...................................	$ ___ /night	$ ___ /night	$ ___ /night
i) Package Price per night (see #6).......	$ ___ /night	$ ___ /night	$ ___ /night
j) Best Deal?			

Guide to RENTAL CAR BARGAINS

This worksheet will help you save on your next car rental by identifying the best rates at competing car rental agencies. Since rates vary significantly in every market, it is a good idea to contact as many companies as possible.

Car Rental Reservations

Rate quotes from a single source:

Expedia
www.expedia.com

Travelocity
www.travelocity.com

Preview Travel
www.previewtravel.com

Rental Agencies:

Alamo
800-327-9633
www.goalamo.com

Dollar
800-424-1282
www.dollarcar.com

Payless
800-729-5377
www.800-payless.com

Avis
800-331-1212
www.avis.com

Hertz
800-654-3131
www.hertz.com

Thrifty
800-367-2277
www.thrifty.com

Budget
800-527-0700
www.budgetrentacar.com

National
888-CAR-RENT
www.nationalcar.com

Step 1

Use the phone numbers listed above to research prices. If you have access to the internet, you can get all the information you need in less than one minute by logging on to one of the major travel web sites (www.previewtravel.com, www.travelocity.com, or www.expedia.com). Simply click on the car rental icon, identify the city, class of automobile and dates you will need the car and you will get an immediate price quote from **Hertz, Avis, Dollar** and all the other major firms.

Step 2

When making your reservation, remember to:

- Decline unnecessary insurance coverage;

- Refuse the "gasoline purchase option" and return the car with a full tank of gas;

- Check on any surcharges for additional drivers, drop-off charges, mileage charges, and airport fees.

Step 3

If you are traveling overseas, reserve your car before you leave the U.S. You will save at least 50% on the rental rate compared to what you will pay if you wait to make your reservation abroad.

Step 4

For the best deals, consider one of several travel agencies that specialize in overseas car rentals at wholesale prices:

Auto Europe
800-223-5555
www.autoeurope.com

DER Travel Service
800-937-1234
www.dertravel.com

Step 5

Consider these before you rent:

- Make sure the prices you are quoted are guaranteed in U.S. dollars;

- Be certain to inquire about mileage charges, drop-off fees, insurance requirements and licensing terms;

- Remember that the smallest cars are likely to be extremely small (two passengers/little luggage capacity) and will have neither air conditioning nor an automatic transmission; and

- Think about starting your trip in a country where rates and taxes are cheapest. The same subcompact that will cost you $150/wk. in Belgium will cost nearly $300 in Sweeden.

T
R
A
V
E
L

RENTAL CAR BARGAINS WORKSHEET

	Package #1	Package #2	Package #3
Company	_____	_____	_____
Daily Rate	_____	_____	_____
Weekly Rate	_____	_____	_____
Weekend Rate	_____	_____	_____
Mileage Charge?	_____	_____	_____
Second Driver Charge?	_____	_____	_____
Late Charge	_____	_____	_____
Airport Service	_____	_____	_____
How far is drop-off site from airport?	_____	_____	_____
Any bargain or promotional rates?	_____	_____	_____

Best Choice _____

HERE'S THE

 Here's the proof that our hidden travel secrets really work. For each suggestion noted, we surveyed the market for the lowest fares available using conventional sources, and then we set out to beat those prices with instructions from our worksheets. All inquiries were made on April 29, 1992.

Travel Suggestion: Use a "Split Ticket" instead of flying direct.

Example: One-way trip from NY to Houston, May 9, 1992.

Lowest Direct Fare	Best Split-Ticket Fare
$ 590 (Delta Airlines)	$ 238 NY to New Orleans (American Airlines)
	$ 289 New Orleans to Houston (Southwest Airlines)
SAVINGS:	$ 142

Travel Suggestion: Use a "Hidden City" instead of flying direct.

Example: One-way trip from St. Louis to Denver, May 15, 1992.

Lowest Direct Fare	Best Hidden-City Fare
$ 358 (Continental Airlines)	$ 187 (Continental Airlines) St. Louis–Denver–Phoenix
SAVINGS:	$ 171

Travel Suggestion: Use a "Back-to-Back" Ticket to avoid Saturday night stay rules.

Example: Round-trip between Las Vegas and Detroit, Departs Detroit, Monday, May 18, 1992. Returns to Detroit, Thursday, May 21, 1992.

Best Fare Without Mandatory Saturday Night Stay	Best Back-to-Back Fare
$ 1,066 (Northwest Airlines)	Detroit–Las Vegas–Detroit $ 428 Las Vegas–Detroit–Las Vegas $ 428 Total Fare for 2 Tickets $ 856
SAVINGS:	$ 210

Travel Suggestion: Buy international airline tickets from a consolidator.

Example: Round-trip from New York to Rome.

Lowest Airline Fare	Lowest Consolidator Fare
$ 1,074 Delta Airlines	$ 440 Alitalia (via Airlink Travel)
SAVINGS:	$ 634

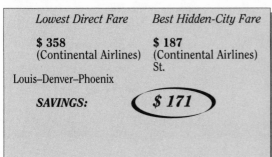

TRAVEL

Travel Suggestion: Fly as an international courier.

Example: Round-trip flight from New York to Singapore.

Lowest Consolidator Fare	Lowest Courier Fare
$ 449 Singapore Airlines via TFI Travel	$ 290 Singapore Airlines via Now Voyager
SAVINGS:	$ 159

Travel Suggestion: Buy airline tickets through a travel agency that rebates airline commissions.

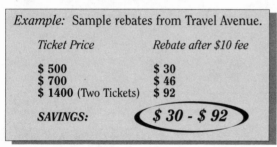

Example: Sample rebates from Travel Avenue.

Ticket Price	Rebate after $10 fee
$ 500	$ 30
$ 700	$ 46
$ 1400 (Two Tickets)	$ 92
SAVINGS:	$ 30 - $ 92

Travel Suggestion: Join a travel club for hotel discounts.

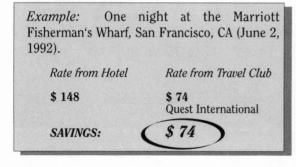

Example: One night at the Marriott Fisherman's Wharf, San Francisco, CA (June 2, 1992).

Rate from Hotel	Rate from Travel Club
$ 148	$ 74 Quest International
SAVINGS:	$ 74

Travel Suggestion: Negotiate for a low-priced hotel room after 8 pm.

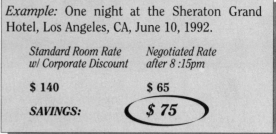

Example: One night at the Sheraton Grand Hotel, Los Angeles, CA, June 10, 1992.

Standard Room Rate w/ Corporate Discount	Negotiated Rate after 8 :15pm
$ 140	$ 65
SAVINGS:	$ 75

Travel Suggestion: Plan vacation stays to take advantage of hotels low-season rates.

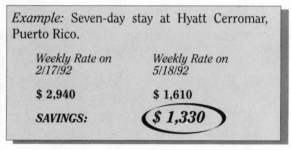

Example: Seven-day stay at Hyatt Cerromar, Puerto Rico.

Weekly Rate on 2/17/92	Weekly Rate on 5/18/92
$ 2,940	$ 1,610
SAVINGS:	$ 1,330

Travel Suggestion: Use a high-volume travel agency that specializes in sea vacations to reserve a cruise.

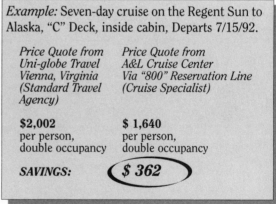

Example: Seven-day cruise on the Regent Sun to Alaska, "C" Deck, inside cabin, Departs 7/15/92.

Price Quote from Uni-globe Travel Vienna, Virginia (Standard Travel Agency)	Price Quote from A&L Cruise Center Via "800" Reservation Line (Cruise Specialist)
$2,002 per person, double occupancy	$ 1,640 per person, double occupancy
SAVINGS:	$ 362

Travel Suggestion: Call *all* the car rental companies to identify the lowest rental rate at your destination.

Example: Four-day car rental from Cleveland Airport on May 5, 1992 (mid-size automobile).

Alamo	$ 141.96	
Avis	188.00	Most expensive
Budget	147.84	
Dollar	123.60	Least expensive
Thrifty	135.52	
Hertz	163.96	
National	147.60	

SAVINGS: **$ 64.40**
(Dollar vs. Avis)

Chapter Three

How to Buy Quality Fashions for Less

Whenever I go shopping for clothes, there are always sales, but rarely any bargains. Is it my imagination, or is something fishy going on?

It isn't your imagination. When it comes to clothing, the word "sale" has become meaningless. Department stores and other fashion retailers routinely overprice their merchandise, then take markdowns to create the *illusion* of value.

To illustrate, let's say department store "x" normally prices a wool sweater at $40. To hype customer interest, they pre-price the garment at $50, then immediately offer a sale at 20% off. The net price is still $40, but shoppers think they are getting a bargain.

Phony discounting is a fact of life at every level of fashion retailing. Outlet malls are just as guilty as the upscale clothiers. In fact, the practice is so widespread we advise that you ignore discount claims entirely.

If I can't rely on the word "SALE," how do I spot bargains?

First, keep in mind that price alone rarely guarantees a bargain. A $100 men's suit certainly costs less than a $250 model, but the cheap suit is not necessarily a better value.

The True Cost of Quality	
$ 100 Suit	**$ 250 Suit**
Useful Life: 1 Year	Useful Life: 5 Years
Cost to Own: $ 100/yr	Cost to Own: $ 50/yr

Low-priced merchandise is often poorly constructed and made from inferior-quality fabrics. Chances are, the $100 suit will last only one or two seasons before it wears out. The better-quality suit, even though it costs twice the price, will perform for at least 5-10 years. Viewed this way, the higher-priced suit is a better *deal*.

True bargains are a combination of quality and value. To find them, learn the features that distinguish superior clothing. Buy when these better garments are discounted.

How can I spot high-quality clothes?

One of the easiest tests for quality is to read the fabric label. Quality clothes are almost always made with natural fibers such as *wool, cotton* or *silk*. These natural fibers are incredibly durable, plus they have a soft, rich look that no chemist has yet duplicated. It is best to avoid manmade fibers, except in fabric blends containing at least 50% natural fibers.

Another simple way to judge a garment is to inspect the quality of craftsmanship. Well-made clothes have tight, even seams and firmly secured buttons. Fabric patterns, such as pinstripes or prints, also align perfectly at the crotch, shoulders, waist, etc.

In many cases, you can learn to spot quality garments faster if you become familiar with how they look and feel. To practice, go to a department store and try on their most expensive shirt, pants, suit, dress, etc. Feel the fabric. Examine the workmanship. Now, try on the cheapest garment in the department. Note the contrasts. Over time, you'll be able to spot quality clothing instantly.

When is the best time to find quality merchandise at low prices?

It stands to reason that the best time to buy anything is when supplies are high and demand is low. With clothing, this means buying at the *end* of a fashion season. Few people, for example, want a winter coat at the first signs of spring, so that is precisely when the buying opportunities are best. Stores must make room for the next season's shipments so they cut prices of their remaining stock to the absolute minimum. By waiting for the end-of-season clearances, you'll save 30-40%, whether you shop at K-Mart or

Saks 5th Avenue. If you buy timeless styles and colors, your purchases will be every bit as fashionable next year.

Fashion Seasons		When to Buy
Winter	*(October-January)*	mid February
Spring	*(February-April)*	early May
Summer	*(May-July)*	mid August
Fall	*(August-October)*	late October

Where is the best place to shop?

It all depends on how much time you have and how good a deal you want. Your options include the usual mall shops and department stores, outlet centers, internet web sites, mail-order catalogues and consignment boutiques.

By far, the largest selection and most consistent quality can be found at the mall. It can also be a decent place for bargains, but you must be certain to restrict your shopping to the after-season clearance sales. During other times of the year, mall stores are likely to have the highest prices of all your shopping options.

If you can't time your purchases to coincide with the big sales from the major retailers, the next-best option would be outlet centers where you can still find decent inventory and lower everyday pricing. Beware, however, that quality at outlet stores can be an issue, so examine every garment carefully for flaws and imperfections.

Internet sites for major retailers are the cyberspace equivalent to outlet stores. In fact, there are few retailers who don't have internet addresses where you can shop for at least a limited selection of what you would otherwise find in a regular store (see the Internet Resource Guide included in this chapter). There are limitations to buying clothes on the internet, however. Selection can be a real problem. Most sites limit you to a handful of choices in a given category. In addition, it is extremely time consuming to use the internet if you're only browsing. Downloading a description of each garment can be a real chore, and you can't tell much from the small pictures. Best to use the web when you know exactly what you're after – a pair of **Dockers** or **Levis** in a certain size and color, for example. In most cases, you can expect to pay on the internet what you would if you visited a factory store in an outlet mall, but remember that you have to factor in the cost of shipping and handling – plus the added cost and inconvenience if a garment doesn't look or fit right.

Catalogues are more convenient than shopping on the web since it is much easier to browse without waiting for constant downloads. Convenience comes at a price, however. It costs lots of money to design, print and mail brochures, which is why an item in a catalogue is almost never cheaper than what you would pay if you bought it in a regular store. The fixed costs of catalogue marketing make it unlikely you will find many items "on sale," and you always need to factor in shipping costs as well.

If convenience is not a factor, your best option for the lowest prices will almost always be consignment stores – boutiques which specialize in the resale of high-quality, previously worn fashions. These are not thrift stores for hand-me-downs. At consignment stores, you can find better-quality suits, overcoats, dresses, accessories — even furs — at unheard-of prices. That's because these clothes are not worn-out relics donated to charity. They are first-rate items sold by their original owners. Many consignment items have been worn for only one season by their usually affluent owners. The consignment store acts as a middleman, receiving a commission when the garment is sold.

It is not unusual to find men's suits, which originally sold for $500 or more, priced at $150. The better the garment, the more likely it will eventually find its way to a consignment shop. The only drawback to these stores – and it can be a big one – is that the selection is never predicable. Because every garment on consignment is unique, you must not only find a garment you like, but also one that fits. One way around the problem is to become familiar with the consignment store's manager. Once they know your size and needs, many are quite willing to call you when interesting merchandise arrives.

You don't sound very enthusiastic about outlet malls and factory stores. Don't they have the lowest prices?

Outlet malls were once a consistent source for bargains. That's because the outlets were a legitimate way for manufacturers to quietly dispose of their excess merchandise without competing against their largest customers— department stores.

Regrettably, what started out as a simple idea has now become big business. Outlet malls are opening at double the rate of traditional shopping centers. In some cases, there are too many malls for the limited amount of discounted merchandise. To keep up with demand, many manufacturers now make products specifically for their outlet stores. In many cases, this "outlet merchandise" is lower priced than what you would find in a department store because the manufacturer has made subtle changes in the quality of the fabrics and the quality of construction. The garments may look the same as the mall merchandise, but it won't hold up as well after a few visits to the washer and dryer.

That isn't to say that some outlet stores aren't a good source of bargains and that some of the merchandise you will find is exactly the same as what is selling in retail stores. The point is that you've got to know labels, fabric content and retail prices if you want to identify real bargains and ignore the junk.

Is the internet changing the way we buy clothes?

The market for selling fashions on the internet is clearly growing, but it is more likely that the web sites will eventually replace printed catalogues than supplant regular stores. That's because shopping for clothes is a visual and tactile experience best done in person. You can't judge the quality of a stitch, the feel of a fabric, or the fit of a sleeve unless you're wearing it! For that reason alone, the vast majority of clothing sales will always be made in person.

Technology is improving to the point that within a few years, vendors will be able to reproduce entire catalogs on the web and display them in a page format similar to a high-quality magazine. The web alternative is so much more cost effective than printing and mailing catalogues that the hard-copy versions will one day be obsolete.

If you are looking for good deals on the web right now, there are a few sites worth exploring. **Designer Direct** (www.designerdirect.com) and **Designer Outlet** (www.designeroutlet.com) are excellent sources for designer overstocks of merchandise from **Calvin Klein, Ralph Lauren, Guess,** etc. at 25-30% off retail.

The web is also great for ordering everyday items like underwear, bras and hosiery, since everyone is familiar with the major brands and the products are more like commodities than unique statements of fashion. Both **L'eggs** (www.pantyhose.com) and **Hanes** (www.onehanesplace.com) have excellent sites where you can save 30-50% off retail prices. You can find similar deals on **No Nonsense** hosiery at (www.legwear.com). One of the best overall sources for bras, socks, underwear and hosiery is the **Chock Catalog** (www.chockcatalog.com), a New York specialty discounter that has been in business for more than half a century.

All of the major retail stores have web sites, including the **Gap** (www.gap.com), **Eddie Bauer** (www.eddiebauer.com) and **Benetton** (www.benetton.com). As we have previously mentioned, selection at these sites is rather limited, but should improve over time. Pricing isn't much better than at the outlet stores or in a mall, but you can save time and aggravation if you know exactly what you're looking for.

A truly amazing site can be found at Piece Unique (www.pieceunique.com). This is an online source for top-of-the-line *haute couture* fashions from **Armani, Chanel, Versace, Prada, Valentino** and **Donna Karan**. We're talking stuff like dress ensembles that retail for $2,000 and up. The twist is that Piece Unique sells items that have been previously worn – often by models in fashion shows in Milan, Rome, Paris and London. That same $2,000 Armani blazer might sell for $700 through Piece Unique – still a hefty sum, but a relative bargain nevertheless.

Are there special rules to follow when buying clothes for kids?

Forget everything you've learned about adult clothing when it is time to buy for children. Easy-care fabrics and durability should be your most important considerations. Polyester and polyester/cotton blends are better for moms and kids since they resist stains and need less ironing than 100% natural fibers.

Markups on children's clothing are especially high at department stores and speciality shops. End-of-season clearance prices are also less appealing. For kids' clothes, your best shopping alternatives are mass retailers such as K-Mart or Walmart. Consignment stores are also an excellent source of bargains, since children outgrow their clothes so quickly.

Clothing Internet Resources

Underwear & Hosiery

Hanes
800-222-0020
www.onehanesplace.com
40-60% discount on regular and irregular hosiery

L'eggs
800-543-1028
www.pantyhose.com
40-60% discount on regular and irregular hosiery

No Nonsense
800-677-5995
www.legwear.com
25-40% discount on regular and irregular hosiery

Chock Catalog
800-222-0020
www.chockcatalog.com
N.Y. discount prices on bras, undergarments and hosiery

Catalog Resources

Catalog City
www.catalogcity.com
Choose from more than 1,000 catalogues in every conceivable shopping category

Catalog Finder
www.catalogfinder.com
Does just what the name implies

Catalog Site
www.catalogsite.com
Order hundreds of mail-order catalogs free

Fashion Trends

Designer Collections
www.firstview.com
View more than 10,000 photos from designer collections as seen at the major shows in Paris, Milan, London and New York

Advice
www.stylexperts.com
Up-to-the-minute suggestions on what's hot in fashion and how to create "the look"

More Advice
www.lookonline.com
Photos, the latest news and everything you need to know about the latest sytles

Discount Designer Fashions

Designer Direct
www.designerdirect.com
25-30% off retail prices for Calvin Klein, Ralph Lauren, DKNY, Guess, Levis, Tommy Hilfiger, etc.

Designer Outlet
www.designeroutlet.com
Top-name designer overstocks at greatly reduced prices

QVC
www.iqvc.com
The best deals from one of the best sources for discounted fashions

Women's Formalwear
www.shop.shop.com/milano/
50% off prices direct from the manufacturer

Haute Couture
www.pieceunique.com
Online source of new and pre-owned luxury designer garments from the best resale boutiques in the world. This is the place where to find a $3,000 Chanel suit worn once by a model in Paris for $700. Designers include Armani, Versace, Prada, Valentino and Donna Karan.

Department Stores/Catalogs

Bloomingdales
www.bloomingdales.com
Limited selection and not as much fun as being there in person

Nordstrom's
www.nordstrom.com
One of the better web sites among the larger stores

Macy's
www.macys.com
Very similar to the Bloomingdales site in terms of selection and ease of use.

Neiman-Marcus
www.neimanmarcus.com
Not the place to look if you're trying to find a bargain

May Stores
www.maycompany.com
More of a resource than a place to buy for the chain which owns Hechts, Lord & Taylor, Strawbridge & Clothiers, May Company, Filene's Basement and Foley's

Sears
www.sears.com
Still a work in progress and nothing like the old Sears catalog. Easier to buy a set of socket wrenches than a new dress.

Spiegel
www.spiegel.com
The leading mail-order catalog also leads the way online

J.C. Penney
www.jcpenney.com
Better than Sears but not as good as Spiegel

Virtual Mall

Benetton
www.benetton.com

Brooks Brothers
www.brooksbrothers.com

Bugle Boy
www.bugleboy.com

Dockers
www.dockers.com

Eddie Bauer
www.eddiebauer.com

continued on next page

Virtual Mall continued

Espirit
www.espirit.com

Gap
www.gap.com

Guess
www.guess.com

Hugo Boss
www.hugo.com

J. Crew
http://jcrew.com

L.L. Bean
www.llbean.com

Landsend
www.landsend.com

Lee
www.leejeans.com

Levis
www.levi.com

Liz Claiborne
www.lizclaiborne.com

Nicole Miller
www.nicolemiller.com

Nike
www.nike.com

Victoria's Secret
www.victoriassecret.com

Specialty

Surfwear
www.oceanpacific.com
Surfing apparel

Dancewear
www.mondor.com
Leotards, leggings, etc.

Fitnesswear
www.look-it.com
Tights, shorts, T's, sweats

Pro Team Wear
www.logosports.com
NFL, NBA, NHL, MLB clothing

Outdoor Wear
www.theoutdoor.com
Hiking, camping, climbing, fishing, hunting clothes

Step by Step

Guide to BUYING MEN'S & WOMEN'S FASHIONS

Most shoppers tend to buy clothing impulsively. They look for items which catch their eye without giving much thought to quality, practicality or cost.

This worksheet will make your shopping habits far more organized. By following a few simple rules, you can consistently save 30-60% off retail prices while actually improving the quality of your wardrobe. Most households spend $1,500–$3,000 a year on clothes. Following these suggestions, you should save as much as $700–$1,800 per year!

The key to the system is knowing what to buy and when to buy it. In most cases, you buy summer clothing in early Fall, Winter clothes at the start of Spring, etc. You also buy for the long term. Higher-quality, classically-tailored clothing is built to last, which means you get more wear for the dollar.

Don't hesitate to carry the worksheet with you when you shop. As crazy as it may seem, it is easy to forget some of the basic buying tips when you are in a store.

Step 1

Open your closets and remove all the clothes you never wear. Surplus clothes are a wasted asset that takes up valuable space and actually cost you money. Convert these useless items into tax credits by donating them to a favorite charity that helps the homeless. You will be doing a valuable service to the community, and the charitable write-off can help offset your future clothing purchases.

Step 2

Once your closets are free from clutter, take an inventory of what remains. Which items do you own to excess? Which garments are in short supply? How many articles need to be replaced? The purpose of the inventory is to underline your future wardrobe requirements and discourage you from buying clothes you really don't need.

Step 3

Summarize your clothing needs based on your informal survey. Where possible, specify style and color. For example, a blue blazer is a classic addition to any man's or woman's wardrobe. By listing a specific item, you can narrow your shopping focus when you are in a store and avoid impulse purchases.

Step 4

Refer to the chart to determine the best sources for the items you need and the best time to shop for them.

Step 5

Regardless of the clothing item you need, go first to one of the better department stores in your area.

Your goal on this visit is to develop a standard for comparing prices and quality. Most department stores rarely stock poorly made fashions, so you should get an excellent idea of how better garments look and feel. Department store prices also tend to be higher, except during clearance sales, so you can generally use them as a benchmark to compare against "discount" and "sale" prices.

While you are doing your research, make sure to examine the most expensive and least expensive versions of the clothing you need. Take special care to compare the quality differences between the two extremes. Usually, the most noticeable distinction is the type of fabric used, but you may also perceive differences in styling construction, etc.

Step 6

Visit malls, discounters and consignment shops, as appropriate, according to your shopping plan in Step 4. Also refer to the list of discount sources included with this chapter for suggestions on where to shop.

Regardless of your destination, remember that timing is critical. **Plan your shopping trips to coincide with the end-of-season clearance sales.**

Step 7

Wherever you find an item you like, be sure to do a quick check for quality based on the checklist on page 68.

Step 8

If the garment you like passes the quality test and is priced 30-60% below what you believe to be the retail price, you've found a deal!

Before you reach for your wallet, however, you may want to consider a little extra negotiating. Many stores are willing to "sweeten" the deal, particularly if you're buying several items. Trying to get something extra will not always work and is certainly not required, but if you're feeling bold, you may try the following suggestions:

Women's Clothes

Business Suits & Dresses
- Department Stores . . . . .Clearance Sales in Feb, Apr, Aug, Oct
- Discount Stores . . . . . . .same as above
- Consignment Shops . . . .Anytime

Casuals
- Department Stores . . . . .Clearance Sales in Feb, Apr, Aug, Oct
- Consignment Shops . . . .Anytime
- Internet . . . . .Anytime
  - Designer Direct (www.designerdirect.com)
  - Designer Outlet (www.designeroutlet.com)
- Discount Stores . . . . . . .Anytime
- Consignment Shops . . . .Anytime

Shirts & Blouses
- Department Stores . . . . .Clearance Sales in Feb, Apr, Aug, Oct
- Discount Stores . . . . . . .Anytime

Bras & Undergarments
- Mail Order . . . . .Anytime
  - Chock Catalog (www.chockcatalog.com) 800-222-0020
  - Hanes Place (www.onehanesplace.com) 800-522-1151

Shoes
- Department Stores . . . . .Clearance Sales in Feb, Apr, Aug, Oct
- Discount Shoe Stores . . .Anytime

Panty Hose
- Mail Order . . . . .Anytime
  - L'Eggs (www.pantyhose.com) 800-543-1028
  - Hanes (www.onehanesplace.com) 800-522-1151
  - No Nonsense (www.legwear.com) 800-677-5995

Accessories
- Consignment Shops. . . .Anytime

Sweaters & Overcoats
- Department Stores. . . . .February Clearance Sales
- Consignment Shops. . . .Anytime

Bathing Suits / Athletic Wear
- Department Stores . . . . . .August Clearance Sales
- Discount Clothing Stores. .August Clearance Sales

Men's Clothes

Suits & Sports Coats
- Department Stores. . . . .Feb & Aug Clearance Sales
- Discount Men's Stores. . .Feb & Aug Clearance Sales
- Consignment Shops. . . .Anytime

Ties
- Department Stores . . . . .Feb & Aug Clearance Sales
- Discount Men's Stores . .Anytime

Dress Shirts
- Department Stores . . . . .Feb & Aug Clearance Sales
- Discount Men's Stores . . .Anytime
- Mail Order/Internet Sales .Anytime
  - Huntington Clothiers (http://hc.stores.yahoo.com) 800-848-6203
  - Paul Frederick Shirt Co. (www.PaulFrederick.com) 800-848-6203

Casual Wear
- Department Stores . . . . .Clearance Sales in Feb, Apr, Aug, Oct
- Discount Stores . . . . . . .Anytime

Shoes
- Department Stores . . . . .Feb & Aug Clearance Sales
- Discount Shoe Stores . . .Anytime

Underwear & Socks
- Mail Order . . . . .Anytime
  - Chock Catalog Co. (www.chockcatalog.com) 800-222-0020
  - Hanes (ww.onehanesplace.com) 800-522-1151

Sweaters & Overcoats
- Department Stores . . . . .February Clearance Sales
- Consignment Shops . . . .Anytime
- Discount Stores . . . . . . .February Clearance Sales

Bathing Suits / Athletic Wear
- Department Stores . . . . .August Clearance Sales
- Discount Clothing Stores August Clearance Sales

FASHIONS

How to Bargain

- Make sure you're talking with some-one who's got the authority; i.e., a manager, department supervisor.

- Be inconspicuous. Don't use a loud voice or try to negotiate around other customers.

- Start by asking for a straight price reduction of an extra 10%.

- Alternatively, ask when the garment will go on sale and if they will sell it to you for the sale price now.

- If you can't get a lower price, ask for an accessory (i.e., scarf) or other garment to be included at no charge or a reduced rate.

Sample Dialogue:

❝ *Excuse me. I like this garment very much, but it is a little out of my budget. I was wondering whether you might consider working out a deal with me for _____.”* *(an extra 10% discount)*

(if the answer is "no") "When is this garment going on sale? Would you be willing to consider selling it to me at the sales price today?

(if they answer is still "no") "How about if I buy a shirt or tie along with my purchase? Would you be willing to include it at no extra charge? What about throwing in the alterations for a discount? ❞

Checklist for Quality Fashions

✔ Price

For some clothing, price is an excellent indicator of quality, since better fabrics cost more. The following guidelines will help you avoid poorly-made garments that won't last.

Target Price Ranges

Women's Suits $200-450 at retail stores, $125-275 at discounters and outlets, and $50-125 at consignment stores.

Men's Suits $200-375 at retail stores, $150-250 at discounters and outlets, and $75-125 at consignment stores.

Sport Coats $125-175 at retail stores, $100-125 at discounters and outlets, and $50-75 at consignment stores.

Women's Blouses $75-125 at retail stores, $50-80 at discounters and outlets.

Men's Dress Shirts $30-50 at retail stores, $20-30 at discounters and outlets, $25-30 by mail.

Women's Shoes $80-100 at discounters and outlets. *Note: Women's shoes wear out faster than men's shoes, so watch your budget. Spending more does not guarantee longer wear.*

Men's Shoes $100-200 at retail stores, $85-150 at discounters. *Note: Men's shoes can be re-soled to last 3-5 years, so it pays to buy high-quality, durable brands.*

Men's Ties $15-25 at retail stores, $10-20 at discounters and outlets. *Note: Ties stain easily and can wear quickly, so don't buy the most expensive.*

✔ Fabric

Check the fabric content of each item by reading the inside label. Does it meet the following minimum guidelines?

Suits Men's or Women's 100% wool (best) or 50% wool/ polyester blend (minimum)

Shirts Men's 100% cotton (best) or 50% cotton/polyester blend (minimum)

Blouses 100% cotton or 100% silk (best) or 50% cotton or silk/ polyester blend. *Note: 100% silk blouses must be dry-cleaned, which adds considerably to your cost of ownership. Cotton or silk/polyester blends are more practical.*

Dresses and Separates 100% synthetic or wool/cotton/synthetic combinations are all acceptable.

Ties Men's-100% silk

Shoes Men's & Women's 100% leather uppers and soles

✔ Workmanship

Before trying on the garment, examine it carefully.

Stitching Are seams neat and evenly spaced with no signs of loose threads?

Buttons Are they attached securely? Are the holes tight and carefully sewn?

Collar Is there a felt backing (suits only) to keep the collar even and smooth?

Pattern Do pinstripes, plaids, or other patterns align properly at the seams?

Lining If there is a lining, is it sewn carefully? You should be able to pinch between the outer fabric and inner lining. Fully-lined garments are best.

Surplus Is there enough material in the waist, sleeve or pants cuff to allow for proper alteration?

✔ Fit

Try on the garment in a well-lighted room with a full-length mirror.

Overall Comfort Is there adequate room for comfortable arm and shoulder movement. Does the crotch pinch or feel too loose?

Shoulders Does it fit smoothly across your shoulders with no bulges or creases?

Waist With proper alteration, will the waist rest comfortably on your natural waistline and fit firmly but not too tight?

Legs Are the pants too tight around the thighs or calves? With proper alteration, will the pant leg hang straight, hitting the top of your shoe with no break?

Front When the jacket (if any) is buttoned, is the look smooth, without creases or folds?

Pleats Do pant pleats (if any) hang straight and closed?

Sleeves With proper alteration, will the sleeves fall at your wrist bone, revealing 1/4 to 1/2 inch shirt cuffs?

✔ Current Condition

(Consignment Merchandise Only) Check previously-owned garments for signs of unacceptable damage or wear.

Moth Holes	Thinning Crotch Area
Frayed Zippers	Frayed Cuffs
Worn Elbows	Rips or Tears
Pilling on Shirt Collars	Perspiration Stains
Ink Stains	

✔ Designer Label

Many discount stores remove designer labels so you never know who made the garment. Fortunately, stores cannot remove all labels, one of which (by law) must contain a manufacturer ID number. If the garment you're examining is missing its designer label, check the ID code to see if it matches one of the high-quality manufacturers listed on *page 70*. If it does, chances are you have found an exceptionally good bargain.

Manufacturer Codes

Women's Clothing		**Men's Clothing**	
Abe Schrader	RN 1559	Alexander Dunhill	RN 60846
Anne Fogarty	RN 48648	Alexander Julian	RN 63329
	RN30669	Bill Blass	RN 38344
Anne Klein	RN 40803	Botany 500	RN 33734
Ann Taylor	RN 61422		RN 34313
Aquascutum	RN 50871	Burberry	RN 31750
	RN 50603	Calvin Klein	RN 54718
Austin Hill	RN 41199	Chaps	RN 45408
Bill Blass	RN 59126	Deansgate	RN 40301
	RN 38344		RN 45773
Bonnie Cashin	WPL 10113	Gant	RN 16157
Bloomingdales	RN 01279	Geoffrey Beene	RN 33293
Burberry	RN 31750	Haggar	WPL 00386
Calvin Klein	RN 41327		WPL 11685
	RN 42642	Halston	RN 49619
Donkenny	RN 43594	Hart Sch., Marx	RN 37207
Evan Picone	RN 35685	Hickey Freeman	RN 55075
Fredricksport	WPL 06168	Levi's	RN 3665
Foxmoor	RN 68525	London Fog	RN 47396
The Gap	RN 54023		RN 47398
Jaeger	RN 22362	Pierre Cardin	RN 41858
J.G. Hook	RN 51898	Polo	RN 41381
Halston	RN 49619	Woolrich	WPL 06635
Harve Bernard	RN 40679	Yves St. Laurent	RN 48545
Herman Marcus	RN 32121		RN 48743
Howard Wolf	RN 12324		
Lane Bryant	WPL 12910		
Leslie Fay	RN 43857		
	RN 14962		
Lilli Ann	RN 29563		
	RN 14962		
The Limited	RN 54874		
	RN 55274		
	RN 55276		
	RN 55283		
	RN 55285		
	RN 55287		
Liz Claiborne	RN 52002		
Pierre Cardin	RN 41858		
Yves St. Laurent	RN 48545		

If you want to find the RN number for a manufacturer not listed, contact the *Federal Trade Commission* at **213 575-7974.**

HERE'S THE PROOF

 Using the **Fashions-for-Less Buying System** really works! Our strategy encourages end-of-season shopping habits at consignment shops, discount outlets and department stores with an emphasis on quality. Here are just a few of the real life bargains from shopping trips in the Washington, D.C. area.

Consignment Bargains

Item:
Liz Claiborne Designer Dress "Dinner Date Collection"

Retail Store:
Hecht's Department Store,
Ballston Centre Mall,
Arlington, VA ....$ 152

Consignment Store:
Quality Consignments Plus,
Fairfax, VA...$ 34

SAVINGS ....$ 118

Item:
Jessica McClintock Wedding Gown

Retail Store:
Jessica McClintock Bridal Gallery
The Gallery at Tyson's II
McLean, VA ....$ 1,450

Consignment Store:
*Encore Resale Dress Shop,
Washington, DC*....................................*$ 275*

SAVINGS..$ 1,175

Item:
Coach Leather Handbag

Retail Store:
Coach Leather Store,
Tysons Corner Center,
Vienna, VA...$ 275

Consignment Store:
Quality Consignments Plus,
Fairfax, VA...$ 45

SAVINGS ....$ 230

Item:
Men's London Fog Overcoat w/ Lining

Retail Store:
Hecht's
Landover Mall, Landover, MD ....$ 215

Consignment Store:
McLean Nearly New Boutique
McLean, VA...$ 75

SAVINGS ....$ 140

Item:
Rosendorf-Evans Full-length Ranch Mink Coat

Retail Store:
Rosendorf-Evans Furs,
Tysons Corner Center
Vienna, VA..$4,500

Consignment Store:
Quality Consignments Plus,
Fairfax, VA...$ 900

SAVINGS ....$ 3,600

FASHIONS

End-of-Season Clearance Bargains

Item:
Ladies' Wool Overcoat

Retail Store:
Nordstrom's Pentagon City
Arlington, VA

In-Season Price .... $ 275

End-of-Season Price .... $ 179

SAVINGS .... $ 96

Item:
**Nino Ceruti Men's Suit,
100% Worsted Wool**

Retail Store:
Bloomingdale's, White Flint Mall
Kensington, MD

In-Season Price .... $ 325

End-of-Season Price .... $ 195

SAVINGS .... $ 130

Item:
Rare Edition Young Girl's Dress

Retail Store:
Hecht's, Fair Oaks Mall, Fairfax, VA

In-Season Price .... $ 42

End-of-Season Price .... $ 28

SAVINGS .... $ 14

Mail-Order Bargains

Item:
**L'Eggs Sheer Energy
Control Top Panty Hose**

Retail Store:
Giant Supermarket
Herndon, VA .... $ 3.34/pair

Mail-Order
L'Eggs Showcase of Savings .... $ 1.93/pair

SAVINGS .... $ 1.41/pair

Factory-Outlet Bargains

Item:
Liz Claiborne 2-piece Women's Suit

Retail Store:
Bloomingdale's, Rockville, MD .... $ 329

Outlet Store
Liz Claiborne Outlet .... $ 139

SAVINGS .... $ 190

Chapter Four

How to Drive a Bargain

How do I get the best deal on a new car?

Wait a second! The fact is that buying a new car is one of the worst financial transactions you can make, regardless of where or how you buy it.

The reason new cars are such a bad deal is "depreciation". Everybody knows that cars lose their value over time, but most people don't realize how much of that loss occurs during the first two years of ownership. A new car loses as much as 20% of its value in twelve months and up to 40% after two years on the road. The actual loss varies, depending on the specific car, but the general trend is the same whether you drive a small compact or luxury sedan. It represents a real loss of your hard-earned money, regardless of when you eventually sell or trade-in.

Why do new car values drop so fast?

At least 20% of the new car price covers advertising and promotion, transportation expenses and profits for the dealer and manufacturer. None of these overhead costs can be recouped when you re-sell — hence the immediate price drop. Depreciation rates slow significantly after the initial 24-month price decline.

If a new car is such a bad investment, why do people still buy them?

The emotional appeal of a new car is hard to resist. Billions of advertising dollars and decades of car worship have made automobiles the chief status symbol in the U.S. Many people simply cannot resist the temptation to drive home in something new and shiny. We suspect there would be far fewer sales of new cars if consumers sat down to consider the true financial consequences. Instead, there seems to be a preoccupa-

Depreciation Rates for New Cars
(After Two Years)

Make & Model	Original Price	Value after 2 Years	% Loss
97 Chevrolet Blaze	$ 22,000	$ 16,000	- 28%
97 Jeep Grand Cherokee	$ 25,000	$ 17,000	- 32%
97 Ford Mustang Convertible	$ 20,700	$ 13,000	- 38%
97 Toyota Camry LE	$ 20,000	$ 15,000	- 25%
97 Dodge Caravan LE	$ 25,000	$ 16,000	- 36%

tion with only one question — "How much is the monthly payment?"

Do you mean I should only buy used cars?

Yes. Why pay the premium for a new car if the value is lost almost immediately? A two-year-old used car, at 60% of the original price, still retains 80% of its useful life. Properly maintained, it will last a minimum of ten years and 100,000 miles and probably a lot more.

Buying used also enables you to move up in status, comfort and performance. For the same prices as a brand-new economy car, you could be enjoying the luxury of a previously-owned **BMW** or *Jaguar*. No one will ever know when you bought the car or what you paid for it. In fact, people will assume you purchased it right off the showroom floor.

Which Would You Prefer?

For the price of these "new" cars	You could drive these "used" cars
1999 Ford Taurus	1994 Lexus LS 400
1999 Volkswagen Jetta	1993 Jaguar XJS
1999 Pontiac Bonneville SE	1994 BMW 740i
1999 Chevy Malibu LS	1997 Lincoln Town Car

How much should I spend?

Probably less than you have in the past. It makes absolutely no sense to put a substantial portion of your savings into an asset that is guaranteed to lose money. Even with used cars, it isn't a question of how much you can afford, but rather, how much you want to lose.

Car dealers or banks figure the maximum amount you can afford based on a monthly payment which typically does not exceed 20% of your monthly net income. As an example, a family earning $50,000 could qualify for a monthly car payment of approximately $650, an amount which equates to a car worth approximately $30,000.

There is a big difference between the maximum loan you qualify for and what you should be spending on a car, however. A better suggestion is to base your decision on what you can afford after all of your other expenses are taken into account, including scheduled contributions to a retirement plan. In most cases, the less you spend on a car, the better.

Will a used car cost more in repairs?

Yes, but don't let the occasional repairs bother you. Independent studies by a major transportation consulting firm indicate that even with a greater frequency of repairs, used cars still cost less to own than new cars. Most of the problems you are likely to encounter such as brake repairs or replacing tires, hoses, belts, batteries, water pumps, etc., are relatively cheap to fix. Even if you assume that a used car will cost an extra $1,000 or $1,500 in repairs, you've still got a bargain compared to what you would have spent on a new car.

To mitigate the chance of excessive repairs, select your used car carefully. Try to limit your choice to cars which are three or four years old, with a documented history of maintenance and an odometer reading of 40,000 or less. In addition to your own careful inspection, also make sure you take the car to a reliable mechanic for a thorough evaluation before you buy.

We have included a step-by-step inspection checklist with this chapter that makes it easy to evaluate a used car, even if you have never looked at an automobile engine in your life. Bring the checklist with you whenever you go shopping.

Who is the best source for used cars?

By far, the single best source for used cars is someone just like yourself. Cars sold by individuals are almost always priced lower than from other sources and since private sellers are not experienced sales persons, you can often out-bargain them if you come prepared.

If you buy from a new car dealer, you will usually pay 10-20% more than you would from a private party. However, dealers are selling more and more cars which are previously-leased. Formerly-leased cars are usually well-maintained and offer good value. If you're interested in a previously leased car, you will find the best selection at a new car dealer that specializes in that particular make. Leased cars are generally newer and better maintained than the average used car. Expect to pay 10-15% more from a dealer than you would from a private party. An alternative to new car dealers are the growing number of used car auto superstores, such as *CarMax* (www.carmax.com) or *AutoNation* (www.autonation.com). Most of the superstores' inventory comes from

large auto leasing companies, banks and rental agencies. Unlike a typical dealer, the superstores promise "no haggle" pricing, but the prices tend to be about the same as what you would find elsewhere.

Independent used car lots offer cheaper prices than the auto superstores and new car dealers, but the quality of the cars is sometimes questionable. The bulk of the inventory on these independent lots is comprised of high-mileage cars purchased at auctions or bank foreclosures and vehicles with a history of mechanical problems or accidents.

Now, if you *really* want the best deal on a quality used car, try to find a friend in the car business who would be willing to let you attend a wholesale used-car auction as his or her guest. These auctions, which are not generally open to the public, are the primary source of used cars that wind up on dealer lots. Again, these auctions are not generally open to the public. However, if you can find the right connections, you can probably save $3,000 to $5,000 on the price of your next car. There are many different companies that conduct these wholesale auctions. One of the largest is *Manheim Auto Auction* (www.manheim.com). Another source for these auctions can be found through the *National Association of Auto Auctions* web page (www.naaa.com). Remember, only licensed dealers can bid at these auctions.

For additional information about more traditional ways of locating and purchasing used cars, refer to the step-by-step instructions at the end of this chapter. You'll learn how to spot private sellers in the classified ads, what questions to ask in order to pre-qualify a car over the phone, how to determine a fair market price and conclude a negotiation to your advantage.

Should I pay cash, or finance?

Always pay cash if possible. Interest payments are not tax deductible so there is no advantage to making monthly payments. Besides, financing creates the illusion of affordability, masking the true magnitude of your investment.

The Six Rules of Car Financing

1. Keep the loan amount to the absolute minimum. *Pay cash for as much of your purchase as possible — at least 40%. This is not a bank requirement, but rather a self-imposed limit which keeps your budget within reason, given your current finances.*

2. Keep the term short. *Limit the loan term to no more than two years. If you can not afford the monthly payments in 24 installments, then you can not afford the car.*

3. Use a home-equity loan if you can. *Interest on home-equity loans is tax deductible, which makes the effective interest rate lower than most car loans.*

4. Try credit unions before talking to banks or car dealers. *Auto loans are usually more affordable at credit unions than at other lenders.*

5. Don't judge a loan by the size of the monthly payment. *What counts is the annual percentage rate (APR) and the total interest you will pay over the life of the loan.*

6. Shop Competitively. *Rates and terms vary significantly, depending on the source. It pays to get quotes from at least 4 to 6 lenders before making a decision.*

Better to buy a cheaper car for cash than a more expensive model on credit.

If you simply don't have the money, there are certain rules you should follow to make sure you get the best deal on a car loan.

What if I still want to buy a new car?

A good deal on a new car doesn't change the fundamental economics against it. However, if you are adamant about buying a new car, you can negotiate a price which is far lower than most people pay. The trick is to beat the dealership at their own game by learning how they price cars and inflate costs for unsuspecting customers.

A good sales person will try to confuse you by tying three separate transactions into one neat package. He'll talk about the price of a new car, the value of your trade-in and the terms of a car loan as if they were parts of a single equation. Before you know it, he'll be explaining low monthly payments or a great factory rebate offer, while at the same time talking you into expensive dealer add-ons or a low trade-in allowance. It is very easy to get confused when you are evaluating so many different variables, which is exactly what the salesman wants.

You must control the agenda if you want the best deal. That means dividing the car-buying process into distinct steps, each of which you negotiate separately.

Step one is agreeing on a price for the new car. Forget the sticker or even the first offer the salesman gives you. Go right to the heart of the matter by finding out what the dealer actually paid for the car and then adding a reasonable mark-up. For more information about new car buying hints see the Step-by-Step instructions at the end of this chapter.

To figure out dealer cost, you should first identify the specific car you like and make sure you understand which options you may want. If you have access to the internet, log on to the **Edmund's** web page (www.edmunds.com). With just a few mouse clicks, you can find out exactly what your dealer paid for a particular model, including various options. You can also find out whether the dealer is receiving any special incentives from the manufacturer which increase the dealer's profit margins. You can find similar information on dealer costs from another web site called **Intellichoice** (www.intelli choice.com), although they will charge you a small fee ($4.95) for the same information **Edmund's** gives you for free. If you do not have access to the internet, **Consumer Reports** (800-888-8275) will provide you with written car pricing information, including dealer costs, by phone or fax for $12 per report. The **Consumer Reports'** service claims to be more up-to-date than its rivals, but we have found the information comparable to **Edmund's**.

Once you know the dealer cost, less certain allowances and credits which are further explained in the step-by-step instructions at the end of this chapter, you are in a position to negotiate a

fair deal. In most cases, you should expect to pay approximately $200 to $400 above the dealer invoice, although if a particular model is in great demand, the final amount will be higher.

Make sure your price does not include dealer-installed options. These are services or accessories installed at the dealership, not the factory, which are added to the price of the car by separate invoice. Examples include rustproofing, glazing, body moulding, pinstripes, fabric care and extended warranties. These are high-profit services which cost the dealer next to nothing but vastly inflate the price of the car. None are necessary, but if they have already been added to your car, negotiate a price based on what it cost the dealer to install them, not an inflated number the salesman quotes you.

Only after you have a firm price on the new car should you shift your attention to a possible trade-in or financing. These are separate transactions and should be treated as such.

The *True* Cost of Dealer-Installed Options		
Item	Retail Price	Actual Dealer Costs
Paint Protection (Glazing)	$ 399	$ 50
Rustproofing (Undercoating)	169	25
Interior Protectant	90	25
Body Molding	80	25
Accent Stripes	100	35
Dealer Prep	75	0

Keep in mind that the salesman will try to low-ball you on the trade-in or sell

AUTOMOBILES

you an expensive financing package, especially if you've already negotiated a low price for the new car. To avoid being taken, do some independent research about the current market value of your car, including shopping around to other sources. Likewise, if you need a loan, investigate the options from other lenders before visiting the dealer. Judging the merits of the salesman's offer is then a simple matter of comparing his terms to those you found elsewhere.

For more information about new-car buying hints, see the Step-by-Step instructions at the end of this chapter.

Should I lease or buy?

Buy. Leases are very seductive, but they should be avoided for several reasons. First, leases are extremely complicated transactions that are difficult to analyze. It is nearly impossible to determine in advance the full cost of a lease since it is influenced by factors which cannot be known at the outset, such as real vs. projected depreciation schedules, excess mileage assessments, wear-and-tear penalties and termination fees. These back-end expenses, not the monthly payment, are usually the factors which turn most lease deals to the advantage of the dealer or lease company. What's worse, after two or three years of monthly payments, you still don't own a car. Of course, you can return the car to the dealer and walk away when the lease term expires, but then what will you do for transportation? Chances are you will lease another new car ... and another ... forever locking yourself into a cycle of monthly payments. The other option when your lease is over is to buy the car for a predetermined price established when the car was still new. This purchase option is almost always slanted in favor of the dealer, so that you effectively lose twice on the same car. About the only time a lease is truly a cost-effective alternative to purchase is when you use a car exclusively for business and can deduct the lease payments on your income tax.

How do I find an honest mechanic?

It's getting harder. A study conducted by the Department of Transportation conservatively estimates that 40% of auto repair costs are completely unnecessary. Consumer losses from repair fraud exceed $30 billion per year!

To minimize the chance of a rip-off, you must take a more active role in how and where your car is serviced. Rule number one is to learn the difference between repair facilities and which type to choose for your particular problem. Dealerships are the top of the pecking order. You will find the best-trained mechanics and the most up-to-date equipment there, but also prices which are usually 20-40% higher than anyplace else. If your car suffers a mechanical failure under warranty, the dealer is your obvious choice for service since it costs you nothing. However, for routine maintenance and non-warranty work, going to the dealer is like paying a brain surgeon to remove a hangnail.

What are the routine jobs? Brakes, tune-ups, mufflers and exhaust systems, cooling systems, transmissions, wheel alignments, oil changes, tires, batteries, shocks, etc. All of these are relatively simple repair and/or maintenance tasks that can be done easily and for less money at franchise specialists (i.e., **Midas, Jiffy Lube, AMCO, Tune Masters**) or a local garage.

If your problem is more serious and your car is no longer under warranty, we recommend you bypass both the dealer and the franchise shop. For major work, you want the skills of a mechanic specifically trained on your type of car who charges lower labor rates than the dealer. Check your Yellow Pages for independent garages that service particular types of cars. You will find specialists that work almost exclusively on **Hondas** or **Toyotas, Nissans** or **BMWs**, even **Fords** and **GM** products. In most cases, these facilities are staffed by mechanics who at one time worked at a dealership before going into business for themselves. You will usually get dealer-quality work here but at labor rates which are 20-30% lower.

Of course, choosing the right type of repair facility doesn't guarantee that you have found an honest one. Unfortunately, you can be taken at a franchise or chain store just as easily as you can at a dealer or independent garage. Experts recommend 4 steps to cut the risks.

For more detailed suggestions about avoiding repair scams, as well as hints for routine maintenance and discount sources for replacement parts, consult Part IV: How to Repair Your Car Without Getting Ripped-Off.

Is my warranty still valid if I get my car serviced someplace other than the dealer?

Yes. It is illegal for a dealer or manufacturer to require you to service your car at their facility. You can have routine, non-warranty work, such as tune-ups, oil changes, etc., performed anywhere. Simply keep receipts and a log book to prove you maintained the car to factory-recommended specifications.

How to Avoid Auto Rip-Offs

1. **Check out the facility's reputation.** Contact the local Better Business Bureau for complaints on file. Also seek out recommendations from friends, relatives and neighbors.

2. **Ask the mechanic to inspect the car in your presence.** Don't just drop off the keys. Looking at the problem first-hand minimizes the chances of fraud.

3. **Learn the familiar signs of a potential rip-off.** Scare tactics, suggested repairs unrelated to your initial problem, expensive overhauls of brakes, engines and transmissions, etc., as well as add-ons to advertised maintenance specials should always make you suspicious.

4. **Get a second opinion.** If your first repair estimate is $150 or more, don't authorize the work without first getting another garage to look at the car. Rival mechanics love to prove their competitors are incompetent. If your car can be fixed for less, the second mechanic will usually say so to win you as a future customer.

AUTOMOBILES

Guide to CHOOSING THE BEST USED CAR

The process of buying a used car starts with your decision about the right make and model. You obviously want reliable and comfortable transportation within a budget that makes sense. This worksheet helps you determine that budget, as well as how to evaluate the quality and performance characteristics of every car on the road today.

Think creatively. When buying a used car, you can often afford a make and model that would otherwise be beyond your budget. To help you appreciate the possibilities, we've listed a selection of late-model, previously-owned vehicles in a number of different price ranges in the chart on page 83. Remember, however, that prices are constantly changing and you should always check for current numbers with an up-to-date source. If you have access to the internet, you can check used-car prices at the *Edmund's* web site (www.edmunds.com) or the *Kelley Blue Book* site at (*www.kbb.com*). Hardcopy versions of the *Kelley Blue Book* are also available at most public libraries.

CHOOSE THE BEST USED CAR WORKSHEET

Used Car Buying Resources

Internet Ratings, Reviews, Pricing

Edmund's
www.edmunds.com

Intellichoice
www.intellichoice.com

Consumer Reports
www.consumereports.com

Kelley Blue Book
www.kbb.com

Autoconnect
www.autoconnect.com

Internet Sales (New & Used)

Car Max
www.carmax.com

Auto Nation
www.autonation.com

Autobytel
www.autobytel.com

Carpoint
www.carpoint.com

Autoweb
www.autoweb.com

Autovantage
www.autovantage.com

Auto Auctions

Manheim Auto Auction
www.manheim.com

National Association of Auto Auctions
www.naaa.com

Safety Recalls

DOT Auto Safety Hotline
800-424-9393

CHOOSE THE BEST USED CAR WORKSHEET

Step 1

Answer these questions to determine how much you can afford.

1. **What is your annual household income after taxes?**

   Net Household Income $ _____

2. **How much of a monthly payment can you afford for your new purchase?**

Finance companies determine affordability using the assumption that monthly car payments (total per household) should not exceed 20% of net household income. This is only a guideline, which may also be influenced by other factors. In our view, the 20% guideline permits too large a percentage of household income to be devoted to monthly car payments. A more conservative estimate would be 10% of net household income.

Leading Industry Guideline

_____ x .20 = _____
Net Household Income   *Maximum Monthly Payments per Household for all cars*

We recomend:

_____ x .10 = _____
Net Household Income   *Maximum Monthly Payments per Household for all cars*

Step 2

Using the chart at right, what is the approximate loan amount you can afford

Keep in mind that these guidelines are only approximations. The amount you actually qualify for will be based upon your specific financial circumstances and credit history. For more information on qualifying for a car loan, see the step-by-step instructions later in this chapter.

Approximate Loan Amount _____

Monthly Payment Converter

Monthly Payment	Approximate Loan Amount
$100	$ 4,000
$200	$ 9,000
$300	$13,000
$400	$17,000
$500	$22,000
$600	$26,000
$700	$32,000

* Assumes typical 48-month financing @ conventional interest rates between 3% and 8% per year and 10% down-payment. These are approximate amounts intended for rough calculations only.

CHOOSE THE BEST USED CAR WORKSHEET

Step 3

If you are not planning to finance your purchase and prefer a more conservative method for calculating how much you should invest in a car, consider our recommendation to limit the current value of the cars you own to no more than 10% of your current household income.

_____ x *.10* = _____
Net Household   Maximum recommended
Income   value of cars in household

_____ - _____ = _____
Recommended   Current value of   Recommended
value of cars in   cars in house-   budget for new
household   hold   purchase

Step 4

Determine which used cars in your price range are appealing to you?

Consult online reviews, recommendations and current prices at one of several web sties including **Edmund's** (www.Edmund's.com), **Intellichoice** (www.intellichoice.com), **Consumer Reports** (www.consumerreports.com), **Carpoint** (www.carpoint.com) or **Autoconnect** (www.autoconnect.com).

If you do not have access to the web, hard-copy versions of these reports can be obtained at any public library. To help stimulate your thinking regarding used cars, we have prepared a select list of cars you can afford based on 1999 prices. To get a completely up-to-date estimate of current prices, consult the sources listed on page 81.

CHOOSE THE BEST USED CAR WORKSHEET

Selected Used Cars You Can Buy for a Fraction of the Original Price

Under $10,000

'93 Olds 98
'93 Lincoln Continental
'93 Cadillac DeVille

'93 Toyota Camry LE
'93 Ford Mustang Convertible
93 Volvo 940

'93 Dodge Caravan LE
'93 Mazda 929
'93 Ford Explorer XL

$10,001 to $14,000

'95 Buick Riviera
'95 Audi 90
'95 Volvo 940 Sdn
'95 Mazda Millenia
'95 Alfa Romeo 164 LS
'95 Infiniti J-30
'94 Audi 100s

'94 Infiniti J-30
'94 Lincoln Town Car
'94 Mazda 929
'94 Saab 9000
'95 Honda Accord LX
'95 Ford Explorer XL
'95 Toyota Camry LE

'95 Dodge Caravan LE
'95 Chevy Blazer Sdn
'93 Toyota 4-Runner
'97 Ford Mustang Conv.
'93 Jeep Gr. Cherokee
'93 GMC Sierra K-2500
'94 Buick Park Ave.

$14,001 to $18,000

'97 Acura 3.0 CL
'97 Mazda Millenia
'97 Mitsubishi Diamante
'96 Olds 98
'96 Buick Park Ave.
'96 Volvo 850
'96 Olds Aurora
'95 Cadillac DeVille

'94 Acura LS-2
'94 Audi C5 Quattro
'94 Cadillac Eldorado
'94 Volvo 850 Turbo
'93 Jaguar XJS
'93 BMW 525
'97 Accord
'95 Lincoln Town Car

'97 Ford Explorer XL
'97 Toyota Camry LE
'97 Dodge Caravan LE
'97 Chevy Blazer 4 Dr.
'97 Jeep Gr. Cherokee
'95 Toyota 4-Runner
'97 GMC Sierra K-2500

$18,001 to $22,000

'97 Buick Park Ave.
'95 Mercedes Benz C220
'97 Saab 9000
'96 Cadillac Fleetwood
'93 Jaguar XJS Conv.

'95 Acura Legend
'97 Lincoln Town Car
'95 Audi Cabriolet Conv.
'96 Lexus ES-300
'97 Toyota 4-Runner

'97 Cadillac Catera
'95 BMW 325i Conv.
'96 Acura 3.2
'93 Lexus LS 400

$22,001 to $26,000

'97 Audi A-6 Sdn
'94 BMW 740i
'97 Volvo S-90
'93 Mercedes Benz 300TE

'95 BMW 325i Conv.
'94 Jaguar XJS 4.0
'97 Volvo 850
'95 Jaguar XJS

'97 BMW 328 i-4
'94 Lexus LS 400
'96 Infiniti Q-45
'97 Lexus ES 300

$26,001 to $30,000

'97 Cadillac Eldorado
'97 Mercedes C 280

'97 Cadillac DeVille
'94 Mercedes E 420

'97 Lexus GS 300

estimated 1999 market prices

AUTOMOBILES

CHOOSE THE BEST USED CAR WORKSHEET

Step 5

Complete the chart by obtaining information about mechanical reliability, fuel efficiency and projected insurance costs.
One of the best sources for this information can be found at the **Autoconnect** web site (www.autoconnect.com) under "new and used car information." Simply follow the prompts to search for the information you need. To estimate annual fuel use, use the formula below:

Used Auto Comparison Worksheet

Year, Make & Model   _____ _____ _____

Desired Options (if any)   _____ _____ _____

Wholesale Value*   _____ _____ _____

Retail Value[1]   _____ _____ _____

Annual Fuel Cost Estimate[2] _____ _____ _____

Annual Insurance Premium Estimate[3] _____ _____ _____

Reliability Ratings and Manufacturer's
Recalls[3]   _____ _____ _____

                             _____ _____ _____

Expert Reviews[4]   _____ _____ _____

                             _____ _____ _____

                             _____ _____ _____

[1]Consult Edmunds or Kelley Blue Book.

[2]Use the formula __15,000__ x $1.20   Example: __15,000__ x $1.20 = $900
                     Hwy MPG   20 MPG

[3]Consult Edmunds web site or contact the Department of Transportation Auto Hotline at 800-424-9393.

[4]List performance, reliability, and other standards.

CHOOSE THE BEST USED CAR WORKSHEET

Step 6

Based on your research, prioritize your search for the car which best suits your needs and budgets.

Best
Choice: _____

Step 7

Review the automotive classifieds in your local newspaper every day for several weeks and complete this chart.

Date	*Make/Model*	*Features*	*Asking Price*	*Telephone No.*
____	_____	_____	$_____	_____
____	_____	_____	$_____	_____
____	_____	_____	$_____	_____
____	_____	_____	$_____	_____
____	_____	_____	$_____	_____

Step 8

Compare advertised prices with the data you've already compiled on the previous worksheet.
You'll know immediately whether the asking price is reasonable. Private sellers should be asking prices slightly higher than the pricing guides. Dealers will probably be asking slightly more than the "retail" price. (Dealers are always hoping to find a buyer who hasn't done their homework.)

CHOOSE THE BEST USED CAR WORKSHEET

Step 9

Phone the dealers. In addition to checking the newspaper classifieds, you will also want to call local dealers who are likely to stock the used car you are trying to find. In many cases, dealers are an excellent source of cars which have been previously leased. You can also use the internet to do this type of search, but frankly, it is easier to get out the *Yellow Pages* and start dialing.

Step 10

Scan the internet. The web sites all work the same way. Each of them has signed up a number of car dealers around the country. The dealers pay a monthly fee so that their inventory of cars is listed on the buying service. When you log on to the web site and describe the car you're looking for, the search engine scans the combined inventories of participating dealers for potential matches. Thus, these web services are not all-knowing cyber-sleuths capable of scanning the universe for cars matching your requirements. Instead, they are little more than sophisticated classified advertisements decorated nicely for the internet. There's nothing wrong with these services, but to get a complete picture of the inventory of cars available in your area, you've got to search them all.

Used Car Web Sites

Carpoint
(www.carpoint.com)

AutoWeb
(www.autoweb.com)

Autovantage
(www.autovantage.com)

Autobytel
(www.autobytel.com)

CHOOSE THE BEST USED CAR WORKSHEET

Step 11

Once you have scanned the newspapers and the internet, you should pre-screen over the telephone any cars which appeal to you.

Sample Dialogue

" *Hello. I'm calling about the ad (or listing) you placed. If it is still available, I'd like to ask you a few questions.* **"**

Phone Survey
(private sellers only)

	A	B	C	D
•(private sellers only) How long have you owned the car?				
• What is the current odometer reading?				
• Can you describe the specific features of the car, including any special options?				
Color?				
How many doors?				
Power steering?				
Auto transmission?				
Air conditioning?				
Stereo?				
Power windows?				
Upgraded interior?				
Special trim?				
Wheel package?				
Other?				
• Is there any rust?				
• What specific repairs have been done to the car?				
• Are there any current mechanical problems with the car?				
• Has the car been in any accidents? If so, describe the damage.				
• What is your asking price?	$	$	$	$
• Is your price firm, or will you consider a reasonable offer?				
• When is the car available for inspection?				
• Where are you located?				

AUTOMOBILES

CHOOSE THE BEST USED CAR WORKSHEET

Step 12

Arrange for a personal inspection of any car which meets these initial criteria:

- The asking price does not exceed the NADA "retail" price and the owner indicates he/she is willing to negotiate;

- Actual mileage does not exceed 40,000 miles/year;

- There is no rust; and

- No major repairs, such as a transmission, valve job, etc., are indicated. (Minor repairs/replacements, such as new tires, brakes, tune-ups, etc., should not discourage you.)

Conduct your personal inspection in daylight hours using the worksheet that follows.

CHOOSE THE BEST USED CAR WORKSHEET

Personal Inspection Checklist

THE EXTERIOR	Car A	Car B	Car C	Car D

A. Rust?

Check for any visible signs of rust corrosion. Look closely at doors and fenders, as well as underneath the car. Any "bubbling" of painted surfaces indicates rust working through the metal. Reject any car with visible signs of rust. It is the one defect which usually cannot be repaired.

B. Tires?

Examine the tread on all four tires and the spare. Wear should be even and appropriate for the mileage of the car. If the odometer reading is less than 20,000 miles, but the tires are nearly bald, you should be suspicious. Perhaps the odometer has been changed. Worn tires on a car with 30,000 or more miles should not be a cause for alarm. If new tires are needed, adjust your offer by the replacement cost (approximately $75 per tire).

C. Fit and Finish?

Inspect the paint as well as the fit of doors, fenders, etc. Mismatched or discolored body panels are an indication the car may have been damaged in an accident.

D. Lights?

Ask the owner or your friend to activate turn signals, emergency flashers, brake lights, headlights and high beams. Do they all work properly? A burned out bulb is easy to fix, but it could also indicate an expensive electrical problem.

E. Oil Leaks?

Check the driveway and garage for signs of oil leaks. If you notice stains that look new, be sure to follow-up with your mechanic.

AUTOMOBILES

Personal Inspection Checklist

	Car A	Car B	Car C	Car D

F. Engine Appearance?

Open the hood and check the appearance of the engine and battery. You're not an expert, but examine the belts and hoses to make sure they are not worn or frayed. A car with a low odometer reading should have a relatively clean-looking engine.

G. Shock Absorbers?

Ask your friend to push down forcefully on the front and rear fenders. If the car continues rocking after the pushing stops, the shock absorbers may need replacing.

H. Exhaust?

Stand behind the car and ask your friend to start the engine. Take a good look at what comes out of the exhaust pipe. The fumes should be almost invisible. Blue smoke indicates that the engine seals are failing – an expensive repair. Black smoke indicates that a tune-up is needed – a less critical problem.

THE INTERIOR

A. Odometer?

Make sure the odometer reading corresponds to the mileage quoted to you over the telephone. Misaligned numbers may indicate tampering.

B. Accelerator?

Look at the accelerator and brake pedal. If a car has less than 40,000 miles, the pedals should look almost new. If the rubber pads are worn, it is possible that the odometer has been changed.

Personal Inspection Checklist

	Car A	Car B	Car C	Car D

C. Carpet, Seats, Dash?

Check for rips, tears and stains. If you are a non-smoker, note that it is very difficult to rid a car of the smell of cigarette smoke if the previous owner used tobacco frequently.

THE TEST DRIVE

A. Ask the owner if you can take a test drive.

Don't be surprised if he/she insists on going with you.

B. Electrical System?

Turn on the ignition switch. Before starting the car, check that the windshield wipers, radio, air conditioning, heat, defroster, interior lights, clock, and power windows/locks/seats all work properly.

C. Engine Start?

Start the engine. It should start easily on the first turn.

D. Clutch/Transmission?

Release the parking brake and put the car in gear, slowly pulling away from the curb or driveway. Automatic transmissions should transition smoothly – no jumps or groans. Manual gears should move freely, without grinding, and the clutch should feel firm.

E. Engine Noise?

Listen for any "knocking" or other unusual noises from the engine.

AUTOMOBILES

Personal Inspection Checklist

	Car A	Car B	Car C	Car D

F. Brakes?

On a quiet residential street with no cars behind you, make several quick stops and a few rolling stops. The car should stop quickly without any pull to the left or right. A slight squeak is not unusual, but severe noise or rubbing sounds could mean the brakes need an overhaul.

G. Engine Temperature, Oil Pressure?

After driving for several minutes, check the engine temperature and oil pressure gauges to make sure they are in the normal range. If you can't find the gauges, the car may be equipped with warning lights which only illuminate at signs of trouble.

H. Highway Performance?

On a major highway, increase your speed to 55 MPH. The car should ride smoothly without excessive rattling, vibrations or other unusual sounds. Briefly take your hands off the steering wheel. The car should continue in a relatively straight path without pulling left or right.

I. Engine Off?

Return the car to the seller's driveway and turn off the engine. It should stop immediately. Continued idling is an indication of improper engine tuning or more serious problems your mechanic can identify.

CHOOSE THE BEST USED CAR WORKSHEET

Step 13

Once you have completed your own personal inspection, ask yourself whether you are still seriously interested in the car. If the answer is "no", do not proceed further. On the other hand, if you do like the car, your next step is to take the vehicle to your mechanic for a professional inspection.

Asking the owner for permission can be tricky. Think of it from his or her perspective. You are a stranger. The inspection is an inconvenience, plus there is no guarantee you will buy the car.

All you can do is ask. In some cases, you can agree to leave your car and keys with the owner while you're gone, or the owner may wish to accompany you; anything goes so long as you can get the car to your mechanic.

The owner may refuse under any circumstances. To try and convince him, you may need to negotiate a purchase price which is conditional on the inspection. In other words, you agree to buy the car for a certain price if everything checks out. If the mechanic finds any problems, you have a right to back out of the deal. If the conditional offer is your only way of persuading the owner, proceed to the next section on negotiation. We have included a sample contract you can use which includes the inspection contingency. When you have an agreement, return to this section and proceed with the professional inspection.

Professional Inspection Checklist

✔ Arrange a time with your selected mechanic to drop off the car. It is always best to call in advance so your time at the garage is kept to a minimum. Expect to pay $25 to $50 for a thorough inspection, unless you are a frequent customer, in which case the mechanic may do it without charge.

✔ Report any problems you've noticed during your own inspection and ask your mechanic to list any defects, excessive wear or expected replacements that will be necessary in the near future.

✔ Ask the mechanic to do the inspection in your presence, so he can show you any problems first-hand.

✔ At a minimum, he should :

- Road test the car;
- Take off all four wheels and examine the brakes;
- Examine the levels and condition of all engine fluids;
- Inspect the exhaust system while the engine is running;
- Check all hoses and belts;
- Check alignment; and
- Check engine on a diagnostic analyzer.

✔ Ask for his general opinion of the car, as well as his specific estimate for any repairs that are needed. A written estimate will help you in determining your offer, and will provide leverage during negotiations.

AUTOMOBILES

CHOOSE THE BEST USED CAR WORKSHEET

Step 14

Negotiate and close the deal by following these steps:

1. Always determine the maximum price you will pay for a car (negotiating limit) before you make an offer.

   a. What is the current "wholesale" and "retail" value of the car according to the *Kelly Blue* Book (www.kbb.com) and *Edmund's* (www.edmunds.com)?

   Wholesale Value   Retail Value

   b. What is the average market value of the car?

   $$\frac{Wholesale\ Value + Retail\ Value}{2} = \underline{\hspace{3cm}}$$
   Average Market Value

   c. How much does the mechanic estimate it will cost to repair any problems with the car?

   Cost of repairs   _____

   d. Determine your negotiating limit by subtracting repair costs from the average market value.

   Average Market Value − Repair Costs = _____
   Negotiating Limit

2. Determine your opening bid by subtracting 15% from your negotiating limit.

   Negotiating Limit x .15 = _____
   Opening Bid

3. Memorize your negotiating limit and your opening bid before you speak with the seller.

   _____   _____
   Opening Bid   Negotiating limit

Winning Negotiating Techniques

- **Call the seller from the mechanic's garage and tell him that you are returning with an offer.**

  Create an air of expectation by not revealing your price until you are again face-to-face.

- **If you have already negotiated a contingent contract, call to say that you are on your way back, but that the mechanic "found some problems."**

  Let the tension of waiting to find out the problems build during your absence.

- **Upon your return, offer the seller your opening bid. Be prepared for any response.**

  The seller may be shocked by your offer, but he/she may also accept it. More likely, you will get a counteroffer.

- **Use the mechanic's inspection to your advantage.**

  Show the seller your receipt detailing the estimated repairs. Explain that your offer is low because of all the money you've got to spend. If the car does not need repairs, talk instead about how your money is tight and that you can't afford a higher price.

- **Wait! Let the owner respond, even if there is an uncomfortable silence.**

  Always let the other side respond to your statement, even if it takes awhile. There is a good chance they will make a lower counteroffer.

- **Always raise your offer by a smaller percentage than the seller lowers his price.**

  Resist the temptation to split the difference. In most cases, the fewer concessions you make, the more the other side will give up to keep the deal alive.

- **Make your final offer no higher than your negotiating limit, after two counter-proposals.**

  Emphasize that it is positively your last offer.

- **Be true to your word. Stop the negotiations if your final offer is not accepted.**

AUTOMOBILES

CHOOSE THE BEST USED CAR WORKSHEET

Step 15

When you have an agreement, put the terms in writing, using a sample contract like that below.

(Includes Inspection Contingency)

MODEL SALES CONTRACT
(Sample Language)

This letter shall serve as a sales contract between _____ ("Buyer") and _____ ("Seller") for the purchase of an automobile identified as a _____ (make/model), license number _____ , vehicle I.D. number _____ ("The Vehicle").

The Seller, as the legal owner of the Vehicle, agrees to its sale to Buyer for the total price of $ _____. Buyer shall secure the sale with an initial deposit ("Deposit") of 5% of the sales price, $ _____, payable by personal check. The balance of the sales price shall be payable by certified check.

The Sale is contingent upon Buyer's acceptance of the Vehicle following an inspection by a qualified mechanic of Buyer's choice. If the Vehicle is not acceptable to the Buyer as a result of the inspection, for any reason, this contract of sale shall be considered null and void and the Deposit shall be returned to Buyer in full. This contract is also contingent upon Seller conveying clear and legal title of the Vehicle to Buyer at the time of final purchase. In the event clear title cannot be conveyed, Seller shall refund Buyer's Deposit in full.

Agreed to, this _____ day of _____ *(month)*, 200_____.

By:

_____   _____
Buyer   *Seller*

_____

CHOOSE THE BEST USED CAR WORKSHEET

Step 16

If the seller is a private party, ask him or her to produce the title proving ownership, as well as a current vehicle registration, before you sign the contract.

Title Checklist

✔ **Is the name of the person you're dealing with the same as the name on the title?**

If not, you must get the title holder's signature or the sale is invalid.

✔ **Are there any liens from a bank or finance company?**

You should contact any lien holder in the owner's presence to confirm the amount as well as procedures for settling the lien. Never allow any cash to change hands until you are assured of a clear title (no liens).

✔ **Check the title at the Department of Motor Vehicles to make certain there are no recent changes. *Most DMV offices will confirm registration over the phone.***

✔ **Does the vehicle I.D. number correspond to the title?**

Check to make certain the numbers match.

Step 17

Pay for the car with a cashier's check, never cash.

The check is a written record to document your purchase in case it is ever challenged.

CHOOSE THE BEST USED CAR WORKSHEET

Step 18

Complete the following checklist
before you take final possession.

Final Sale Checklist

❑ Keys for ignition, doors, trunk,
gas cap, and glove box?

❑ Owner's manual?

❑ Repair records (if any)?

❑ Spare tire and jack?

❑ Warranties that are still valid?

❑ Title signed over to you?

❑ Touch-up paint (if any)?

Guide to CHOOSING THE BEST NEW CAR

If you insist on buying a *new* car, this worksheet will show you how.

Do not deviate from the prescribed steps in any way. Car dealers will try to change your agenda to maximize their negotiating leverage. It is important that you dictate the pace and the progression to maintain control of the sales process.

We assume you have already decided which make and model to buy. If that is not the case, refer to the Automobile Buying System on page 80. The same principles apply.

BUYING A NEW CAR WORKSHEET

New Car Buying Resources

Internet Ratings, Reviews, Pricing

Edmund's
www.edmunds.com

Intellichoice
www.intellichoice.com

Consumer Reports
www.consumerreports.com

Carpoint
www.carpoint.com

Autoconnect
www.autoconnect.com

Internet Sales

Autobytel
www.autobytel.com

Autoweb
www.autoweb.com

Autovantage
www.autovantage.com

Carpoint
www.carpoint.com

Cars Direct
www.carsdirect.com

Priceline.com
www.priceline.com

Financing

Bank Rate Monitor
www.bankrate.com

Car Finance.com
www.carfinance.com

Trade-in Pricing

Edmund's
www.edmunds.com

Kelley Blue Book
www.kbb.com

AUTOMOBILES

BUYING A NEW CAR WORKSHEET

Step 1

Determine the dealer's cost.

Your first trip to any dealer should be for information purposes only. When you are approached by a salesman, be very clear that you do not intend to buy a car today and will not even discuss prices.

Look at as many models of the car you like as the dealer has in stock. Decide which, if any, options you like, whether you prefer two or four doors, etc. When you find a car that includes all of the options you want, copy the information from the manufacturer's sticker on the left side of the New Car Pricing Worksheet.

After you have completed the information on the left side of the form, leave the dealership and go straight home to your computer and get on the internet. Log onto **Edmund's** web site (www.edmunds.com) and check out the dealer's invoice cost for the car you want. You may obtain the same information for a fee ($4.95 per report) from **Intellichoice** (www.intellichoice.com) or by calling **Consumer Reports** at 800-888-8275 ($12.95 per report).

Look up the entry for the car you want and select the dealer invoice data that corresponds to the information you

"Holdback" Payment from Manufacturer to Dealer*

Automaker	Holdback	Automaker	Holdback
Acura	3 %	Audi	none
BMW	2 %	Buick	3 %
Cadillac	3 %	Chevrolet/GMC	3 %
Chrysler	3 %	Dodge	3 %
Ford	3 %	Honda	2 %
Hyundai	2 %	Infiniti	3 %
Jaguar	2 %	Jeep/Eagle	3 %
Lexus	2 %	Lincoln/Mercury	3 %
Mazda	2 %	Mercedes-Benz	3 %
Mitsubishi	2 %	Nissan	3.5 %
Oldsmobile	3 %	Plymouth	3 %
Pontiac	3 %	Porsche	none
Saab	3 %	Saturn	none
Subaru	2 %	Toyota	2 %
Volkswagen	2 %	Volvo	$300

* The holdback is calculated in most cases on the Manufacturer's suggested list price, which is also known as the "sticker" price.

copied from the manufacturer's sticker. Copy this information on the right side of the New Car Pricing Worksheet.

Domestic manufacturers pay dealers a supplementary "holdback" fee which is not reflected in the dealer invoice. To find the dealer's true cost, you must subtract this holdback from the dealer cost you have already calculated. Note that a dealer holdback is not the same as a manufacturer's factory rebate. A rebate is a buyer's incentive that has nothing to do with what a dealer pays for the car.

Step 2

Research your auto financing options.

Contact at least six lenders in your area that offer new-car loans. Be sure

to include your current bank as well as any credit unions to which you may belong. If you own your own home and have sufficient equity, you should also investigate home-equity loans. Home-equity loans are tax deductible, which means you will probably pay a lower net interest rate than if you use

BUYING A NEW CAR WORKSHEET

a conventional auto loan to finalize your purchase.

Use the survey on the next page to compare alternate lending Auto Financing Options sources.

You can also use the internet to survey car loan options. For an overall survey of loan rates, use the **Bank Rate Monitor** site at (www.bankrate.com). For a specific rate quote, log on to (www.carfinance.com).

New Car Pricing Worksheet

	Manufacturer's Sticker*	**Dealer Invoice** *Completed from your research*	
Model			Model
Standard Features			Standard Features
Engine Size			Engine Size
Manufacturer's Suggested Retail Price (Base Only)			Base Price
Option Packages by Name			Option Packages by Name
Individual Options			Individual Options
			Subtotal (a)
			Dealer Holdback (b)
			Dealer Incentive (c)
Destination Charge			Destination Charge (d)
Total Manufacturer's Suggested Retail Price			True dealer cost [a-(b+c)+d]

Copy this information from the window sticker.

AUTOMOBILES

BUYING A NEW CAR WORKSHEET

Auto Financing Options

	Lender 1	Lender 2	Lender 3	Lender 4	Lender 5	Lender 6
What is your minimum down payment?						
What is the current annual percentage rate?	_____ %	_____ %	_____ %	_____ %	_____ %	_____ %
Is this a fixed or adjustable interest rate?	___ fixed ___ adjust.	___ fixed ___ adjust.	___ fixed ___ adjust.	___ fixed ___ adjust.	___ fixed ___ adjust.	___ fixed ___ adjust.
If adjustable, what are the adjustment terms?						
Do you charge loan origination, processing or other fees?						
What would my actual monthly payment be on a hypothetical $10,000 loan for three years?						
For four years?						
How long does it take to get approved for a loan?						
Will you pre-qualify me before I actually buy a car?	Yes / No	Yes / No	Yes / No	Yes / No	Yes / No	Yes / No

After reviewing your choices, which outside lender offers the best financing option?

Best Financing Source   _____

Annual % Rate   _____

Term   _____

BUYING A NEW CAR WORKSHEET

Step 3

Research the trade-in value of your current car.

To find out, consult the **Kelley Blue Book** at your local library or reach them online at www.kbb.com. Make sure you calculate the proper allowances for condition, mileage and option features.

_____
Current Retail Value

_____
Current Wholesale Value

Step 4

Begin the process of identifying the best price for your new car in person or via the internet.

Shopping Online

If you are shopping online, you will want to connect with several of the auto-buying services that give participating dealers in your area the opportunity to compete for your business. Use the "New Car Buying Resource" chart on page 101.

Remember that because each service represents only a portion of the dealers in your area (or maybe none at all) you will need to use more than one site to get a truly representative sample.

On each site, you will be asked for specific information about the car you want to buy, including color, options and the distance you are willing to travel from your home to do business. You will also be asked for information so that dealer(s) may contact you.

Keep in mind that while the internet allows you to present your business to a number of car dealers at the same time, the actual process of negotiating and buying a car is basically the same whether you do it in person or in cyberspace. Beware, however, that if you start your negotiating on the internet and over the phone, it is probably unwise to visit the dealership in person and talk to a salesperson on the showroom floor. Most internet transactions are performed by salaried personnel at the dealership, not the commissioned sales force. Once you visit with a salesman at the dealership, you may be triggering a commission that limits the dealer's ability to offer you a better deal via the internet.

AUTOMOBILES

BUYING A NEW CAR WORKSHEET

Shopping in Person

If you plan to shop in person instead of online, remember these "rules" as you set out.

Shopping Tips

1. **Leave the kids at home.**

2. **Bring your spouse but agree in advance that only one person will do the negotiating.**

3. **Show no emotion.**

4. **Bring a calculator and the information you've assembled on your New Car Pricing Worksheet and Auto Financing Options chart which you have just filled out in this chapter.**

When you walk into the showroom, get right to the point. Tell the salesperson you have already done a lot of research and are prepared to buy a car today if the price is acceptable.

Be quite specific about the car you want, including desired options. Tell the salesperson you do not want any other options, including any installed by the dealer, and are willing to order the car from the factory, if necessary, to get the car you want.

Allow the salesman to make the initial offer. Since you already know the true dealer cost, you will probably be amused at the price.

Patiently explain that you have already determined the price you will pay and name that figure, based on your earlier research, adding approximately $300 - $500 to the dealer's true cost for the car. Emphasize that yours is a cash offer and that you will save a discussion of financing options for later.

At this point, the salesman will probably laugh and explain to you that your price is impossible. He may even bring out the actual dealer invoice to "prove" that the dealer paid more for the car. He will complain that you probably used one of those "price" books which is out-of-date or inaccurate, and a dozen other comments too numerous to mention.

If you listen carefully, he will probably try to justify the higher price with additional charges, such as "dealer prep," dealer-installed options, etc., which are not reflected in the invoice.

You can respond that in the case of prep charges, the manufacturer already pays the dealer a fee for these services, so you will not pay twice. As for dealer-installed options, remind the salesperson that you are not interested in them. They can either take them off the car, or sell the car "as is" for your stated price.

You will recall that the true cost of dealer-installed options is much lower than what the dealer claims. If you do want any of these services, you should pay a price in line with the true costs.

Under no circumstances should you buy an extended warranty, life insurance, or a dealer-installed stereo system. (You can buy a better stereo for half the price at a discount audio store.)

BUYING A NEW CAR WORKSHEET

At this point, expect the salesman to shake his head and tell you that you are not being reasonable. He will probably excuse himself to talk with his sales manager, leaving you alone in his office.

Don't say anything while he is away. Many offices are bugged.

You should not be surprised if the salesman returns with the aforementioned sales manager not far behind. The manager will try to reason with you. He will tell you that it is impossible for the dealership to meet your price. He will probably repeat many of the same arguments you have already heard, but don't be surprised if you start to lose your nerve. Now is the time to reassert your power. "Fine," you say. "Give me your best and final offer. If it isn't acceptable, I'll go elsewhere."

Don't be surprised if the manager tells you that in order to get a lower offer approved, it needs to be in writing with a deposit check attached. This is a common trick of experienced salesmen. Once you put your name on the line and hand over money, even with a contingency, it becomes harder to leave. Tell the manager, "No way."

Make it clear you will sign nothing less than an offer that has already been initialed and approved by the dealership.

Once again, you will probably be left alone while the salesman and his manager mull their next move. You may get a third salesman this time, or the same cast of characters. In any event, chances are they will tell you they can't meet your terms. At this point, prepare to leave. You'll probably be stopped before you reach the door with an even better offer. If not, move on to the next dealership and try again.

Remember...

- Don't pay more than $500 over dealer cost.
- Don't include a factory rebate in any of your calculations.
- Don't pay for options you don't want or need.
- Don't buy dealer-installed options, services or extended warranties.
- Don't pay for dealer prep.
- Don't sign anything until the dealer provides a written offer approved by management.
- Don't make a deposit unless you have an approved deal.

Step 5

Ask about financing options. Only after you have a signed agreement on the price of the new car should you discuss financing.

Let the salesperson explain the various loan packages available, but remember that regardless of what you are told,

only three numbers are relevant for comparison:
- Term
- Total interest paid over term.
- Fees (if any)

Once you know the APR, term, interest charges and fees, if any, choosing the best financing should be as easy as comparing your alternatives.

	Dealer Financing	Other Financing
Term	_____	_____
Total Interest Charges	_____	_____
Fees	_____	_____

Step 6

Decide the merits of a trade-in.

If you have negotiated the lowest price possible on a new car, don't be surprised if the dealership attempts to make a bigger profit on your trade-in.

If you have done your homework before you visited the showroom, you should have a very good idea of what your car is worth.

If the dealer is offering you anything less than the wholesale price as indicated by the **Kelley Blue Book**, you should seriously considering selling your car on your own. Keep in mind that if you sell yourself, you should expect to realize a sales price which is somewhere between the wholesale and retail prices quoted in the **Kelley Blue Book**.

Guide to AUTO REPAIRS

Face it, you will never know enough about cars to compete with a professional mechanic.

Nevertheless, you can take precautions to limit the chance of incompetent or fraudulent service.

The worksheet below shows you how to check out a mechanic in advance, what to say when you bring in your car, how to confirm whether the repairs are truly needed and how to avoid some of the more common repair scams.

Our recommendations do take time, which for many readers is a valuable commodity. However, when you realize that a major car repair can cost you as much as 20-40% of your monthly income, making sure you get your money's worth is time well spent.

AUTO REPAIR WORKSHEET

Step 1

Based on the type of work you need performed, where is the best place to take your car for service?

Type of Work	Recommended Facility
Oil Change	Quick Lube Franchises / do it yourself
Any Mechanical Problems while car is under warranty	Dealer
Brakes	Franchise Service Center or Local Garage
Electrical System	Garage Specializing in Your Car Type, or Dealer
Emmissions System	Dealer
Muffler & Exhaust System	Franchise Muffler Shop
Cooling System (Radiator)	Local Garage
Tune-up	Local Garage or Tune-up Franchise
Battery	Department Store or Local Garage
Wheel Alignment	Tire Store
Engine Diagnostics	Garage Specializing in Your Car Type
Shock Absorbers	Franchise Service Center
Automatic Transmission	Franchise Transmission Shop
Manual Transmission	Garage Specializing in Your Car Type

A U T O M O B I L E S

Step 2

Look in the *Yellow Pages* under "Automobile — Repairs" and select 3 or 4 garages to call based on the type of work needed. Call each facility using the suggested dialogue.

Tailor your questions, depending on the type of facility and the work you need. For example, it is not necessary to inquire about a dealer's billing rates if the work is covered by warranty. Likewise, you don't need to go through an exhaustive Q&A if all you need is an oil change.

(Continue with survey.)

Note: *Always pay by credit card. If you have a future problem related to the repair and the garage refuses to fix it, you can always challenge the bill through your credit card company. If you pay cash or by check, you do not have this valuable protection.*

Mechanic's Survey

	Garage 1	Garage 2	Garage 3	Garage 4
A. What is your standard labor rate per hour?				
B. Do you bill based upon the real time for the job or according to a flat-rate manual?	___ Real Time ___ Flat Rate	___ Real Time ___ Flat Rate	___ Real Time ___ Flat Rate	___ Real Time ___ Flat Rate
Note: *Real time is preferable.*				
C. What will it cost to make the needed repairs on my car?				
D. What is included in this price?				
E. Are your mechanics paid a commission based on the cost of the repair? **Note:** Commission mechanics have a greater incentive to exaggerate your repair needs.				
F. Do you give a free estimate of repairs without obligation?	___ Free Estimates	___ Free Estimates	___ Free Estimates	___ Free Estimates
G. What are your hours and how late can I pick up my car?				
H. Do you take credit cards?				

AUTO REPAIR WORKSHEET

Step 3

When you have completed your survey, contact your local **Better Business Bureau** and/or the local consumer affairs office in your town. Ask if they have any complaints on file against the particular garages you're considering.

Note that many complaints go unreported so inquire about several garages, in order to compare the relative number of complaints. Keep in mind that shops which do a very large volume of business are likely to have more complaints on file.

Step 4

Based on your phone survey and complaint investigation, select the garage that best suits your needs.

Tips When Dealing with a Mechanic

- **Be conscious of your dress and manner.** Play down your status and do not appear rushed, inconvenienced or disinterested.

- **Describe symptoms, don't make a diagnosis.** You may suggest a repair that is unnecessary.

- **Ask for an estimate before authorizing any repairs.** You should be entitled to a free estimate of what it will cost to find and fix the problem. Whenever possible, try to be present during this inspection.

- **Ask whether needed parts are in stock or must be ordered.** Also inquire whether the parts are new or rebuilt, a genuine factory replacement or other brand, and the price difference between them.

- **Request that used parts be retained for your inspection.** Even if you never look at them, the note on your work order helps to keep the mechanic honest.

AUTO REPAIR WORKSHEET

Step 5

Be prepared for a follow-up call from the mechanic.

Chances are you will get a phone call from the repair shop indicating that more work is needed than was originally planned. Sometimes, these requests to do additional work are legitimate. In many cases, however, the "added work" is really a chance for the mechanic to earn an extra profit. Here are a few signs that you may be the victim of a repair scam.

- **The Scare Tactic.** You are told that if you do not repair a problem immediately, your car could be permanently damaged.

- **The Unforseen Problem.** You are informed that they have uncovered a previously undiscovered problem that needs immediate attention—and will add to your repair costs.

- **The Come-on.** You took your car in for a $49.95 advertised special and they try to talk you into a $250 overhaul or additional maintance you didn't request.

- **The Surprise.** You are told that you need new brakes, shocks or other part, even though you never noticed a problem.

Step 6

Stand your ground.

Don't be intimidated, scared or rushed into additional repairs. Do not authorize additional work unless you can inspect the problem yourself or get a second opinion from another garage (see Step 3).

Step 7

Get a second opinion.

Do not hesitate to take your car to another garage for a second opinion, particularly if the first mechanic's estimated repairs exceed $150.

Sample Dialogue:

Hello. I just took my car to the shop around the corner. They told me that I needed a new_____, but frankly I'm not sure I believe them. I will be happy to pay for your diagnostic time, but I would like you tell me whether their recommendation is accurate.

AUTO REPAIR WORKSHEET

Step 8

Consider buying new tires over the internet andhaving your local garage install them.

In many cases, you can save $100 or more when you replace four tires. You can contact these sources by phone or the internet.

Discount Tire Sources

Discount Tire
800-589-6789
www.tire.com

Tire Rack
888-362-8473
www.tirerack.com

Suggestion: *If you buy a new car, avoid the dealer add-ons which inflate your costs without adding value.*

Suggestion: *Factor gas mileage into your total ownership costs before deciding which car to buy.*

	Car "A"	Car "B"
Miles/Gallon	20 MPG	32 MPG
Total Miles Driven	80,000 miles	80,000 miles
Total Gas Consumption	4,000 gallons	2,500 gallons
Cost Per Gallon	$ 1.05	$ 1.05
Total Cost	$ 4,200	$ 2,625
Savings		$ 1,800

16-14

Suggestion: *Buy your tires from a mail-order internet source instead of a local tire store.*

1999 Ford Mustang

With Dealer Add-Ons	**Without Dealer Add-Ons**
Manufacturer s Suggested Retail Price $ 16,470	*Manufacturer s Suggested Retail Price* $ 16,470
Rustproofing $ 275	—
Body Molding $ 80	—
Accent Stripes $ 114	—
AM/FM/CD Stereo System $ 816	*AM/FM/CD Stereo System* $ 395*
Dealer Prep $ 85	—
Extended Warranty $ 425	—
Total Price $ 18,265	*Total Price* $ 16,865
	Savings $ 1,400

*Stereo purchased from discount audio store

Tire: Yokohama AVS S4   Size: 215-65-15

	Discount Tire Store (Reston, VA)	Tire Rack
Tires	$ 480.00	$ 315.00
Installation	incl.	35.00*
Taxes	21.60	0
Total	$ 501.60	$ 350.00

* mounting & balance at local mechanic

Savings $ 151.60

Suggestion: Buy a two- or three-year-old used car for nearly the same price as a new car, but move up in style, comfort and luxury.

Used Car	New Car
1995 Jeep Cherokee Laredo 4WD	1999 Jeep Cherokee Laredo 4WD
$ 14,200	$ 26,100
Current Market Value (based on blend of wholesale/retail price)	Dealer invoice + destination charge $500 dealer mark-up

Savings if you buy used $11,900

16-12

Chapter Five

Pay Lower Premiums for Your Insurance

How do I get a better deal on insurance?

Two easy steps should save you at least $500-$1,500 per year on your insurance bills.

First, increase the deductibles on all your policies (where applicable). By agreeing to pay a slightly larger share of any claims you may have, you can reduce your premiums as much as 20-30% while still retaining protection against serious losses.

Also, resist the temptation to shop from a single source. Prices for identical coverage can vary by as much as 60%, but the differences are not always predictable. One company can be the price leader for a particular policy, but less competitive for another. You've got to make several inquires to be assured of the lowest possible premiums.

If I raise my deductibles, won't I pay more when I have a claim?

Not in the long run. It's true that with a higher deductible, you pay a slightly larger percentage of any loss. However, chances are you will go several years without an accident or even decades

without serious illness, burglary or fire. During these periods, the money you save by paying lower premiums add up. This surplus should be more than enough to cover your deductibles when and if you do have a claim. As our illustration shows, even with a serious loss, the policy with a higher deductible saves you money over time.

High Deductibles Save You Money*		
$100 Deductible Policy	vs.	$500 Deductible Policy
$ 800	Annual Premium	$ 610
$ 4,000	Total Premium Paid for 5 Years	$ 3,050
1	No. of Claims During Period	1
$100	Deductible you must pay	$500
$ 4,100	Net Cost of Insurance (5 yrs)	$ 3,550
--	Total Savings	$ 550

*Standard policy

Do you have specific advice on how to get low rates for auto insurance?

Yes. It is easy to cut the fat out of an auto policy because you can adjust your coverage in so many ways. As we have already mentioned, raising deductibles is high on the list of priorities. Most policies carry a standard deductible of

Cars that Will *LOWER* Your Rates				Cars that Will *RAISE* Your Rates		
Ford Escort Honda Civic (4 dr)	Mitsubishi Mirage Plymouth Horizon	Subaru Justy Toyota Tercel	**$ 10,000** **or** **Less**	Eagle Summit Ford Escort GT Ford Mustang	Ford Festiva Honda Civic (2 dr) Hyundai Sonata	VW Golf VW GTI VW Jetta
Chevy Beretta Dodge Caravan Dodge Spirit	GMC Safari Van Plymouth Acclaim	Plymouth Voyager Toyota Camry	**$ 10,000** **to** **$ 15,000**	Chevy Camaro IROC Chevy Lumina APV Chrysler Lebaron Dodge Daytona Dodge Monaco Eagle Talon	Ford Probe Geo Prizm Honda Prelude Jeep Cherokee Mazda 626	Mazda Miata Mitsubishi Montero Nissan 240 SX Pontiac Firebird Toyota Corolla
Buick LeSabre Chevy Suburban Chrysler New Yorker Ford Bronco	Ford Crown Victoria Ford LTD Wagon Mercury Cougar Mercury Grand Marquis	Mercury Sable Olds 88 VW Vanagon Volvo 240	**$ 15,000** **to** **$ 20,000**	Mustang Convertible Saab 9000	Nissan Pathfinder Toyota 4-Runner	VW Cabriolet
Acura Legend Buick Electra Buick Reatta	Chrysler 5th Ave Jeep Wagoneer	Lincoln Continental Toyota Cressida	**$ 20,000** **to** **$ 30,000**	BMW 325	Totota Supra	
Cadillac Fleetwood	Jaguar XJ6	Volvo 760	**$ 30,000 +**	Audi BMW 525, 750	Cadillac Allante Chevy Corvette	Mercedes 500 Series Porsche (all models)

$100 for collision damage and a $50 or $100 deductible for comprehensive claims (vandalism, road hazards, acts of nature, etc.). Raising the collision deductible to $500 makes good sense, while the comprehensive deductible should be increased to at least $250. These changes will probably save you $100-$400 per year for each automobile insured. If your car is more than 7 years old, or worth less than $4,000, you may wish to drop comprehensive/collision protection entirely.

Another way to save is by eliminating coverage which is duplicated in other policies you own. Medical protection, for example, is completely unnecessary if you and your passengers are already covered by health insurance. Dropping this repetitive coverage should save you $20-$50 per year.

Finally, reconsider the type of car you are driving. Insurers maintain detailed files on the accident history and repair costs for every vehicle made.

Everything from paint color to horsepower is considered. Driving the right car can lower your premiums 10-25%, compared to comparably-priced models with poor accident histories.

Raising your deductibles, eliminating unnecessary coverage and choosing the right vehicle can dramatically lower your rates, to be sure. But there are also many factors which are beyond your control. Many insurers base their rates in part on factors including your credit history, education, and marital status. Where you live is also a huge consideration. In general, you will pay more in urban areas than you would living in the suburbs or the country. It is also important to keep in mind that insurers have different philosophies about the type of drivers they choose to cover. You will never be told this directly, but you can see the practice at work simply by shopping a number of companies. Some insurers will only cover drivers with accident-free records. Others discourage drivers in certain age groups. You can tell how badly an insurance company wants your business simply by comparing their rates to the competition. If an insurance company doesn't want you as a customer, their rate quotes will speak loud and clear.

If you want a fairly comprehensive comparison of what insurance companies are charging in your area, you may want to consider a new service offered by the authors of **Consumer Reports** magazine. Their auto insurance pricing service offers specific rate comparisons among competing insurers in Arizona, California, Colorado, Florida, Georgia, Illinois, Louisiana, New Jersey, Nevada, New York, Ohio, Pennsylvania, Texas, Virginia and Washington. The service costs $12 per vehicle and can be ordered by calling 800-224-9495. You can also contact your state insurance department. Many states publish a free survey of local auto insurance rates.

If you want to do the leg work yourself, simply pick up the phone and call several insurance agents in your area, especially those representing the companies listed on the Best Bets chart which are generally known for decent service and competitive prices.

Best Bets for Auto Insurance

Allstate
(check local phone directory)

GE (Colonial Penn Franklin)
800-335-2166

Geico
800-841-3000

Safeco
800-255-9990

Liberty Mutual
800-526-1547

Mercury Insurance
800-579-3467

State Farm
(check local phone directory)

USAA*
800-282-2060

Progressive Insurance
800-888-7764

available exclusively to military families and their dependents

What about shopping for auto insurance on the web?

The day is coming when shopping for auto insurance on the web will be the rule, rather than the exception. However, the process has not yet matured to the point where you can be certain your internet search is truly thorough. At this time, only a handful of insurers are successfully marketing auto insurance via the world wide web. For the moment, the leader is probably **Progressive Insurance** (www.progressive.com). The **Progressive** site asks you for relevant personal information like your age, the type of car you drive, your driving history and how many miles you drive each year. Once you submit the information, **Progressive** responds with an online rate quote, but they take the process one step further by also including rates from some of their competitors. The company promises that the comparisons are accurate, but remember the source—and check out the competition yourself.

Other insurers that provide online rate quotes include **Reliance Direct** (www.reliancedirect.com), **Geico** (www.geico.com) and **AIG** (www.aig.com). Expect more companies to follow suit in the foreseeable future, but keep in mind that just because you find an insurance quote on the internet doesn't guarantee a good deal.

What are the keys to a better deal on homeowner's insurance?

Just like auto insurance, you can save plenty by modifying the deductibles on your homeowner's policy. With few exceptions, you should be carrying a deductible of at least $500.

Also be certain you are not over-insuring your property. Remember that homeowner's insurance will only cover the costs of rebuilding your house. It makes no sense to include the land value of your property when considering the right amount of coverage to buy.

Usually, insurers are more inclined to give you a better deal on homeowner's coverage if they also insure your automobiles. Therefore, you should seek rate quotes from the same sources you are considering for your car insurance. Be sure that when you shop, you tell the agent that you want any discounts which apply to an auto/home policy combination. You're also likely to earn credits for installing deadbolt locks, smoke alarms, security systems and even outdoor lighting.

Should I buy life insurance?

The only reason to buy life insurance is if your death would cause significant financial hardship for your family. If there is no one depending on your earning power, or your estate is not so large or illiquid that your heirs will need instant cash for taxes and funeral expenses, you probably don't need life insurance.

If you are in the market for coverage, keep it simple. Most experts recommend term insurance as the best value for young or middle-aged families. Non-smokers can easily buy $250,000 of coverage for less than $250 per year at age 35. At age 55, the annual premium, in most cases, still averages less than $600.

More elaborate types of life insurance, such as "whole life" or "universal life" pay a death benefit, but part of your premium also works like an investment which you can redeem or borrow against during your lifetime.

In most cases, you will do better purchasing term insurance coverage and putting the money you would have spent on universal or whole life insurance into an alternative investment like a stock mutual fund.

You won't hear many insurance agents touting the benefits of term insurance. Agents earn roughly five times the commission for selling whole life policies as they do on a term policy.

You can minimize the influence of agents, and in some cases bypass the commissions, by shopping for term coverage on your own. Consider contacting **Quotesmith** by phone or at their web site (800-556-9393/www.quotesmith.com). **Quotesmith** provides price quotes from up to 375 different companies, the largest database in the industry. They guarantee that their service will identify the lowest term-life quote or they will pay you $500. Other quote services include **Select Quote** (800-289-5807/www.selectquote.com), **Insurance Quote Services** (800-972-1104/www.quote.com) and **First Quote** (800-583-0231/www.1stquote.com). None of these other services is as comprehensive as **Quotesmith**.

If my family needs life insurance, how much coverage is enough?

In most cases, experts recommend buying enough life insurance to provide your beneficiaries with 75% of your current income as long as it is needed. In most cases, this will translate into a policy with a death benefit equal to 7-10 times your current salary.

Obviously, these are only guidelines. If your spouse already earns a high income, you may need less coverage; more protection may be necessary if you have an exceptionally large household with additional dependents.

Should I consider buying an annuity policy for retirement?

Probably not. You can achieve the same result with greater control by investing your own money. Besides, with most annuities, any cash left in your account when you die goes to the insurance company, not your heirs.

An annuity makes sense if you worry about outliving your retirement income or your ability to manage your assets in later years. In this case, paying a fixed charge up-front, in exchange for a guaranteed monthly income benefit for life could be attractive.

What about the insurance policies advertised by direct mail or on late night TV?

Almost without exception, these policies are a bad deal. Most pay meager benefits or duplicate coverage you already have.

A classic example is the supplementary hospitalization policy that "pays you cash" if you are hospitalized for any reason. Most conventional health insurance policies already cover 100% of hospitalization charges. The cash benefits from the supplementary plan amount to pocket change.

Another predictable rip-off is life insurance you can buy "regardless of your health." Any company willing to sell life insurance to anyone, even cancer patients, must find a way to make money after paying claims. In most cases, they do so by charging above-average rates for below-average benefits.

What other types of insurance should be avoided?

Stay away from policies which only cover specific risks. Flight insurance, cancer insurance, trip cancellation insurance, mugger's insurance, etc., may seem cheap, but these types of policies are actually the most expensive type of insurance you can buy. That's because they only cover you against a specific event or for a very limited period of time. Blanket policies (auto/health/homeowner's/life) are a much better choice because they protect you against virtually all risks at all times.

You should also avoid frivolous policies which protect you against very minor risks. Typical examples would include weather insurance, road hazard insurance, contact lens insurance, pet insurance, etc. In all of these cases, you pay a high price for the protection you receive, while the chances of a claim are very low.

One type of supplemental coverage that *is* a good deal is a personal umbrella liability policy. Most companies who sell auto and homeowner's insurance offer the protection, which usually provides an additional $1 million in coverage if you are found liable in certain types of civil court proceedings stemming from an accident, libel or slander charges. Umbrella liability policies are cheap (less than $150 per year) and extremely important if you have assets which

exceed the protection offered by standard auto and homeowner's insurance policies. President Clinton used such a policy to defray some of his court costs from the Paula Jones case.

Does the financial strength of an insurance company really matter?

Yes. Since 1989, more than 120 insurance companies in the U.S. have gone bankrupt. Additional failures could push the system to the breaking point, although to date there have been few, if any instances, where a policyholder did not receive payment on a valid claim. Even so, there is simply no reason to choose an insurance company with a weak balance sheet when you can find plenty of safe alternatives.

To find out whether a particular insurance company is financially sound, ask your insurance agent for the company's **A.M. Best** rating, a reference to the company's financial strength. Insist on a rating of "A" or better. If you want to find out an insurer's rating on your own, you can find it by consulting the **A.M. Best Guide to Insurance**, which can be found at your local library. **A.M. Best** also has a web site (www.ambest.com) where you can buy a rating report for $4.95. Most insurance agents, however, can provide you with the same information free of charge.

What if I have any problems collecting on a claim?

Don't be intimidated. The last thing in the world an insurance company wants is an extended dispute with a customer. Juries dislike insurance companies, and fighting a claim often costs the company more than the amount in dispute.

The key to prevailing with an insurance company is to keep meticulous records and document all your communications in writing. You always want "proof" of your version of events.

When you have a problem with an insurance company, you should start by complaining to a claims adjuster or supervisor. If that does not work, ask about formal appeal procedures or voluntary arbitration. Complain all the way to the president of the company if you have to, but do not accept any settlement which is less than you deserve under the terms of your policy.

If you still get the run-around, next contact the Department of Insurance in your state. When you write them, make sure you summarize your complaint in a cover letter and include copies of your policy and relevant documents. The level of assistance that these insurance departments provide varies from state to state, ranging from excellent in California or New York, to non-existent in parts of the Midwest or South.

As a last resort, do not hesitate to file in small claims court or seek an attorney's advice if the dispute is over a sizeable amount of money. Threatening legal action is often a quick way of encouraging the insurance company to reconsider its position or propose a compromise.

What about health insurance, long-term care and medi-gap policies?

They are covered in our chapter on health care.

Guide to
LOWER AUTO INSURANCE RATES

This worksheet will help you evaluate your current auto insurance policy and eliminate the unnecessary coverage that contributes to high costs. Also included are step-by-step instructions for locating the lowest-priced insurance companies in your area. The 20 minutes it will take you to complete the form should save you a minimum of $200-500 per year.

AUTO INSURANCE WORKSHEET

Auto Insurance Contacts

Low Cost Insurers

Geico
800-861-8380
www.geico.com

State Farm
(see local phone directory)
www.statefarm.com

GE Auto Insurance
800-335-2167
www.geautoinsurance.com

Mercury Insurance
800-579-3467
www.mercuryinsurance.com

Safeco
800-255-9990
www.safeco.com

Allstate
(see local phone directory)
www.allstate.com

USAA*
800-282-2060
www.usaa.com

Reliance Direct
800-619-1600
www.reliancedirect.com

Progressive Insurance
800-288-6776
www.progressive.com

AIG Auto
800-807-9458
www.aigonline.com

Erie Insurance
800-458-0811
www.erieinsurance.com

* Available exclusively to active or retir military officers and their families

Rate Comparisons

Consumer Reports Auto Insurance Pricing Service
800-224-9495

Quotesmith
800-556-9393
www.quotesmith.com

1-2-3 Insurance
www.123insurance.com

AUTO INSURANCE WORKSHEET

State Insurance Departments

Alabama	205 269-3550	Montana	406 444-2040
Alaska	907 465-2515	Nebraska	402 471-2201
Arizona	602 255-5400	Nevada	702 885-4270
Arkansas	501 686-2935	New Hampshire	603 271-2261
California	213 736-3582	New Jersey	609 292-8170
Colorado	303 620-4341	New Mexico	505 827-4548
Connecticut	203 297-3800	New York	518 474-2121
Delaware	302 736-4251	N. Carolina	919 733-2004
D.C.	202 727-7434	N. Dakota	701 224-2440
Florida	904 488-0030	Ohio	614 644-2673
Georgia	404 656-2056	Oklahoma	405 521-2828
Hawaii	808 548-5450	Oregon	503 378-4271
Idaho	208 334-2250	Pennsylvania	717 787-5173
Illinois	217 782-4515	Rhode Island	401 277-2223
Indiana	317 232-2395	S. Carolina	803 737-6160
Iowa	515 281-5705	S. Dakota	605 773-3563
Kansas	913 296-7830	Tennessee	615 741-2241
Kentucky	502 564-3630	Texas	512 322-3470
Louisiana	504 342-5300	Utah	801 530-6400
Maine	207 582-8707	Vermont	802 828-3301
Maryland	301 333-6300	Virginia	804 786-3741
Massachusetts	617 727-3333	Washington	206 753-7301
Michigan	517 373-0240	W. Virginia	304 348-3394
Minnesota	612 296-6848	Wisconsin	608 266-0430
Mississippi	601 359-3569	Wyoming	307 777-7401
Missouri	314 751-3365		

AUTO INSURANCE WORKSHEET

Step 1

Call your insurance company. Ask them to summarize your current policy, based on the questions listed below. If more than one car is insured, note the coverage and cost for each vehicle separately.

Questions to Ask Your Agent

			Vehicle 1	Vehicle 2
LIABILITY	A.	What do I pay per year for LIABILITY COVERAGE? .... (Liability Coverage protects you against the claims of others if you cause an accident.)		
	B.	What are the policy limits for:		
		• Property Damage..		
		• Injuries (per person)		
		• Injuries (per accident)		
COLLISION	C.	What do I pay per year for COLLISION COVERAGE? .... (Collision Coverage pays for damage to your car from accidents.)		
	D.	What is my deductible for Collision Coverage?		
COMPREHENSIVE	E.	What is my deductible for COMPREHENSIVE COVERAGE? .... (Comprehensive Coverage pays for damage or loss of your car due to vandalism, theft or acts of nature.)		
	F.	What is my deductible for Comprehensive Coverage?........................		
MEDICAL	G.	What do I pay per year for MEDICAL COVERAGE? .... (Medical Coverage pays for medical bills for you and your passengers if you are injured in an accident.)		
TOWING/ RENTAL	H.	What do I pay per year for TOWING COVERAGE and reimbursement for CAR RENTALS in connection with repairs to my vehicle.		
UNINSURED MOTORIST	I.	What do I pay per year for UNINSURED MOTORIST COVERAGE? .. (Uninsured Motorist Coverage reimburses you for claims against a driver who is not insured, if he/she is the cause of an accident.)		
		Total Cost of Insurance		

12.1.1

AUTO INSURANCE WORKSHEET

Step 2

Streamline your existing policy by raising deductibles and eliminating unnecessary coverage.

	Current Policy		Streamlined Policy	
	Vehicle 1	Vehicle 2	Vehicle 1	Vehicle 2

LIABILITY COVERAGE

No changes are suggested in standard coverage. The minimum coverage needed is $50,000 in property damage, $100,000 in injury claims (per person) and $300,000 in injury claims (per accident). You will need more coverage if your assets exceed $300,000.

	Current Policy		Streamlined Policy	
	property	*property*	*property*	*property*
	injuries/person	*injuries/person*	*injuries/person*	*injuries/person*
	injuries/accident	*injuries/accident*	*injuries/accident*	*injuries/accident*

COLLISION COVERAGE

Protection cannot exceed the value of your vehicle. If your car is worth less than $3,500, most experts suggest eliminating collision coverage entirely. If your car is worth more than $3,500, collision coverage is suggested, but make sure your deductible is at least $500.

	Current Policy		Streamlined Policy	
	yes / no	yes / no	yes / no	yes / no
	coverage?	*coverage?*	*coverage?*	*coverage?*
	deductible	*deductible*	*deductible*	*deductible*

COMPREHENSIVE COVERAGE

Protection cannot exceed the value of your vehicle. If your car is worth less than $3,500, most experts suggest eliminating comprehensive coverage entirely. If your car is worth more than $3,500, comprehensive coverage is suggested, but make sure your deductable is at least $250.

	Current Policy		Streamlined Policy	
	yes / no	yes / no	yes / no	yes / no
	coverage?	*coverage?*	*coverage?*	*coverage?*
	deductible	*deductible*	*deductible*	*deductible*

MEDICAL COVERAGE

Medical Coverage is unnecessary if you and your passengers are covered by a conventional health insurance policy.

	Current Policy		Streamlined Policy	
	yes / no	yes / no	yes / no	yes / no
	coverage?	*coverage?*	*coverage?*	*coverage?*

TOWING/RENTAL REIMBURSEMENT COVERAGE

Towing and Rental Reimbursement Coverage is not particularly expensive, but the coverage is insignificant. Keep this protection or drop it at your own discretion.

	Current Policy		Streamlined Policy	
	yes / no	yes / no	yes / no	yes / no
	coverage?	*coverage?*	*coverage?*	*coverage?*

UNINSURED MOTORIST COVERAGE

Uninsured Motorist protection is optional if your vehicle is covered by collision coverage and you have regular health insurance. Consider dropping this coverage if uninsured.

	Current Policy		Streamlined Policy	
	yes / no	yes / no	yes / no	yes / no
	coverage?	*coverage?*	*coverage?*	*coverage?*

12.1.2

AUTO INSURANCE WORKSHEET

Step 3

Obtain all relevant information about
the drivers and cars you wish to
insure.

Driver(s)

Name	Birth date	Soc. Sec. No.	Driver's License No.	Accidents	Traffic Tickets

Automobile(s)

Make	Model	Year	Current Odometer Reading	Miles Driven Per Week

Step 4

Who is the principal driver for each
car? To save money, always assign the
youngest and highest risk driver to the
oldest, least valuable vehicle.

Car	Principal Driver

AUTO INSURANCE WORKSHEET

Step 5

Contact your state Department of Insurance to see if they publish a survey of auto insurance rates. If available, ask that one be mailed to you, then use it to identify the lowest-priced insurers in your area.

Alternatively, you should consider a price survey from the **Consumer Reports Auto Insurance Pricing Service** (800-556-9393) [$4.95 per report]. You can also obtain a free quote comparison by contacting **Quotesmith** (www.quotesmith.com 800-556-9393).

Step 6

Log on to the internet or call several of the following companies to obtain direct quotes based upon the streamlined policy coverage you identified in Step 2.

Internet Insurance Contacts

Geico
800-861-8380
www.geico.com

GE Auto Insurance
800-335-2167
www.geautoinsurance.com

Mercury Insurance
800-579-3467
www.mercuryinsurance.com

Reliance Direct
800-619-1600
www.reliancedirect.com

Progressive Insurance
800-288-6776
www.progressive.com

AIG Auto
800-807-9458
www.aigonline.com

AUTO INSURANCE WORKSHEET

You should also considering contacting several companies with a reputation for good service and low prices who work through insurance agents. Make sure you inquire about discounts for insuring more than one car, combining your auto insurance with homeowner's coverage, as well as any other price reductions for which you qualify. You should do the same with any of the internet companies you've contacted.

Sample Dialogue:

❝ *Hello. I'm shopping for car insurance and would like a price quote over the phone. I need 50/100/300 liability coverage*, $500 deductible coverage for collision**, $250 deductible coverage for comprehensive** and no medical coverage.* **❞**

* *Remember your coverage should be higher if you have more than $300,000 in assets to protect*

** *Drop collision and comprehensive coverage if your car is worth less than $3,500.*

State Farm
(see local phone directory)
www.statefarm.com

Safeco
800-255-9990
www.safeco.com

Liberty Mutual
800-526-1547
www.libertymutual.com

USAA*
800-282-2060
www.usaa.com

Erie Insurance**
800-458-0811
www.erieinsurance

* *Only available to military personnel and their families*

** *Don't bother applying if you don't have a perfect driving record*

Guide to LOWER HOMEOWNER'S INSURANCE RATES

This worksheet will help you lower the cost of your homeowner's insurance. Use it to determine the correct amount of coverage for your house, furnishings and other valuables, as well as liability protection for you and your family. The step-by-step instructions show you how to locate insurance companies offering the lowest rates for comparable policies. If you are typical of most readers, the 10-15 minutes you spend completing this form should save you $75 to $150 a year in lower premiums.

If you rent your home, a special renter's policy is available. Proceed directly to Step 7.

HOMEOWNER'S INSURANCE WORKSHEET

Homeowner's Insurance Contacts

Low-Cost Insurers

State Farm
(see local phone directory)
www.statefarm.com

Allstate
(see local phone directory)
www.allstate.com

Farmers Insurance
(see local phone directory)
www.farmers.com

Safeco
800-255-9990
www.safeco.com

Liberty Mutual
800-526-1547
www.libertymutual.com

USAA*
800-282-2060
www.usaa.com

* only available to military personnel and their families

Erie Insurance
800-458-0811
www.erieinsurance.com

Flood Insurance

National Flood Insurance Program
800-427-4661
www.fema.gov

HOMEOWNER'S INSURANCE WORKSHEET

Step 1

Call your insurance company.
Ask them to summarize your current policy based on the questions listed below.

Summary of Existing Coverage
Questions to Ask Your Insurance Agent

A. What is the current amount of my coverage for structural damage? _____

B. How much protection do I have for damage or theft of my personal belongings and household furnishings? _____

C. How much protection do I have for liability claims? _____

D. What are the limits of my coverage for loss or theft of the following items?

 • jewelry and furs _____

 • stamps, coins or currency _____

 • silverware _____

 • art or collectables _____

 • guns _____

 • other valuables (specify)

 • _____ _____

 • _____ _____

 • _____ _____

 • _____ _____

E. What is the deductible I must pay before you will honor a claim? _____

F. Do you pay for the **replacement cost** of my personal property or the **cash value** of these items minus depreciation? _____

G. What is my annual premium? _____

H. Do I have supplemental protection against earthquakes or floods? _____

Step 2

Estimate what it would cost to (a) rebuild your home and (b) replace its contents if it were destroyed.
If your home is of average construction, you should estimate between $60 and $80 per square foot of finished area.

If you own a unique home with special features or an older property that would be particularly expensive to replace, it may make sense to ask an appraiser for a more precise estimate.

To determine costs to replace personal property, do a quick inventory of your belongings, then estimate the cost to replace them at current prices.

HOMEOWNER'S INSURANCE WORKSHEET

Estimated Costs

Rebuild Your Home		Replace Your Personal Property	
		Carpeting	_____
		Window Coverings	_____
Size of home (sq. ft.)	_____	Furniture	_____
Type of construction (brick, wood, aluminum siding)	_____	Clothing	_____
No. of bedrooms	_____	Jewelry & Furs	_____
No. of baths	_____	Silverware	_____
Patio or deck?	_____	Art	_____
Fireplace?	_____	Other Collectables	_____
Finished basement?	_____	Guns	_____
Finished attic?	_____	Major Appliances	_____
Heating/ AC system	_____	Home Electronics	_____
Garage?	_____	Kitchen Items	_____
Special Features?	_____	Tools	_____
_____	_____	Musical Instruments	_____
_____	_____	Miscellaneous	_____
Total Cost to Rebuild	_____	**Total Replacement Value of Personal Property**	_____

HOMEOWNER'S INSURANCE WORKSHEET

Step 3

Compare the amount of coverage under your existing policy to the actual cost of rebuilding your home and replacing its contents.

Note if you are over- or under-insured for structural damage, personal property or any particular items which are only covered to stated maximums.

	Amount of Current Coverage	Actual Cost of Replacement
A. Structural damage	_____	_____
B. Personal property losses		
Total coverage	_____	_____
Jewelry & furs	_____	_____
Silverware	_____	_____
Stamps, coins, currency	_____	_____
Art & collectables	_____	_____
Guns	_____	_____
Other valuables	_____	_____
_____	_____	_____
_____	_____	_____

Step 4

Contact at least 5 insurance companies, including the company that insures your automobile.*

Ask them to quote you a specific rate for a homeowner's policy based on the actual replacement costs for items you wish to insure.

* You can usually obtain a multi-policy discount if you insure your home and auto with the same company.

Allstate	800 484 6317
Amica	800 662-6422
Nationwide	800 582-1236
Safeco	800 341-3600
State Farm	309 766-2311
USAA	800 531-8080

“ *Hello. I'm shopping for homeowner's insurance and would like a price quote by phone. My home is approximately ___ sq. feet and I estimate the cost of rebuilding at $ _____. I want Replacement coverage for my personal property with a $500 deductible. I (will / will not) need supplementary coverage for certain valuables (specify as necessary). I want liability coverage equal to my net worth, which is $_____. Please note that I have fire extinguishers, deadbolt locks and a burglar alarm system for which I would like a discount if one is available.* Also, I would like to know what kind of discount I might receive if I also insured my auto(s) with your company.* ”

Homeowners' Insurance Pricing Survey

	Policy #1	Policy #2	Policy #3	Policy #4	Policy #5
Company					
Phone Number					
Agent's Name					
Structural Coverage					
Personal Property Coverage					
Supplemental Coverage (if any)					
Coverage Based on a Replacement Value	YES / NO	YES / NO	YES / NO	YES / NO	YES / NO
Deductible					
Supplemental Coverage for Earthquakes or Floods					
ANNUAL PREMIUM					

HOMEOWNER'S INSURANCE WORKSHEET

Step 5

Compare price quotes to your existing policy. Do you save any money with another company?

Current Policy	_____
Best Rate Quote	_____
Annual Savings	_____

Step 6

If the new policy saves you more than $50 per year, replace your existing coverage.
Repeat the process every 12 months to guarantee you are always paying the lowest rate possible.

Step 7

If you rent your home and the replacement cost of your personal belongings is $5,000 or more, you should buy a renter's version of homeowner's insurance.
The policy reimburses you for damage or theft of these items, plus personal liability protection. Buy only the protection necessary to replace your valuables. Use the chart from Step 4 to shop for the lowest-priced policy.

Step 8

Complete an inventory of your personal property.

When disaster strikes, many homeowners are unprepared. One of the biggest mistakes is not keeping a complete inventory of your personal possessions. You will need such a list to document your losses to an insurance company and it is next to impossible to compile one from memory. Fill out this inventory as thoroughly as possible, then keep a copy in a safe place, such as a safe deposit box or fire-proof file cabinet

Personal Property Inventory

Item	Manufacturer	Style No.	Purchase Price	Approx. Date Purchased	Serial Number (if any)

LIVING ROOM

- *Furniture*

- *Other*

DINING ROOM

- *Furniture*

- *China*
- *Silverware*
- *Other*

FAMILY ROOM

- *Furniture*

- *CDs, Records & Tapes*
  (estimate total collection and replacement value) _____

Personal Property Inventory

	Item	Manufacturer	Style No.	Purchase Price	Approx. Date Purchased	Serial Number (if any)
BEDROOM 1						
• Furniture						
• Clothing						
• Other						
BEDROOM 2						
• Furniture						
• Clothing						
• Other						
BEDROOM 3						
• Furniture						
• Clothing						
• Other						
BEDROOM 4						
• Furniture						
• Clothing						
• Other						

Personal Property Inventory

Item	Manufacturer	Style No.	Purchase Price	Approx. Date Purchased	Serial Number (if any)

KITCHEN

- Refrigerator
- Disposal
- Range
- Microwave
- Misc. Appliances

- Pots & Pans
- Dishes/Glsswr
- Other

ENTERTAINMENT EQUIPMENT

- TVs

- VCR
- Stereo
- CD player
- Tape player
- Camcorder
- Speakers
- Camera
- Binoculars
- Other

GARAGE

- Power Tools

- Lawn mower
- Misc.

Personal Property Inventory

Item	Manufacturer	Style No.	Purchase Price	Approx. Date Purchased	Serial Number (if any)

MUSICAL INSTRUMENTS

HOME FURNISHINGS
- Carpet
- Other flooring
- Drapes/window coverings

MISCELLANEOUS

Guide to
LOWER LIFE
INSURANCE RATES

Life Insurance Contacts

Low-Cost Insurers

Term Life

Veritas
800-552-3553
http://veritas.ameritas.com

Golden Rule
800-950-4474
www.goldenrule.com

First Penn
800-288-6699
www.1stpenn.com

North American
800-800-3656
www.nacolah.com

Valley Forge
800-262-0348
www.cnalife.com

Online Quote Services for Term Insurance

CompuLife
800-798-3488
www.term4sale.com

Quotesmith
800-556-9393
www.quotesmith.com

Right Quote
800-366-1983
www.rightquote.com

Insurance Quote Svces.
800-972-1104
www.quote.com

First Quote
800-583-0231
www.1stquote.com

Universal Life

Veritas Life
800-552-3553
http://veritas.ameritas.com

Amica Mutual
800-234-5433
www.amicamutual.com

USAA Life
800-531-8000
www.usaalife.com

Dial-up Quote Services

Select Quote
800-289-5807
www.selectquote.com

Accu-Quote
800-442-9899

Agent Referral Network CompuLife
800-798-3488
www.term4sale.com

Insurance Sales Net.
800-467-8736
www.800insurme.com

Discount Agents

Northwood-Roche
800-732-2832
www.northwoodroche.com

Cohen Agency
626-431-2994
www.4-1-1.com/cohen

Phillips Agency
714-256-1972
http://hometown.aol.com/insure20/index.html

LIFE INSURANCE WORKSHEET

This worksheet will help you decide whether life insurance makes sense for your family. You may be surprised to learn that you don't need the protection.

If you do need coverage, there are easy-to-follow instructions on estimating the proper amount of insurance, choosing the best type of policy and finding little-known sources that can save you 20-75% on your premiums.

Step 1

Fill out the form at right to determine your family's current living expenses and sources of income.

CURRENT ANNUAL EXPENSES [1]:

MORTGAGE OR RENT: _____

PROPERTY TAXES: _____

AUTO INSURANCE: _____

HOMEOWNER'S INSURANCE: _____

GROCERIES: _____

TELEPHONE: _____

GASOLINE: _____

AUTO REPAIRS: _____

VACATIONS: _____

RESTAURANTS: _____

CREDIT CARDS [2]: _____

ELECTRICITY: _____

WATER: _____

RETIREMENT SAVINGS [3]: _____

COLLEGE SAVINGS [4]: _____

MISCELLANEOUS EXPENSES: _____

TOTAL EXPENSES: _____

CURRENT ANNUAL INCOME (AFTER TAXES)

YOUR INCOME: _____

SPOUSE INCOME: _____

OTHER INCOME [5]: _____

TOTAL INCOME _____

[1] Multiply actual or estimated monthly income and expenses by twelve (12) to determine annual estimates.

[2] Estimate what you currently spend on a monthly basis excluding restaurant meals, vacation travel or gasoline, then multiply this estimate by twelve (12).

[3] Estimate your current contributions to a retirement account. If you do not currently save for retirement, complete the retirement fund worksheet in Chapter 7, then estimate the annual contribution necessary to reach your retirement goal.

[4] Estimate your current contributions to a college savings fund for your children. If you do not currently save for your children's college education, complete the college worksheet in Chapter 7, then estimate the annual contribution necessary to reach your savings goal.

[5] Do not include income from your retirement accounts.

LIFE INSURANCE WORKSHEET

Step 2

Modify expense and income projections to reflect changes after your death.

Expenses will decrease without you, since your family will spend less for food, clothes, gasoline, etc. A rule-of-thumb is that the death of a breadwinner reduces household expenses by 25%, although you can make your own estimate if your personal circumstances are unique.

Family income will also decrease, unless your spouse can make up for your lost contribution. At a minimum, reduce income projections by your current salary.

$$\underline{\hspace{2cm}} - \underline{\hspace{2cm}} = \underline{\hspace{2cm}}$$

Current Family Expenses — *Changes to Expenses After Your Death* = *Future Family Expenses*

$$\underline{\hspace{2cm}} - \underline{\hspace{2cm}} = \underline{\hspace{2cm}}$$

Current Family Income — *Changes to Income After Your Death* = *Future Family Income*

Step 3

Determine whether your future family income will be greater than expected expenses.

If the answer is "yes," you do not need life insurance.

If the answer is "no," life insurance is recommended.

Note: Many agents will try to sell you life insurance even if your family does not need the death benefits. Their sales pitch is that certain types of life insurance, such as **whole life** or **universal life** make excellent retirement plans since part of the policy is a savings plan which earns tax-deferred interest. While it is true that these policies help you postpone taxes, you can achieve the same results yourself by contributing each year to a 401(k) or IRA plan. If these plans are fully invested in growth-oriented no-load mutual funds, your yields will usually far exceed what you could earn with an insurance company. Even better, you're not paying for unnecessary death benefits or built-in agent commissions.

Step 4

Determine how much coverage you need. If you need life insurance, restate your family's projected income and expenses after your death. How much supplementary income is necessary to meet their future needs?

_____	_____	_____
Future Living Expenses	Projected Income	Additional Income Required

(The expression above reads: Future Living Expenses − Projected Income = Additional Income Required)

Step 5

State the ages of your spouse and other dependents, then estimate the number of years they will need supplementary income.

	CURRENT AGE	YEARS NEEDED*
SPOUSE	_____	_____
CHILDREN	_____	_____
OTHER DEPENDENTS	_____	_____

*For spouses, assume supplementary income is needed until age 65, provided that a well-funded retirement plan will take affect thereafter. If such a plan is not in place, supplementary income will be necessary throughout their projected lifetime. The current life expectancy for males is 72; The current life expectancy for females is 79. For children, assume supplementary income is needed until they are self-sufficient at age 22.

Step 6

Assuming you own your home, how many years until your mortgage is fully paid?

Years remaining on your mortgage: _____

Step 7

If you have children who will attend college and for whom you have not already established a college savings plan, estimate how much you will contribute to their college education and when they will need the money.

CHILD:	CONTRIBUTION PER YEAR	NO. OF YEARS	WHEN NEEDED
_____	_____	____	____
_____	_____	____	____
_____	_____	____	____
_____	_____	____	____

Step 8

Fill out the chart at right summarizing your family's supplementary income requirements based on changing expenses. The total income required will give you a good idea of how much life insurance to buy.

You may wonder why the Family Income Retirement chart does not account for inflation. Logic would suggest that goods and services will cost more over time. However, you must also remember that your insurance proceeds will be earning interest. For the purpose of our chart, we assume that the likely inflation rate in the years ahead will be approximately 4.5% per year. We also assume that interest rates will be 6.5%. If you are currently in a 28% tax bracket, 6.5% interest on your savings translates into after-tax income of 4.68%. The inflation rate (4.5%) and the real return on your insurance proceeds (4.6%) offset one another, making adjustments for interest and inflation unnecessary. These are reasonably conservative estimates.

Family Income Requirements

YR	AMOUNT	YR	AMOUNT	YR	AMOUNT
1		11		21	
2		12		22	
3		13		23	
4		14		24	
5		25		25	
6		16		26	
7		17		27	
8		18		28	
9		19		29	
10		20		30	

TOTAL_____

Example:

The Jones family will need $20,000 per year if Mr. Jones dies. In five years, their only child will start college, needing $5,000 per year for tuition and books. In six years, the home mortgage will be fully paid. In nine years, their only child will graduate college and become self-supportive. In 14 years, Mrs. Jones will reach retirement and receive a pension adequate to meet her continuing needs. A supplementary income chart for the Jones family would resemble the following:

Year	Income Needed	Coments
1	$ 20,000	
2	20,000	
3	20,000	
4	20,000	
5	25,000	Child starts college (+$5,000/yr)
6	17,000	Home mortgage paid off (–$8,000/yr)
7	17,000	
8	17,000	
9	12,000	Child graduates (-$5,000/yr)
10	12,000	
11	12,000	
12	12,000	
13	12,000	
14	0	Wife gets pension
TOTAL	**216,000**	

LIFE INSURANCE WORKSHEET

Step 9

Determine which type of policy is best for you.

If you are in good health, under 55 years of age and need insurance for 20 years or less, term life is your best insurance value. You cannot beat the price or the simplicity.

Here's what a healthy adult male might expect to pay for $150,000 of coverage.

Typical Annual Premium for Term Life Insurance
$250,000 Death Benefit

Age	Premium	Age	Premium
35	$ 288	46	$ 560
36	300	47	593
37	318	48	630
38	335	49	673
39	350	50	444
40	368	51	718
41	390	52	770
42	423	53	823
43	448	54	885
44	473	55	945
45	515		

Source: Investors Life Insurance of Nebraska

Term coverage is the best deal because it is pure insurance, without the bells and whistles of other types of policies. It has no accumlated value you can redeem in later years, and there are no hidden fees the insurance company can add for managing your surplus premiums.

No frills = lower costs.

About the only reason not to choose term life is if you need coverage beyond age 70. Most insurers will not guarantee renewals thereafter, which means your policy can be cancelled if you don't pass a physical. Term policies are also prohibitively expensive late in life. Even modest protection can cost several thousand dollars per year.

In these cases, whole life may be a better option. Unlike term insurance, whole life can always be renewed, regardless of your age or health. The size of your premium is also more manageable, since surplus funds you put into the policy in early years help defray the higher cost of insurance later. In the long run, whole life rarely saves you money compared to term coverage, but the level payments and guaranteed protection can make it more convenient if you still need life insurance after retirement.

We have illustrated a typical whole life policy (at right) to give you a better idea how such a plan works. In the scenario below, Bill has purchased a 20-year whole life policy which pays $250,000 in benefits if he dies. Bill's premium is $1,500 per year, even though the cost of maintaining his death benefit (mortality charge) is lower in the initial years of the policy and higher as he gets older. The difference between the annual premium and the rising cost of insurance is offset by his policy's growing cash balance and dividends paid by his insurance company. Should Bill wish to cancel his policy in less than 20 years, he has the option of withdrawing his cash balance.

LIFE INSURANCE WORKSHEET

Bill's Whole Life Policy
Age: 55
Annual Premium: $1,500 / yr
Death Benefit: $250,000

Year	Annual Premium	Accumulated Cash Value	Death Benefit	Annual Dividends on Cash Balance
1	$ 1,500	$ 1,460	$ 250,000	8%
2	1,500	3,020	250,000	8%
3	1,500	4,615	250,000	8%
4	1,500	6,233	250,000	8%
5	1,500	7,869	250,000	8%
6	1,500	9,516	250,000	8%
7	1,500	11,166	250,000	8%
8	1,500	12,802	250,000	8%
9	1,500	14,408	250,000	8%
10	1,500	15,969	250,000	8%

Both term and whole life policies come in a variety of formats so you can tailor your coverage to your specific needs. Among term policies, we recommend the multi-year option, since you get the advantage of level premiums and guaranteed renewals. If you are among the minority who needs a whole life policy, universal life is probably best, since you can change your annual premium or death benefits if your family situation changes.

Types of Life Insurance

Term Life Policies

STRAIGHT TERM
Buy coverage one year at a time. Renewable at discretion of insurance company, unless policy has a guaranteed renewal clause.

MULTI-YEAR TERM
Level premiums during term of coverage (i.e. 5, 10, 15 years).

CONVERTIBLE TERM
May convert policy from term to whole life (one-time option).

Whole Life Policies

TRADITIONAL WHOLE LIFE
Fixed annual premium and death benefits.

SINGLE PREMIUM WHOLE LIFE
Lump sum premium. Eliminates need for annual payments.

UNIVERSAL LIFE
Can vary premiums or make withdrawals of accumulated cash at any time.

VARIABLE LIFE
You decide how your cash balance is invested I.e. stocks, bonds, money market.

VANISHING PREMIUM
You pay higher premiums in earlier years, then let yields on your cash balance pay for future cost of insurance.

Which type of policy is best for your circumstances? _____

LIFE INSURANCE WORKSHEET

Step 10

If you need term coverage, start with an unbiased rate quote from *Compulife* (www.term4sale.com/ 800-798-3488) or *Quotesmith* (www.quotesmith.com/ 800-556-9393). Either service will ask you questions about your age, health, amount of coverage you desire, etc. You will receive online rate quotes from a long list of companies.

In most cases, it is desirable to purchase a term life policy with a level premium over a certain period of time (i.e., ten years.) Be certain to specify the number of years you will need the coverage.

In addition to the quote services, contact several insurers directly. In most

cases, you will be referred to an agent. Once again, provide the relevant information and make note of the price quote on the rate survey.

Inquire from the agent you speak with whether there are ways you might qualify for a preferred premium, based on your health history and other factors. In some cases, the rules for preferred policies are more flexible than they are described on a in brochures or on a website. Keep in mind that any rate quote is only preliminary, pending a medical evaluation and review of your application.

Insurers to Contact for Rate Quotes

Veritas
800-552-3553
http://veritas.ameritas.com

Golden Rule
800-950-4474
www.goldenrule.com

First Penn
800-288-6699
www.1stpenn.com

North American
800-800-3656
www.nacolah.com

Valley Forge
800-262-0348
www.cnalife.com

LIFE INSURANCE WORKSHEET

Step 11 — Term Insurance Rate Survey

Fill out the Term Insurance Rate Survey below listing the rates you have been quoted from various sources.

Company		Company		Company	
Death Benefit		Death Benefit		Death Benefit	
Company Rating		Company Rating		Company Rating	
Yr	Premium	Yr	Premium	Yr	Premium
1		1		1	
2		2		2	
3		3		3	
4		4		4	
5		5		5	
6		6		6	
7		7		7	
8		8		8	
9		9		9	
10		10		10	
11		11		11	
12		12		12	
13		13		13	
14		14		14	
15		15		15	
16		16		16	
17		17		17	
18		18		18	
19		19		19	
20		20		20	
Conditions for Renewal		Conditions for Renewal		Conditions for Renewal	
Physical?		Physical? Yes / No		Physical?	
When?		When?		When?	
Total Premiums		Total Premiums		Total Premiums	

Company		Company		Company	
Death Benefit		Death Benefit		Death Benefit	
Company Rating		Company Rating		Company Rating	
Yr	Premium	Yr	Premium	Yr	Premium
1		1		1	
2		2		2	
3		3		3	
4		4		4	
5		5		5	
6		6		6	
7		7		7	
8		8		8	
9		9		9	
10		10		10	
11		11		11	
12		12		12	
13		13		13	
14		14		14	
15		15		15	
16		16		16	
17		17		17	
18		18		18	
19		19		19	
20		20		20	
Conditions for Renewal		Conditions for Renewal		Conditions for Renewal	
Physical?		Physical? Yes / No		Physical?	
When?		When?		When?	
Total Premiums		Total Premiums		Total Premiums	

LIFE INSURANCE WORKSHEET

Step 12

If you need universal, whole life or annuity productscontact an insurance agent. It is not advisable to shop for these products without a licensed insurance agent or broker. If you do not know a reputable agent in your area, get a referral from the following services.

We recommend that you discuss your needs with at least three different agents and obtain price quotes from all of them.

Agent Referral Networks

CompuLife
800-798-3488
www.term4sale.com

Insurance Sales Network
800-467-8736
www.800insurme.com

Step 13

Contact the following insurers who have sales representatives who can answer your questions by phone and provide price quotes directly.

Warning: Any price quote on whole life and universal life products is largely influenced by the interest rate and investment return assumptions that are used to generate the quote. This is because your insurance policy will perform differently depending upon prevailing economic conditions in the years ahead. It is extremely important that you consider various interest and investment rate assumptions to understand how each policy may perform under different circumstances. It is also important that you compare policies from different insurers based upon the same assumptions.

Insurers Who Sell Directly

Veritas Life
800-552-3553
http://veritas.ameritas.com

Amica Mutual
800-234-5433
www.amicamutual.com

USAA Life
800-531-8000
www.usaalife.com

Sample Dialogue:

" *Hello. I am in the market for life insurance and I was hoping you could help me. I've decided* that I am interested in permanent coverage and would like you to explain my various options for the whole life and universal life products you sell. I'm in the market for a policy that pays a death benefit of $_____, and I will need the coverage for _____ years. I realize that the policy performance is *predicated on certain assumptions. So I would like you to give me a price quote assuming current interest rates and yields, as well as low and high estimates based on interest rates at ___ % and ___% and investment returns of ____% and ____%. When you quote me rates, I would like to see the annual premium, the cost of insurance (mortality charge) and the projected cash balance for each year I own the policy.* **99**

Step 14

Once you have conducted a thorough search of your options, complete the Whole Life/ Universal Life Rate Survey on page 149, again making certain you are comparing policies based upon identical assumptions. Note that the policy with the lowest price may not necessarily be the best investment.

LIFE INSURANCE WORKSHEET

Whole Life Rate Survey

Company				Company				Company		
Company Rating				**Company Rating**				**Company Rating**		
Interest Rate Assumption %				**Interest Rate Assumption** %				**Interest Rate Assumption** %		
Yr	Annual Premium	Cost of Insurance	Cash Balance	Yr	Annual Premium	Cost of Insurance	Cash Balance	Yr	Annual Premium	Cost of Insurance	Cash Balance
1				1				1			
2				2				2			
3				3				3			
4				4				4			
5				5				5			
6				6				6			
7				7				7			
8				8				8			
9				9				9			
10				10				10			
11				11				11			
12				12				12			
13				13				13			
14				14				14			
15				15				15			
16				16				16			
17				17				17			
18				18				18			
19				19				19			
20				20				20			
	Total	Total	Final Balance		Total	Total	Final Balance		Total	Total	Final Balance

Step 15

Once you have identified the most attractive option(s) from either the Term Life Insurance Rate Survey or the Whole Life/Universal Life Rate Survey, you may wish to consider a little-known opportunity to lower the price you pay for the policy you want even further.

In most cases, approximately 50% of the first-year premium you pay for term life coverage, and as much as 80% of the first-year premium you pay for other types of life insurance, is paid to your insurance agent in the form of commissions. For example, were you to buy a term life policy for an annual premium of $800, the insurance company you buy your policy from will pay your agent as much as $400. In two states, Florida and California, state law permits agents to rebate to you some or all of their commission. If you live in either state, you can simply ask your agent whether he would consider sharing a portion of the commission as a further inducement to do business. As you might imagine, most agents are not particularly enthused by the prospect of cutting their fee, but it does happen, particularly if there is a lot of money at stake. If you don't feel comfortable negotiating with the agent,

you might just consider contacting one of the insurance agencies below that guarantees a sizeable rebate:

Agents Who Rebate Commissions

Northwood-Roche
800-732-2832
www.northwoodroche.com

Cohen Agency
626-431-2994
www.4-1-1.com/cohen

Phillips Agency
714-256-1972
http://hometown.aol.com/insure20/index.html

The discount program from these agencies is available regardless of where you live. The only "catch" is that you must be physically located in California at the time you sign the final policy contract. You might think that flying halfway across the country to sign your name might seem a bit extreme, but when you consider that in some cases the rebate savings can amount to hundreds or even thousands of dollars, the notion isn't as far-fetched. In fact, many people have been known to turn the trip into a mini-vacation using the money they've saved.

If you think we are exaggerating about the money you can save on your insurance, think again. Here are just a few real life examples of how much you can save using the suggestions in this chapter.

Suggestion: Lower your auto insurance rates by raising your deductibles.

Example: We asked State Farm Insurance to quote us a policy for a 1996 BMW 325, driven by a 35-year-old male in Fairfax, Virginia. In one case, we asked for a $100 deductible on collision coverage. In the other, we requested a $500 deductible. Choosing the higher deductible saved $237 per year.

Policy A ($100 Deductible)	Policy B ($500 Deductible)
$ 756.44 Annual Premium	$ 518.78 Annual Premium
Savings	**$ 237.66**

Suggestion: Shop several insurance companies for the lowest prices.

Example: We asked nine major insurance companies the cost of insuring a 1997 Honda Accord and a 1995 Olds Cutlass Supreme in Detroit, Michigan. We specified identical coverage for a family of four, all with clean driving records. The price differential between highest and lowest priced policies was an astounding $4,039!

Company	Annual Premium
Allstate	$ 5,746
State Farm	$ 3,372
The Hartford	$ 3,622
Travelers	$ 2,950
Geico	$ 2,809
Liberty Mutual	$ 2,497
USAA	$ 1,994
Nationwide	$ 1,707

Potential Savings **$ 4,039** *per year*

We conducted a similar survey among five companies for homeowner's coverage on a $150,000 house in Grand Rapids, Michigan. Again, the coverage was identical. In this case, the price differential between the highest and lowest priced policies was more than $400.

Company	Annual Annual
Travelers	$ 907
Nationwide	$ 767
Allstate	$ 569
State Farm	$ 503

Potential Savings: **$ 403** *per year*

Suggestion: Only insure the cost to rebuild your house, not the total market value.

Example: We asked The Hartford Insurance to quote us standard coverage for a home located in Gaithersburg, Maryland. We asked for the annual premium based on the home's total value ($220,000) as well as for 85% of the cost to rebuild. By covering only rebuilding costs, the annual savings is more than $126 per year.

Policy A ($220,000)	Policy B ($160,000)
$ 457 Annual Premium	$ 331 Annual Premium

Annual Savings: $126

Suggestion: Use an insurance quote service to identify the lowest price on term coverage.

Example: We searched the quote service for rates on a $500,000, 20-year level-term policy for a 49-year-old male non-smoker, residing in Massachusetts and rating "preferred" health status. The difference between the lowest and highest quotes was more than $470 per year!

	Ameritas	Jefferson Pilot Financial
Death Benefit	*$500,000*	*$500,000*
Term	*20-yr, level premium*	*20-yr, level premium*
Health Rating	*preferred*	*preferred*
Annual Premium	*$1,125*	*$1,595*

Total Savings $ 9,400

($470 x 20 yrs.)

Chapter Six

The Bargain-Hunter's Guide to Jewelry

Where do I find the best deals on jewelry?

Pawnshops and small, independently-owned jewelers are the best source for high-end diamonds, emeralds and upscale watches. Television shopping channels (**QVC** and **HSN**) are the best choice for less formal pieces and semi-precious stones. Avoid department stores and national jewelry chains. Mall jewelers often double or triple wholesale costs to cover national advertising, high rents and other overhead. The shopping channels deal in higher volumes without the high overhead, passing on the savings to you.

Is it risky to buy at a pawnshop?

It depends on what kind of pawnshop. At established shops with a long history in the area, the savings opportunities far outweigh the risks. You can improve your chances of a bargain by following three important rules:

Pawnshop Buying Tips

1. Never visit a pawnshop until you have first researched prices at three or more retail jewelers.

2. Shop only at pawnshops doing business from the same location for at least five years.

3. Stick to a predetermined budget regardless of how enticing more expensive items may appear.

You may be interested to know that 1 in 10 Americans visited pawnshops last year according to statistics compiled by the International Association of Pawn Brokers. The trend is growing.

Are there other ways to find bargains without going to such extremes?

Look in the Yellow Pages for jewelers who advertise that they both buy and sell jewelry. These merchants are typically family owned and almost never located in expensive shopping areas where the overhead adds to the price. Jewelers who buy from individuals pay less for their merchandise, so they can in turn pass savings on to their retail customers. The bargains are particulary good on loose stones.

If you live near Los Angeles or New York, or plan to vist anytime soon, you can find excellent prices in the downtown shops that comprise an area known as the "jewelry district." In these concentrated areas, there are literally hundreds of wholesale and retail jewelry outlets where you can find almost any type of item at wholesale prices. If you are planning a large purchase ($2,000 and up), it may be worth a long-distance trip.

Jewelry Districts

New York Jewelry District
47th Street between 5th and 6th Avenues

Los Angeles Jewelry District
Hill Street (Downtown), between
6th and 7th Streets

Isn't old jewelry less desirable than new merchandise?

Not at all. Fine jewelry, especially gemstones, are virtually indestructible. A new diamond looks exactly the same to the naked eye as a stone which is 10, 20 or even 50 years old. You should have no reservations about buying previously-owned stones. In fact, thousands of customers do so every year without even knowing it. It is common practice for jewelers to re-mount old diamonds in new settings without disclosing it to their customers.

Do I need to know anything special when I buy a diamond?

Diamonds are the easiest gems to buy because their price can be determined objectively using an international grading system based on size, color, clarity and cut. Once you know a particular stone's grade, you can easily compare it to comparable stones from different jewelers. The key is to make certain the grade you are told accurately describes the stone. One way to make certain is to insist on a written appraisal, preferably by an independent source such as the **Gemological Institute of America** (GIA). A GIA certification assures you that a stone is accurately graded, although the certification adds to your cost.

What about other gems?

There is unfortunately no universal grading system for emeralds, rubies, sapphires or other precious gems, so determining market price is far more difficult. A grading system was tried several years ago but failed because it was impossible to classify the infinite variety of gem colors. Generally, the clarity of a stone and the richness of its color will determine its value, but these features cannot be graded. Because there is no objective standard to measure against, it is easy for a novice gem buyer to overpay. Make sure you look at many stones from a variety of dealers before making a purchase.

Any advice on pearls?

Unlike gems, pearls are produced by living creatures (oysters). They are actually mineral deposits secreted by the oyster around an irritant (sand, gravel, etc.) that has become lodged inside the animal's shell. Natural pearls are formed by nature. Cultured pearls are created with man's help, usually by injecting a small rounded bead into the oyster, around which the pearl deposits form. It is impossible to distinguish between a natural and cultured pearl unless you use an X-ray machine.

Pearls are graded by size, color, roundness, smoothness and lustre. In that way, they are similiar to diamonds and relatively easy to price. The most expensive pearls are round and pinkish in color with a deep iridescent lustre.

I am constantly seeing synthetic diamonds and other "imitation" jewelry advertised on shopping channels. What do you think of this kind of jewelry?

Compared to the real thing, synthetic stones are indeed a bargain. For decades, the very rich have worn fake diamonds, preferring to leave their expensive originals locked away in a safe deposit box. There is no reason for you to spend $500, $1,000 or more for an expensive diamond cocktail ring or other extravagance when a fake version looks just as good and sells for less than $35. Remember, jewelry is a fashion accessory, not an investment.

Guide to
JEWELRY
AT A DISCOUNT

Internet Resources

Home Shopping Channels

QVC
www.qvc.com

HSN
www.hsn.com

Gold Jewelry

Sarraf
213-612-4690
www.sarraf.com
(wholesale prices from jeweler in L.A. Jewelry District)

4-Jewelry
www.4jewelry.com
(internet-only jewelry source)

Jeweler's Warehouse
800-661-5393
www.jewelersware-house.com

Diamonds

Diamonds U.S.A
800-577-9118
www.diamonds-usa.com

Fine Watches

Alan Marcus & Co.
800-654-7184
www.alanmarcuso.com

Links to other jewelry discount sources

Rappaport Company
www.diamonds.net

Step 1

The best sources for jewelry bargains are pawnshops and independent jewelers who both buy and sell. Using the Yellow Pages, locate several of these sources in your area.

PAWNSHOPS
JEWELERS   BUY   /   SELL

_____   _____

_____   _____

_____   _____

If you prefer, you can also shop TV shopping channels such as *QVC* and *HSN*. If you have a particular item in mind, try their web sites at www.qvc.com and www.hsn.com. Keep in mind that the most popular items usually sell out on the air and never make it back to the web site. Other web sites listed above may also prove useful.

Step 2

Never visit these sources without first educating yourself about jewelry prices and quality at the retail level. Begin by visiting your local mall and learning as much as possible about the type of jewelry you wish to purchase. Be as specific as possible. You can't compare prices unless you know exact specifications for size, weight and quality.

Diamonds

All diamonds are graded according to 4 measures of quality, making price comparisons easy.

A sample description for a diamond would read as follows: "1.24 Carat, H Color, VS1, Brilliant Cut."

You can obtain an up-to-the-minute report on the current wholesale value of any type of diamond on the world market by purchasing a copy of **The Rappaport Report**. This informative guide publishes the current wholesale price for diamonds worldwide. To order, call 212 354-0575 ($9.00/issue).

Diamonds: Four Measures of Quality

Color — Designated by letter grade.
D - E - F - G - H - I - ..... - Z
(colorless <<< --- >>> yellow)

Clarity — Designated by category.

F	VVS1	VS1	SI1
	VVS2	VS2	SI2
flawless	very, very slightly flawed	very slightly flawed	slightly flawed

(Higher quality <<< --- >>> Lower quality)

Size — Designated by Weight (in Carats).
100 "points" = 1 Carat = 1/5 gram

Cut — No designation (not graded by letter or number). Stones are judged by their overall brilliance and sparkle.

Gold

Gold is measured by weight and purity.

1. Purity is described in number of Karats, spelled with a "K." All gold jewelry must be stamped with a karat designation. Nothing under 10 karats can be labeled as real gold.

2. Gold-*filled* jewelry contains a layer of 10-, 14- or 18-karat gold *mechanically* bonded to another metal surface.

3. Gold-*plated* jewelry contains a coating of gold *electro-chemically* bonded to another metal surface. (*Plated* jewelry contains less gold than gold-*filled* jewelry.)

24 Karat	=	Pure gold
18 Karat	=	18 parts gold, 6 parts metal filler
14 Karat	=	14 parts gold, 10 parts metal filler
10 Karat	=	10 parts gold, 14 parts metal filler

Silver

Silver is measured by weight and purity. Sterling silver contains 92.5% pure silver.

Rubies

Measured by weight (in Carats). Color, clarity and cut are important measures of value but are not graded.

Sapphires

Measured by weight (in Carats). Color, clarity and cut are important measures of value but are not graded.

Emeralds

Measured by weight (in Carats). Valued for color and clarity, but brilliance of cut is less important.

Semiprecious Gems

(Spinels, Garnets, Topaz, Aquamarine, Amethysts) Measured by weight (in Carats). Color, clarity and cut are important measures of value, but because these gems are less expensive, the differences are less important.

Pearls

Pearls are valued by 5 measures of quality, making comparison shopping easy.

Pearls: Five Measures of Quality

Size	Measured in millimeters. Usually, the larger the pearl, the higher the price.
Shape	Measured by "roundness". (To test roundness, rotate a strand of pearls on a flat, smooth surface. Round pearls rotate evenly without wobbling.)
Color	Judged by appearance. Pearls with a pinkish color are more valuable than yellow or grey.
Smoothness	Judged by appearance. Pearls with no surface flaws are more valuable than those with imperfections.
Lustre	Judged by appearance. Look at your reflection in the pearl(s); the sharper the image, the higher the quality.

Step 3

In the form below, write down specific prices you find at the mall stores for the jewelry items which interest you. Remember to note all the criteria used to value a particular gem or precious metal (see Step 2). Do not be shy about taking notes. Tell the salesperson that you are comparison shopping and want to know as much as possible about their merchandise.

RETAIL SOURCE	ITEM	DESCRIPTION (Weight, Color, etc.)	PRICE
_____	_____	_____	$_____
_____	_____	_____	$_____
_____	_____	_____	$_____
_____	_____	_____	$_____

Step 4

After you have completed your research at the retail level, you are ready to go bargain hunting at pawnshops and jewelers who both buy and sell or some of the web sites we've listed. Ask to see specific items that can be easily compared to those you summarized in Step 3. When exact comparisons are possible, the bargains and the rip-offs will be easy to spot. Write down your findings and then move on to the next source. Because these stores have an ever-changing inventory, do not expect to find what you are looking for at every location.

RETAIL SOURCE	ITEM	DESCRIPTION (Weight, Color, etc.)	PRICE
_____	_____	_____	$_____
_____	_____	_____	$_____
_____	_____	_____	$_____
_____	_____	_____	$_____

Step 5

Wherever you buy, ask for a written receipt that includes an exact description of the item you buy. Diamonds should include all the relevant grading characteristics and an appraisal or GIA certificate should be attached if one is available. For expensive items, you will want to take your purchase to an independent appraiser for a confirmation that what is on your receipt is accurate. If it is incorrect, bring the item back to the original place of purchace and demand a refund.

HERE'S THE PROOF

We went to local pawnshops and independent jewelers in the Washington, D.C. area to price several common items. Then we went to local shopping malls to price comparable merchandise. The results suggest just how much money you can save on jewelery by avoiding the malls.

Item	Mall Store	Discount Source	SAVE!
Ladie's 1 Carat Diamond Ring H Color, VS; Clarity 14 Karat setting	Bailey Banks & Biddle Tyson's Corner Center Tyson's Corner, Virginia $7,500	National Pawnbrokers 3100 Lee Highway Arlington, Virginia $3,350	*$4,150*
Ladie's 1/2 Carat Diamond Ring H Color, VS; Clarity 14 Karat setting	Bailey Banks & Biddle $2,650	National Pawnbrokers $795	*$1,855*
Men's Gold President's Rolex Watch	Black Starr & Frost Tyson's Corner Center Tyson's Corner, Virginia $11,000 (sale price) *(regularly $13,750)*	National Pawnbrokers $6,750	*$4,250*
Ladie's 24-inch cultured pearl necklace 6.5 millimeter	Tokyo Pearl Tyson's Corner Center Tyson's Corner, Virginia $1,140	Dominion Jewelers 107 Rowell Court Falls Church, Virginia $795	*$345*
Unisex 14 Karat Gold Chain herringbone pattern weight: 10.5 grams	Antwerp Diamond Exchange Tyson's Corner Center Tyson's Corner, Virginia $367	National Pawnbrokers $135	*$232*
Total Savings (all 5 items)	*$22,657*	*$11,825*	*$10,832*

Chapter Seven

Cut Your Utility Bills in Half

What can I do to lower my energy bills?

If you want to save money, implement an overall conservation program — not a single tip here and there. Listed below are 10 steps every homeowner should take. They are quick, easy to do, and don't require a major investment of your time or money. In most cases, this comprehensive approach should cut your energy bills from $400 to $700 per year!

---

10 Ways to Cut Energy Costs

1. Turn down the thermostat and install a timer on your water heater;

2. Install flow restrictors on all your hot water faucets;

3. Change from incandescent to flourescent bulbs in areas where you use lighting more than 5 hours per day;

4. Re-caulk and seal doors and windows;

5. Insulate single-pane window glass from winter cold using inexpensive plastic film;

6. Upgrade the insulation in your attic;

7. Buy a timer for your heating or central air conditioning system;

8. Use fans–in summer and winter;

9. Shield your air conditioning unit(s) from direct sun; and

10. Keep your thermostat at 68° (or lower) in winter or 75° (or higher) in summer.

What about a more dramatic plan?

You can certainly do more to cut your energy consumption, but you must also take into account what it costs to implement the program. It is not uncommon for people to spend $5,000 on a new central heating system in order to save $500 per year in lower fuel bills, without realizing it will take 10 years for the savings to cover the initial investment. The point is that you can go overboard on energy conservation if you're not careful.

Worksheets included with this chapter will help you to keep it all in perspective. You'll learn how to calculate what you currently spend for heating and cooling your house and what sort of savings you can expect from a major investment in new equipment. You will probably be surprised to learn that in many cases, small inexpensive changes often yield the highest net savings.

Where do I start?

At your water heater. Hot water accounts for up to 40% of all the energy consumed in your home. The good news is that for a one-time cost of about $30, you can retrofit your water heater, saving from $100 to $300 per year in operating costs.

The first move costs you nothing. Simply turn down the thermostat. The average system is set between 140°-160°, which is far too high for washing or bathing. In fact, at these high temperatures, you must turn on the cold tap just to make the water bearable. With just a screwdriver, you can lower the temperature setting to 120°, saving approximately 20-25% in energy costs without affecting comfort or cleaning results. Even so, more than 70% of the water heaters in the U.S. are set higher than necessary.

Estimated Operating Costs for Hot Water Heaters*

Temperature Setting	40 Gallon Capacity	80 Gallon Capacity
Low 120°	$ 372	$ 740
Medium 140°	$ 430	$ 868
High 180°	$ 463	$ 1,040

* Electric Models Only

We also recommend purchasing an automatic timer and water-flow restrictors. The timer can be programmed to turn off your water heater when you don't need it, such as when you are asleep or at work, saving an average of $5 per month. Flow restrictors reduce the amount of hot water you use by 50% without affecting water pressure or temperature. Installation takes seconds and the cost is less than $1 per faucet.

For detailed instructions on how to make the modifications described above, refer to the energy-saving guide at the end of this chapter.

How much electricity do I waste if I leave lights burning in several rooms at the same time?

The typical U.S. household consumes 1,200 kilowatt hours of electricity, or approximately $96 per year, for interior lighting. On a daily basis the cost is only 25¢, so there isn't much harm in keeping an extra light burning occasionally. That isn't to say you can't save money on lighting. New energy-efficient fluorescent light bulbs produce the same

Incandescent vs. Fluorescent Light Bulbs
Electricity Consumed/Year

Incandescent		Fluorescent
$ 12.81	4 hours/day	$ 3.42
$ 19.22	6 hours/day	$ 5.13
$ 25.62	8 hours/day	$ 6.83

75-watt incandescent bulb vs. a 20-watt fluorescent bulb, producing identical amounts of light (1,000 lumens). Cost of electricity @ 8¢/kilowatt hour.

Total Costs for 10,000 Hours of Lighting*

Incandescent		Fluorescent
$ 87.75	Electricity Consumed	$ 23.42
$ 10.00	Cost of Bulb(s)	$ 25.00
$ 97.75	Total Costs of Operation	$ 48.42
--	Total Savings	$ 49.33

Hours of Use	Average Savings Per Year	Years Needed to Break Even on Purchase of Fluorescent Bulbs
2 hours/day	$ 3.60	13.7 years
4 hours/day	7.6	6.8 years
6 hours/day	10.96	4.5 years
8 hours/day	14.50	3.4 years

* A typical bulb will produce approximately 10,000 hours of illumination. During that same period, you will use approximately 13 standard incandescent bulbs. For purposes of analysis, we have assumed incandescent bulbs can be purchased at a discount store for 75¢ each, while a comparable fluorescent bulb will cost $25.

illumination as conventional incandescent lights, but use 75% less power. Where you use lights frequently, a switch to fluorescent bulbs can save up to $18/year in electricity per bulb!

Fluorescent lights also last 7 times longer than incandescent bulbs, although they are considerably more expensive. Whereas an ordinary 100-watt light bulb might sell for 85¢, a comparable fluorescent bulb costs $20. The energy savings still make fluorescent bulbs a good buy, but you must use them at least 5 hours per day for the investment to really pay off. For that reason, we recommend fluorescent lights only in high traffic areas that require illumination on a regular basis.

If I stick with conventional incandescent bulbs, are certain brands better than others?

No. Even though higher-priced "long-life" or "Miser" bulbs are designed to outlast or out-perform standard brands, they wind up costing you about the same money when bulb life, electricity consumption and purchase price are taken into account.

How do I know if I have enough insulation around my house?

Most homes in the U.S. are under-insulated. The Department of Energy has issued recommendations for optimum insulation levels, based on the climate in your region of the country. Using these guidelines, you can determine the precise amount of insulation you should have in your attic, walls and floors, and how much, if any, extra protection you need.

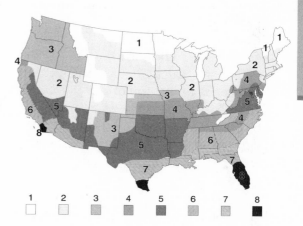

Cost of Incandescent Light Bulbs

	Purchase Price	Life Expectancy	Total Cost of Operation*
GE Long-life 60-watt	$ .85	1500 hours	$ 7.20
GE Miser 60-watt	1.10	1000 hours	7.08
GE Standard 60-watt	.75	750 hours	7.19

* Including electricity

U.S. Department of Energy Recommended Insulation Levels

Insulation Zone	Attics		Floors over unheated basements or crawl spaces	Exterior Walls
	Electric Resistance	Gas, Oil or Heat Pump		
1	R-49	R-49	R-19	R-11
2	R-49	R-38	R-19	R-11
3	R-38	R-38	R-19	R-11
4	R-38	R-38	R-19	R-11
5	R-38	R-30	R-19	R-11
6	R-38	R-30	R-19	R-11
7	R-30	R-30		R-11
8	R-30	R-19		R-11

You will note that the guidelines are expressed in terms of "R-value", which measures resistance to heat loss. To find out how much of a particular type of insulation is needed to produce a given R-value, simply consult the chart below. In most parts of the country, the ideal amount of insulation is approximately 12 inches for attics, 6 inches under cold floors and 3 inches in exterior walls.

Of course, insulation saves energy, but it also costs money to install. Therefore, before you embark on a major insulation project, you should make sure your investment will pay off in energy savings within a reasonable period of time. For specific advice on how to do the cost-benefit calculations, consult the worksheets at the end of the chapter.

How much does re-caulking and weather stripping save in heating and cooling expenses?

The average crack that shows visible light probably adds $15-20 to your heating and air conditioning bill each year. We recommend an annual inspection of all interior and exterior caulking, as well as weather stripping around doors and windows to detect these leaks. For less visible gaps, hold a goose down feather or lighted match up against window and door frames to find signs of air movement. On days when outside temperatures are 50° or less, the feather can detect the flow of cold air into your home.

Heat loss can also be a problem around kitchen and bathroom exhaust fans, mail slots, electric wall outlets and fireplace chimneys. Our worksheets offer practical solutions to solving these and other air infiltration problems. Most remedies cost $3 or less.

Thickness of Insulation to Obtain R-Values

R-Value	Fiberglass Blanket	Rockwool	Perlite
R-11	3.5 inches	3.5 inches	3.75 inches
R-19	6.0 inches	6.0 inches	6.5 inches
R-30	9.0 inches	9.5 inches	10.0 inches
R-38	12.0 inches	12.0 inches	13.0 inches
R-49	15.0 inches	16.5 inches	17.0 inches

Note: Always consult the manufacturer's recommended installation guidelines, since specific products may vary from average performance.

Can I do anything to stop heat loss through my windows?

Glass is a terrible insulator. Compared to 12 inches of attic insulation, a single-pane window loses 4,122% more heat.

The best way to counteract this problem is to place a sealed air barrier between indoor living spaces and the glass which is exposed to outside temperatures. Storm windows are one of the oldest solutions, but they are prone to leaks. A much better option is double or triple-pane glass – 2 or 3 layers of permanently bonded glass with air sandwiched in the middle. Most newer homes come equipped with these new windows, which cut heat loss by 50-67%.

If you live in an older home, window replacements are expensive. Unless you are planning major renovations, switching to double or triple-pane glass is probably not cost-effective if your only aim is to save energy. Fortunately, you can cut window heat loss by a similar percentage for less than $2 per window using plastic window insulating kits sold in hardware and home centers. The kits consist of clear plastic film which you stretch across the inside or outside of your window. The plastic creates the same air barrier as double-pane glass with nearly identical insulation results — but at a fraction of the price. At the end of the cold season, you simply tear down the plastic and throw it away.

I have the exact opposite problem – my windows let in too much heat in the summertime. What should I do?

Again, double- or triple-pane glass provides a significant amount of insulating power. However, in summer months, sunlight passing through your windows heats walls, carpet and furniture in your home, raising inside temperature. The same process causes a closed automobile to get hot when parked in direct sun.

To cut down on radiant heat, you must reduce the amount of direct sunlight that enters your home. Awnings, shutters or shade trees are the most effective barriers, but they may not be practical in your situation. As an inexpensive alternative, keep window shades or drapes drawn during late morning and afternoon hours. You may also want to consider applying reflective film to windows where heat gain is a particular problem. Tinting can cut radiant heat by 30-40%, and damaging ultra-violet rays by nearly 98%. Professional appli-

cations cost $2-3 per square foot of glass area, but in many homes, the problem can be fixed by treating just one or two windows.

Which source of energy is cheaper, electricity or gas?

Without question, gas provides more heat for the dollar. It costs a typical family less than half as much to heat water with gas as it does with electricity, and one-fourth as much to cook meals or dry clothes. Savings on central heating can be equally dramatic, especially when compared to electric resistance heating systems.

Annual Cost of Operating Appliances Electric vs. Gas		
Electric		Gas
$ 458 /yr	Water Heater	$ 200 /yr
100 /yr	Range & Oven	25 /yr
103 /yr	Clothes Dryer	27 /yr
1,021 /yr *	Central Heat	415 /yr

Cost estimates are based on a typical family of four, living in approximately 2,000 sq. ft. of living space. Electricity expenses based on national average of 8¢ per kilowatt hour and natural gas costs of 60¢ per therm (100 cubic yards).

* Resistance Heat system

Should I switch to natural gas?

Not necessarily. In many parts of the country (particularly New England) natural gas is not readily available. Even with lower operating expenses, you may not save much when you consider the cost of installing new gas appliances. Buying a new central heating system, oven/range, water heater and gas dryer will set you back $4,000-$7,500. When you compare the projected energy savings against these up-front investment costs, it can take many years to make your conversion pay off.

Before you make any hasty decisions, we suggest you call your local utility and ask them to analyze your current energy use patterns, as well as what you will save with the new equipment. Then you can decide which changes make sense based on how long you will live in your home. We have illustrated a hypothetical example of such a conversion to give you an idea of what the analysis entails.

Hypothetical Switch from Electricity to Natural Gas

Appliance	Annual Operating Expenses with ...		Cost to Purchase New Gas Appliances (plus installation)
	Electricity	Gas	
Water Heater	$ 458	$ 200	$ 215
Range & Oven	100	25	650
Clothes Dryer	103	27	225
Heating System	985	510	4,500
Cooling System	320	--	no change
Dishwasher	--	--	no change
Clothes Washer	--	--	no change
Total Operating Costs/Yr.	$ 1,966	$ 762	Total Expenses $ 5,590
Annual Savings:	$ 1,204		

Break Even Analysis

Cost of Purchasing and Installing Equipment:	$ 5,590
Annual Energy Savings after Conversion:	$ 1,204
Time needed to recoup investment:	5,590 ÷ 1,204 = 4.64 years

What about the cost of other heating fuels?

It is difficult to give precise estimates because so much depends on regional energy prices and the efficiency of your appliances. However, as a rule, heating oil and liquid propane are more efficient than electricity.

Heat (BTUs)* per Dollar

Natural Gas	146, 000 BTUs
Heating Oil	116,000 BTUs
Liquid Propane	67,000 BTUs
Electricity	38,000 BTUs

Based on 70¢/therm for natural gas, $1.20/gallon for heating oil, $1.35/gallon for propane and 8¢ per kilowatt hour for electricity.

* BTU = British Thermal Unit. A single BTU represents the heat generated by the flame of a single wooden match.

I've read that they are deregulating utility markets. Can I choose which supplier I use and does it make good sense to switch?

It is true that electric utilities are being deregulated in many markets, but the process is proceeding at an uneven pace. Whether you have a choice depends on local and state law. At some point in the future, however, it is likely that most Americans will have a choice. It is too early to tell whether the differences among competing providers will be meaningful to consumers. There is no question that choice works for large commercial users who have benefited from shopping for the lowest utility rates for a number of years. If you live in an area where the electricity market has been deregulated, make sure you ask the following questions before making a change:

1.) How much of a savings can I expect and is it worth it?

2.) What happens if there is a power outage in my area?

3.) If I choose a less-established company, could it mean that power outages coud be more frequent and last longer?

4.) Are there any extra service charges or other fees that I will incur?

If I stick with electricity, can I still lower my heating bill?

Yes. If you currently have a resistance heating system, you can save money by switching to an electric heat pump. The pump does not rely on resistance heat coils, like traditional electric systems. Instead, it works like an air conditioner in reverse, extracting ambient heat from outside air and depositing it inside your home. Even when outdoor temperatures are 40° the heat pump can absorb sufficient warmth to keep your house comfortable. When temperatures drop below 40°, supplementary heating coils provide additional warmth.

In regions with moderate winters, heat pumps can operate at two or three times the efficiency of standard electric heat systems.

Annual Cost to Heat a 2000 sq. ft. Home

Electric Resistance Heat: $ 1,021
Electric Heat Pump: $ 552

Do different thermostat settings have a big impact on my heating bill?

The lower your thermostat setting, the less money you will spend to heat your home. During a 24-hour period, for every degree you lower your thermostat, you cut your heating costs by 3.1%. For example, if you normally keep your house at 72°, reducing the thermostat to 70° saves you 6.2% on your heating bill.

If you lower the thermostat by larger increments while you are asleep or away at work, you will save even more. For example, the U.S. Department of Energy recommends you set your thermostat at 68° while you are awake and active in the home and 60° at bedtime or when you leave for work. These settings will save you 13.4% in energy costs compared to what you would pay to maintain a constant 72°.

Thermostat Setting & Your Heating Bill

Temperature Setting	Additional Costs or Savings
77°	15.5% More
76°	12.4% More
75°	9.3% More
74°	6.2% More
73°	3.1% More
72°	Current Setting
71°	3.1% Less
70°	6.2% Less
69°	9.3% Less
68°	12.4% Less
67°	15.5% Less
66°	18.8% Less

Based on 70¢/therm for natural gas, $1.20/gallon for heating oil, $1.35/ gallon for propane and 8¢/kilowatt hr. for electricity.

BTU = British Thermal Units. A single BTU represents the heat generated by the flame of a single wooden match.

Many people find it hard to remember when to turn down the thermostat. If you want more precise control, you should replace your unit with a digital timer. The timer allows you to program various temperature settings automatically. For example, you could schedule a 10° reduction after you fall asleep at night, and then pre-heat your house thirty minutes before waking up in the morning. Timers take some of the drudgery out of monitoring your thermostat, and add consistency to your savings program.

Are small electric or kerosene heaters economical?

If you plan on sitting in a certain area for an extended period of time and need additional warmth, a space heater is much cheaper to operate than your central heating system. Why pay to heat rooms no one is occupying?

Do the same rules about thermostat settings apply to air conditioning?

The principle is the same, but the process is reversed. If you have a central air conditioning system, you save money (5% per degree) when you raise the thermostat. For example, it takes 20% less electricity to maintain 76° as it does to maintain 72°.

To add to your savings, consider supplementing your air conditioning with portable electric fans. Air moving against your skin makes the ambient temperature in a room feel cooler, even if the actual temperature hasn't changed. For example, if a fan creates a 5 mph breeze in an 82° room, it will feel the same as a still room at 72°. With fans supplementing your air conditioning, you can afford to keep your thermostat setting much higher without sacrificing comfort. In many cases, this dual approach can help reduce your overall cooling costs up to 45%.

Even if you don't use central air conditioning, fans can produce amazing results. Sunlight streaming through your windows and on your roof will raise temperatures inside your home approximately 1° per hour during daytime hours. By 6 pm, outside temperatures have started to cool but the air inside your house stays hot because of insulation and the higher temperatures of walls, carpets, furniture, etc. If you place a box fan, exhausting to the outside, in the window of the hottest room in your house– usually the highest point with a western exposure —and open a window in the coolest room in your house– usually a lower level or basement window with a northern exposure — you will create a breeze which will force hot air out of your home and draw cool air from the outside. Using this technique should make air conditioning completely unnecessary so long as outside temperatures remain below 85°.

Is there anything else I can do to reduce cooling costs?

Yes! Make sure your home is well insulated. It will cost you more than twice as much to air condition a poorly insulated home as a well insulated one.

Annual Cost to Air Condition an 1,800 sq. ft. House in Dallas, Texas

Insulation Rating	Total Cost of Electricity
Poor (R-9)	$ 1,400
Average (R-18)	$ 1,200
Excellent (R-38)	$ 547

Another important step is to shade your windows. An outside temperature of 75° can raise temperatures inside your house as high as 90° if enough sunlight enters through windows. Blocking this sunlight with shutters, awnings, drapes or shade trees can help to reduce your cooling expenses by 15-25%. Also shade your air conditioning unit. Higher temperatures cause your system to work harder and less efficiently. If you can lower the temperature around your system by 10°, you can usually save a comparable percentage of electricity.

Finally, only air condition those areas of your home where you really need it. Close off spare bedrooms or living areas which remain unoccupied for long periods of time.

Are window units more efficient than central air conditioning systems?

The efficiency of each system depends on its design, but it is generally less expensive to operate a window unit because it cools a smaller area. Central air systems have a larger capacity, and so consume more power.

Is there an easy way to figure out what size air conditioner to buy?

For rough computations, you can figure that a fairly well insulated home will lose approximately 15 BTUs* of cool air per sq. ft. of room area in one hour. An 1,800 sq. ft. home would therefore need a system with a capacity of 27,000 BTUs/hour (1,800 x 15). You can do the same calculations for window units. If you need a system for a bedroom measuring 10' by 15' (150 sq. ft.), the proper size air conditioner would be 2,250 BTUs (150 x 15).

To buy a fan, you must do a slightly different calculation. A good model should be able to exchange the air in the room or area you wish to cool at least 40 times per hour. To determine the correct fan size for your needs, measure the room or area

---

Fan Size = Cooling Area x 40 ÷ 60
(CFM) (cubic feet)

Example:

10' by 20' room with 8' ceilings
Total Cubic Feet = 1,600 (10 x 20 x 8)
1600 x 40 ÷ 60 = 1,066 CFM
Correct fan size = 1,000 CFM

---

to be cooled three ways — length, width and ceiling height. Multiplying these numbers will give you the correct volume of air in the room, measured in cubic feet. You can then use your answer to solve for the correct fan size using the formula in the Fan Size chart on page 200.

Is the efficiency of appliances very important?

Yes and No. Overall, the cost to operate appliances like toasters, dishwashers, microwave ovens, etc., is miniscule compared to what you spend on heating and air conditioning. But while more efficient appliances won't save you a fortune on your utility bills, the differences do add up over time. For example, over 10 years, a clothes dryer which is 30% more efficient than the competition can save you $238 in electricity. For this reason, you should always take operating costs into account when shopping for major appliances.

The U.S. Government helps make this comparison easy by requiring manufac-turers to display an energy label on refrigerators, clothes dryers, hot water heaters and air conditioners that discloses energy consumption for one year of typical use. Our energy worksheets will show you how to factor the label information into your buying decisions.

What can I do to reduce my energy bills if I rent my home?

If you rent, you obviously want to avoid spending money on costly improvements. However, most of our recommendations do not require an investment of more than a few dollars. It costs nothing to turn down the thermostat on your furnace or water heater. A tube of insulating caulk costs less than $2 and water-flow restrictors are only 75¢ per faucet. Even plastic insulating kits for your windows can be purchased for under $3.

Do you have any suggestions for reducing my telephone bills?

If your long-distance bill is less than $100 per month, it probably makes no difference which long distance carrier you choose. Any of the "big three" — *AT&T, Sprint* or *MCI-WorldCom* — offer reasonable rates and excellent customer service. On the other hand, if your long-distance bills exceed $100 per month, it pays to consider some of the smaller long-distance firms that offer rates in the range of 7¢ per minute, 24 hours per day, 7 days a week.

Where do you find these companies? Start with the companies listed below. If you need more ideas, consider the telecom page at *Yahoo* (www.yahoo.com)

How Much Do Electric Appliances Cost to Operate?	
Appliance	Cost per Yr.*
Clothes Dryer	$ 79.44
Coffee Maker	11.20
Dishwasher	29.04
Freezer (16 cu.ft.)	145.00
Hair Dryer	2.00
Microwave Oven	15.20
Range w/ Oven	56.00
Color TV	21.76
Vacuum Cleaner	3.68
Washing Machine	8.24

* At national average of 8¢/kwh

or a service called **CheapRates** (www.cheaprates.com). Smaller communications companies who sell long-distances service at a discount pay to be listed on these web pages. When you compare services, remember to look for one that offers six-second billing and no monthly surcharge or minimum fee.

What about cellular service?

Competition has dramatically lowered the cost of cellular calls. Companies are so eager for new customers that they have cut per minute charges as much as 75% over the last two years. The changes have been so dramatic that in many cases, cellular customers who signed up months or years ago may find that they are paying well above current market rates. Don't expect the cellular companies to give you the new rates if you ask for them. In fact, they are perfectly content if you keep on paying the old rates as long as possible.

check is to use the **Wireless Dimension** web site (www.wirelessdimensions.com). It can tell you what various services in your area are charging, as well as other specifics regarding their calling plans.

U
T
I
L
I
T
I
E
S

Long-Distance Discounters
Frontier Communications
800-783-2020
LCI
800-524-5664
Pioneer Telecom
800-555-0396
Advanced Communications
800-257-3908

If you are not sure who has the best deal in your market, an easy way to

Guide to
ENERGY AUDIT AND INSPECTION

This worksheet will help you make minor changes in your home which can dramatically reduce your annual energy bills. So that you can gauge your progress, each step will estimate your likely savings from the proposed change. For best results, conduct the entire inspection at one time. In most cases, you can complete the required steps in two hours or less.

ENERGY AUDIT WORKSHEET

Step 1

Determine your current energy costs.

A. How much do you spend on electricity, natural gas and/or heating oil in an average year? Review receipts or reconstruct your records from old check stubs, then complete the table at right.

MONTH	ELECTRIC BILL	NATURAL GAS/ HEATING OIL BILL
January		
February		
March		
April		
May		
June		
July		
August		
September		
October		
November		
December		
TOTAL		

ENERGY AUDIT WORKSHEET

B. To determine how much you spend each year to heat and cool your home, you must compare energy consumption during prime heating/cooling months to what you spend during periods when such heat/AC is not necessary.

1. Avg. bill for electricity, natural gas or heating oil during heating season _____

2. Avg. bill for electricity, natural gas or heating oil during non-heating/cooling season _____

3. Monthly cost to heat your home in winter (1–2) _____

4. Avg. bill for electricity during cooling season _____

5. Avg. bill for electricity during non-cooling/heating season _____

6. Monthly cost to cool your home in summer (4–5) _____

U T I L I T I E S

Step 2

Conduct an energy audit of your home.

Take a tour of your home noting changes you can make that will lower your energy bills.

✔ Central Heating System

A. What is the average winter thermostat setting during daytime and evening hours? _____

B. What is the average winter thermostat setting when you are asleep? _____

C. What is the average winter thermostat setting when the home is unoccupied? _____

ENERGY AUDIT WORKSHEET

You will save approximately 1% of your annual heating bill for each degree below your current thermostat setting, provided the change is maintained for eight hours each day. Keeping the change for 24 hours will result in a 3% savings. For example, if you turn your thermostat back 2° for the eight hours you are active in the home, 4° for the eight hours you are asleep and 5° when you are away at work, your total savings would be 11% (2% + 4% + 5% = 11%).

D. **Now that you know lowering the thermostat can save you money, establish new temperature settings that are still in your comfort range.**

Time Period	Old Setting	New Setting	Savings (%)*
_____	_____	_____	_____
_____	_____	_____	_____
_____	_____	_____	_____
_____	_____	_____	_____

* *Credit a 1% savings for each degree lower than current setting, maintained for eight hours.*

TOTAL SAVINGS ON HEATING BILL _____ %

E. **How much money do you save at the new settings?**
To make sure you adhere to the new temperature settings, consider installing a new programmable thermostat. (About $20 at most hardware stores.)

_____ X _____ = _____
Current Heating Bill   % Saved at New Temp. Settings   Total Savings

✔ Air Conditioning System

A. **What is the average summer thermostat setting during daytime and evening hours?** _____

B. **What is the average summer thermostat setting when you are asleep?** _____

ENERGY AUDIT WORKSHEET

C. **What is the average summer thermostat setting when the home is unoccupied?**

_____

You will save approximately 1.67% of your annual air conditioning bill for each degree above your current thermostat setting, provided you maintain the change for at least eight hours. For example, if you turn up your thermostat 3° during the eight hours you are active in the home, 4° during the eight hours you are asleep and 5° when you are at work, your total savings will be 20.4%.

D. **Now that you know raising your thermostat can save money, establish new temperature settings that are still in your comfort range.**

Remember that electric fans will make your home feel cooler, even at high temperature settings.

Time Period	Old Setting	New Setting	Savings (%)*
_____	_____	_____	_____
_____	_____	_____	_____
_____	_____	_____	_____
_____	_____	_____	_____

* Credit a 1.67% savings for each degree higher than current setting, maintained for eight hours.

Total savings on air conditioning bill _____ %

E. **How much money do you save at the new settings?**

Again, a programmable thermostat will make it easier to implement your changes.

_____ X _____ = _____
Current A/C Bill   % Saved at New Temp. Settings   Total Savings

UTILITIES

ENERGY AUDIT WORKSHEET

✔ Attic Insulation

A. Climb into your attic or crawl space to inspect the insulation.

B. Measure the thickness of the material with a ruler, then consult the chart below to estimate your home's current insulation level (R-Value).

Current Insulation Level   R-_____

R-Value of Your Current Insulation

Current Insulation	R-Value (Fiberglass)	R-Value (Rock Wool)	R-Value (Perlite)
3.5"	R-11	R-11	R-11
6"	R-19	R-19	R-19
10"	R-30	R-30	R-30
12"	R-38	R-38	R-38
16"	R-49	R-49	R-49

C. According to the chart below, what is the correct amount of attic insulation for your region?

Insulation Zone	If You Have Electric Resistance Heat	If You Have Gas Heat or an Electric Heat Pump
1	49	49
2	38	38
3	38	38
4	38	38
5	38	30
6	38	30
7	30	30
8	30	19

Recommended R-Value   R-_____

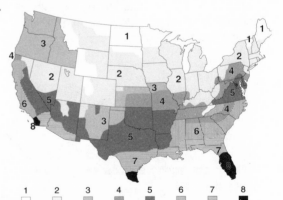

D. Calculate how much, if any, additional attic insulation you need?

1. Recommended insulation (See Chart)   R-_____

2. Current insulation (See Step B)   R-_____

3. Insulation Needed (1 – 2)   R-_____

4. Percentage of Increase
(Needed R-Value ÷ Current R-Value - 1 x 100)

_____ %

E. How much money will you save on heating and air conditioning costs if you upgrade your attic insulation?

Percentage of Increase	Annual Energy Savings
(Insulation)	(Heating and Cooling)
25%	2%
50%	4%
100%	8%
150%	10%
200%	12%
250%	13%
300%	14%

_____ X _____ = _____

Current   % of Energy   Total
Heating and   Bills Saved   Savings
Cooling Bill   After
(See Step One) Insulation
                 Upgrade

F. Years needed to break even on cost of adding new insulation.

_____

✔ **Water Heater**

A. Turn off the power to your water heater at the main fuse box. (Skip this step if you have a gas system.)

B. Remove the coverplate(s) on the front of the heater using a screwdriver.

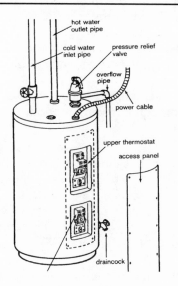

C. What is the temperature setting for each thermostat?

Upper Thermostat   _____

Lower Thermostat   _____

ENERGY AUDIT WORKSHEET

D. **Use the chart below* to estimate the annual cost of operation at current temperature settings.**

Electric Water Heater		Gas Water Heater	
Temperature Setting	Annual Cost of Operation	Temperature Setting	Annual Cost of Operation
120°	$367	120°	$110
140°	$471	140°	$141
160°	$576	160°	$172
180°	$681	180°	$204

*Based on U.S. Department of Energy estimates of average hot water use per household. Electric calculations assume 87% efficient system at 8¢ per kilowatt hour. Gas estimates assume a 70% efficient model at a cost of $5.65 per million BTUs.

Current cost of operation per year   _____

E. **Adjust the thermostat settings to "low" (approximately 120°).**

F. **Close the coverplate(s) and switch on the power at the main fuse box.**

G. **Re-calculate the annual cost of operation at the lower temperature setting.**

Example: Current Setting @ 160°; New Setting @ 120°. According to the chart, it costs $576 to operate a standard electric water heater at 160°, and $367 to operate the same system at 120°. The net savings is $209.

_____ − _____ = _____
Current   Operating   Annual
Operating   Cost at   Savings
Cost   120° Setting
(See table)   (See table)

H. **Calculate your annual savings if you install an automatic timer to turn off your water heater when you are not likely to need hot water.**
Note: Electric timers can be purchased at most hardware stores ($20-35) and are simple to install.x

_____ x 0.167 = _____
Operating   Savings %   Annual
Costs at   After   Savings
120° Setting   Installing
                 Timer

ENERGY AUDIT WORKSHEET

I. Calculate your annual savings if you install automatic-flow restrictors in all your hot water faucets and shower heads.

Note: Flow restrictors can be purchased at most hardware stores for less than $1 and are simple to install.

$$\underline{\hspace{3cm}} \times \underline{\hspace{1.5cm} 0.25 \hspace{1.5cm}} = \underline{\hspace{3cm}}$$

Operating Costs at 120° Setting   Savings % After Installing Flow Restrictor   Annual Savings

J. Add up the savings from all three hot-water conservation steps.

Annual Savings at 120° Setting: _____

Annual Savings After Installing Timer   _____

Annual Savings After Installing Flow Restrictors: _____

Total Savings: _____

✔ Window Glass

A. Inspect the glass in all your windows. How many layers of glass do you see? (Look closely at the corners to see whether you have single, double or triple-pane windows.)

Single Pane	Double Pane	Triple Pane
.9R	1.7R	2.8R

B. How much insulation (R-Value) do your windows provide?

C. How much money can you save by adding clear plastic insulating film to your windows during the heating season?

Number of Window Panes	Savings After Installing Window Film
Single Pane	15% off current heating bill
Double Pane	7% off current heating bill
Triple Pane	3% off current heating bill

$$\underline{\hspace{3cm}} \times \underline{\hspace{3cm}} = \underline{\hspace{3cm}}$$

Current Heating Bill   Savings % After Installing Window Film   Annual Savings

ENERGY AUDIT WORKSHEET

✔ Caulking

A. On a day when outside temperatures are 50° or cooler, inspect interior window seals for air leaks. Move a goose down feather or lighted match around the window frame searching for signs of air movement. Note specific areas where you detect leaks.

Air leaks are usually caused by deteriorating caulk or weather stripping around the window frame. In some cases, the window itself may be warped. See if you can pinpoint the problem with a visual inspection. If this is not possible, recaulk and/or weather strip the entire window.

B. Conduct the same inspection around doors, mailbox openings, kitchen or bath exhaust fans, electric outlets on outside walls, and fireplace chimneys. Note any areas where you can detect air flow.

Air leaks around doors are usually solved by installing metal insulation strips which compress when a door is closed. It is best to stuff loose insulation into mail slots and exhaust fans, keeping them closed for the winter season. The best solution to a drafty fireplace is to install glass doors across the hearth.

C. Move outside and conduct an inspection of outdoor caulking and weather stripping around doors and windows. Note areas where holes, cracking and general deterioration is plainly visible.

Cracks or holes should be filled with high-grade, siliconized caulk.

Window Location	Area of Leak

Area of Home	Location of Leak

Location of Problem	Description

ENERGY AUDIT WORKSHEET

D. Based on your inspection, would you say you have air leaks around 100%, 50%, 25% or 10% of your home's windows, doors, etc.?

Percentage of Leaks   _____ %

E. Estimate how much you can save on your air conditioning and heating bills by correcting these problems.

% of Air Leaks around Doors, Windows, etc.	Estimated Energy Savings after repairs
100%	12%
50%	6%
25%	3%
10%	1%

_____ X _____ = _____

Current Heating/ Cooling Bill	Savings % After Repairs	Total Savings

---

✔ Lighting

A. Walk through your house noting all light fixtures you use for 5 hours or more per day.

Room	Light Fixtures		Wattage of Bulbs		Hrs. of Use/day		Watts Consumed
_____	_____	:	_____	x	_____	=	_____
_____	_____	:	_____	x	_____	=	_____
_____	_____	:	_____	x	_____	=	_____
_____	_____	:	_____	x	_____	=	_____
_____	_____	:	_____	x	_____	=	_____
_____	_____	:	_____	x	_____	=	_____

Total Watts Consumed   _____

ENERGY AUDIT WORKSHEET

B. Calculate the annual cost of operating all these light fixtures.

_____ x 365 days = _____
Total Watts / Day   *Total Watts / Yr.*

_____ x 1,000 = _____

Total Watts / Day   *Total Kilowatts / Yr.*

_____ x_____ = _____

Kilowatts / Yr.   *Cost Per Kilowatt**   *Annual Lighting Cost*

C. Calculate your savings if you replace these incandescent lights with fluorescent bulbs.*

Flourescent bulbs provide the same light for less power. Use the chart provided to identify the correct flourescent replacement for your current bulb(s).

* Ask your electric company for local rates or use the national average of 8¢ / kilowatt hour

Bulb Replacement Recommendations

Current Incandescent Bulb	Correct Fluorescent Replacement
60 watts / hour	15 watts / hour
75 watts / hour	20 watts / hour
100 watts / hour	26 watts / hour

Bulb Replacement Evaluation

A Light Fixture	B Current Incandescent Bulb Wattage	C Recommended Flourescent Bulb Wattage	D Watts Saved Per Hour (B-C)	E Watts Saved Per Day (watts/hr x hours used per day)	F Watts Saved Per Year (Savings per day x 365 days)	G Annual Savings (Savings per year x 8¢)

Appliances

Calculate your estimated savings after completing each of the steps listed below.

Refrigerator

- Pull your refrigerator away from the wall and inspect the rear area around exposed coils and/or motor heating vents. Remove dust or dirt with a vacuum cleaner or brush.

- Close refrigerator and freezer doors on a dollar bill to check for air leaks. If the dollar can be pulled out without much resistance, the rubber gasket around the door should be replaced.

- Use an outdoor thermometer to test the temperature inside the refrigerator and freezer compartments. Adjust thermostats so that interior temperatures are no lower than 40° (refrigerator) or 20° (freezer).

Clothes Dryer

Check the exhaust hose where it enters your wall and again at the outside vent. Remove accumulated lint and debris.

Clothes Washer

Set your wash cycle for "cold" or "warm" wash and "cold" rinse.

Dishwasher

Turn off the drying cycle or disconnect the heating element so your dishes will air dry.

Central Heating/Air Conditioning Filters

Clean or replace dirty air filters.

Appliance	Estimated Savings After Adjustment*	
Refrigerator:	$15 - $25	_____
Clothes Dryer:	$10	_____
Washing Machine:	$80*	_____
Dishwasher:	$12	_____
Air Filters:	$25	_____
Total Savings		_____

* Savings are derived from conserving hot water produced by electric heating systems. If you own a gas water heater, your savings will be approximately $15-20/year.

UTILITIES

ENERGY AUDIT WORKSHEET

Step 3

Summarize your results

How much can you save by making
the simple changes suggested in
the Energy Audit?

System/ Appliance	Recommendation	Savings
Central Heating System	Change Thermostat Setting Clean Filters	_____
AC System	Change Thermostat Setting	_____
Water Heater	Change Thermostat Setting	_____
	Install Timer	_____
	Install Water-Flow Restrictors	_____
Insulation	Insulate to Optimum Levels	_____
Window Glass	Install Plastic Film for Winter	_____
Caulking & Cracks	Re-caulk and seal	_____
Refrigerator	Adjust Temperature, remove dust and check/replace seals	_____
Washing Machine	Use Cold or Warm water wash cycle and cold rinse cycle	_____
Clothes Dryer	Clean Exhaust Hose	_____
Dishwasher	Turn off or disconnect drying mechanism	_____
Total Savings:		_____

ENERGY AUDIT WORKSHEET

Step 4

**Go shopping for the items you need
to make the changes already noted.**

Shopping List

Item	Quantity	Price	Correct Size	Comments
Water Heater Timer	_____	$25 - 35	Match wattage rating on water heater	Easy to install
Water Flow Restrictors	_____	75¢ each	Match size to faucet diameter	Easy to install
Window Insulation Kits	_____	$1-2 per window	Measure window area (sq. ft.)	No tools needed
Flourescent Light Bulbs	_____	$15-25 ea.	Match lumens to correct bulb ratings	Replace incandescent bulbs only when use exceeds 5 hrs/day
Caulk	_____	$2 per tube		Choose siliconized caulk
Weather Stripping	_____	$2 per door or window	Measure bottoms and sides of doors or windows	Choose tension strips made of plastic or metal over felt, foam or sponge rubber
Foam gaskets	_____	50¢ per outlet		Install in electric outlets which face outside walls
Attic Insulation	_____	20-30¢ per sq. ft.	Measure area to be insulated (sq. ft.) before making a major investment	Calculate break-even point
Air Filter(s)	_____	$2 - 5	Measure current filters for correct size.	Clean filters every three months
Heating / AC Thermostat Timer	_____	$40 - 60		Easy to install

Guide to ENERGY TIPS

The easiest way to save energy is to change wasteful living habits. The tips listed below can add 15-20% to your overall savings program.

Air Conditioning and Cooling
- Use the diagram below to expell hot air from your house quickly.

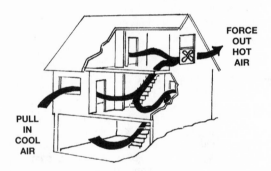

FORCE OUT HOT AIR

PULL IN COOL AIR

- Always close doors and vents to rooms where air conditioning is unnecessary.

- Shade your air conditioner from direct sunlight with an awning or plants to boost operating efficiency 5-10%.

- Keep all window drapes and blinds closed during the day to keep out the Sun's radiant heat.

Heating
- Avoid the use of kitchen or bathroom exhaust fans for extended periods in winter; exhaust fans can expell all the heat in a home in 60 minutes or less.

- Install glass doors on your fireplace to prevent the chimney from drawing warm air out of your house.

- Use a humidifier to make interior temperatures feel warmer. Dry air makes a room feel much colder.

- Use a ceiling fan to distribute heat that has stratified near the top of a room in high-ceiling areas.

- Seal mail slots, kitchen fans and pet doors during winter months using scraps of insulation; keep these closed and inoperative during winter heating months.

- Open drapes or blinds on windows with southern or western exposure to capture radiant heat from the sun during daylight hours.

- Close heat vents and shut doors to rooms where heat isn't required. (**Note:** Do not close off rooms if you own an electric heat pump.)

Hot Water
- Use a dishwasher to save hot water. Doing the dishes in the sink usually consumes more hot water.

- Do full loads in your washing

machine and dishwasher to maximize use of hot water.

- Insulate your hot water pipes if they pass through an unheated basement or crawl space.

- Insulate your water heater if it feels warm to the touch.

- Stop leaky faucets. One drip per second can cost you $3-5 per month in hot water.

- Take showers instead of baths; showers consume 75% less hot water.

Cooking

- Keep oven doors closed as much as possible. You lose 25-35% of the heat when you open the door even for a brief look.

- Turn off an oven 15-20 minutes before the cooking process is complete; residual heat will complete the job.

- Match the correct-sized burner to the pan you are using.

- Cover pots during the cooking process to reduce energy consumption 20%.

- Run the self-cleaning cycle after you have used the oven for cooking to take advantage of residual heat.

- Open the oven door when you finish baking so that the residual heat can warm your kitchen (winter only).

- Use a microwave oven whenever possible. Microwaves operate 40-75% more efficiently than conventional electric ovens.

Refrigerator

- Do not store more than a 1-week supply of soda, beer or other beverage in your refrigerator at any one time. The more bottles you store, the more power your refrigerator will consume to keep them cool.

- Allow hot foods to cool before you refrigerate them. Heat from the containers causes the compressor to work harder.

- Use the refrigerator to defrost frozen foods. The frozen items add free cooling power.

- Keep freezers tightly filled to minimize air flow. Fill an empty freezer compartment with bags of ice if necessary.

- Consider de-activating stand-alone freezers in summer months to cut annual operating costs by up to 40%.

Lighting

- Turn off lights if you leave a room for 15 minutes or more; 15 minutes is the break-even point for conservation and extended bulb life.

- Install light dimmers to adjust lighting levels and energy consumption to the necessary minimum.

- Use reflector bulbs in focused lighting situations, such as desk lamps, hallways, etc. A 50-watt reflector bulb illuminates a narrower area with light comparable to a 100-watt standard bulb, but uses half as much electricity.

Guide to
HOW TO SHOP
FOR APPLIANCES

This worksheet will help you evaluate the current capacity, operating performance and efficiency of new appliances you may wish to buy.

Step 1

Read the Energy Label. By federal law, all new dishwashers, washing machines, dryers, refrigerator/freezers, water heaters and air conditioners sold

ENERGYGUIDE		
Model with Lowest energy cost **$104**	**$139**	Model with Highest energy cost **$202**

in the U.S. must be clearly labeled to show the average cost of operation for one year.

Avg. Life Expectancy of Major Appliances	
Refrigerator	15 years
Freezer	20 years
Dishwasher	11 years
Washing Machine	11 years
Dryer	15 years
Water Heater	12 years
Room Air Conditioner	15 years
Electric or Gas Furnace	20 years
Heat Pump	15 years

Remember that over time, energy costs will far exceed the original purchase price of any appliance.

Always compare the energy labels of different brands you are considering. The best contrast is to project operating costs for the entire life of the appliance. In other words, compare total costs over 15 years for a refrigerator or 11 years for a dishwasher.

Savings Analysis		
	#1	#2
Sales Price	$ 710	$ 805
Energy Label	$ 110	$ 85
Life Expectancy (see chart)	15 years	15 years
Lifetime Energy Costs (Life expectancy x energy label)	$ 1,650	$ 1,275
Total Cost of Ownership (Lifetime energy costs + Sales Price)	$ 2,360	$ 2,080
Best Buy		$ 280

Step 2

Calculate your break-even point before you buy any product or appliance which claims to save you money on your utility bills, be sure to calculate how long it will take to recoup your original investment.

To do a cost-benefit analysis, compare the operating costs of new equipment to what you pay to run your current appliance. Divide the initial purchase price by this annual savings rate to determine the breakeven point of the investment.

Example:	Old Equipment	New Equipment
	Electric Resistance Heating System	High Efficiency Gas Furnace
Operating Cost	$ 1,150/year	$ 475/year
Savings/Year	—	$ 675
Purchase Price & Installation	—	$ 3,275
Break even on Investment	—	4.85 years
		($3,275 ÷ $675)

Step 3

Choose the right size. Always buy appliances with the correct capacity for your current and future needs. Appliances which are too large or too small for the intended job waste energy.

Recommended Sizes of Various Appliances:

Water Heaters

No. of Family Members	Recommended Size of Water Heater (Gallons)	
	Electric	Gas
2	40 gallons	40 gallons
3	40 gallons	40 gallons
4	52 gallons	40 gallons
5	52 gallons	40 gallons
6	52 gallons	52 gallons
7 or more	80 gallons	65 gallons

Refrigerators

No. of Family Members	Recommended Size of Refrigerator (Cubic Feet)
2	12 -14 cubic feet
3	14 -16 cubic feet
4	16 -18 cubic feet
5	18 - 20 cubic feet
6	22 cubic feet

Air Conditioners

Air conditioners are sized according to BTUs (British Thermal Units). You will need 1.8 BTUs of cooling capacity for every cubic square foot of living area to be cooled (cubic ft = length x width x height).

You will also need a unit powerful enough to circulate air throughout the cooling area. To calculate circulation capacity, multiply cooling BTUs by .036. The answer equals the correct CFM rating (cubic feet per minute).

Example:
Room measures 20' x 10' with a ceiling height of 9 '
Cubic area = 1,800 cu. ft.
Correct Unit Size: 1,800 x 1.8 BTUs = 3,240 BTUs
Correct CFM Rating: 1,800 BTUs x .036 = 64.8 CFM

Heating Systems

Heating systems are sized according to BTUs. You will need approximately 2.8 BTUs of heating capacity for every cubic square foot of living area to be heated.

You will also need a unit powerful enough to circulate air throughout the heating area. To calculate circulation capacity, divide heating BTUs by 55. The answer is equal to the correct CFM rating (cubic feet per minute).

Step 4

Electric Fans

Fans are rated in CFMs. To determine the correct fan size for your needs, use the following formula:

Area to be cooled (cubic feet) x 40 Air Exchanges/Hour ÷ 60 Minutes = Required Fan Rating

Example:
Area to be cooled = 1,600 cubic feet
Correct Fan Size: 1,600 x 40 ÷ 60 = 1,066 CFM

Washing Machines

Always choose an extra-large capacity machine capable of handling 18 lbs. of laundry or more. You can always adjust capacity settings to meet your individual wash needs.

Light Bulbs

Manufacturers recommend you size light bulbs for ambiant lighting needs based on a ratio of 1 watt/sq. ft. of area to be lighted. You may also wish to consult the chart below for more specific recommendations:

Lighting Task	Incandescent Bulb	Fluorescent Bulb
Kitchen	100 watts	26 watts
Bathroom(s)	60 watts	NR*
Hallways	40 watts	NR
Dining Area	75 watts	NR
Livingroom/Den	75-100 watts	20 watts
Bedroom(s)	60 watts	NR
Closets	25 watts	NR
Outdoor Fixtures	75 watts	20 watts
Desk Lamps	75 watts reflector or 3-way bulb	NR

* NR = Not Recommended

Choose the right efficiency rating. Central heat and air conditioning systems are given an energy-efficiency rating based on the ratio between operating costs and heating and/or cooling output. The higher the efficiency rating, the lower the operating expenses.

Air conditioners and heat pumps are rated according to a standard known as SEER (seasonal energy efficiency) rating. Always buy a system with a SEER rating of *10 or higher.*

Gas heating systems are rated according to a different standard, known as AFUE (Adjusted Fuel Utilization Efficiency). When purchasing a new system, you should look for an AFUE rating of at least **80%**. Higher-rated systems are also available, but are too costly relative to the additional energy savings.

APPLIANCE BUYER'S WORKSHEET

		#1	#2	#3	#4	#5
(A)	Type of Equipment:					
(B)	Sales Price:					
(C)	Annual Operating Cost (see Energy Label)					
(D)	Lifetime Operating Cost					
(E)	Total Ownership Costs (B + D)					
(F)	Annual Operating Cost of Old Equipment					
(G)	Annual Energy Savings (C- F)					
(H)	Break-even (B ÷ G)					
(I)	Best Buy?					

		#1	#2	#3	#4	#5
(A)	Type of Equipment:					
(B)	Sales Price:					
(C)	Annual Operating Cost (see Energy Label)					
(D)	Lifetime Operating Cost					
(E)	Total Ownership Costs (B + D)					
(F)	Annual Operating Cost of Old Equipment					
(G)	Annual Energy Savings (C- F)					
(H)	Break-even (B ÷ G)					
(I)	Best Buy?					

UTILITIES

HERE'S THE PROOF

Our worksheets show you how to estimate your own savings from our energy conservation program. However, to dramatize the poten- tial, we've illustrated the savings for a typical family of four. As you can see, for an initial investment of $140, a typical family saved an incredible $759 per year.

Current Status	Suggestion(s)	Cost to Implement	Current Operating Costs	New Operating Costs	Annual Savings
Water Heater					
150-gallon capacity	a) Turn thermostat to 120°	$ 0	$ 471	$ 367	$ 104
Current setting = 120°	b) Install flow restrictors	$ 4	$ 367	$ 317	$ 50
Daily use = 60 gal/day	c) Install timer	$ 30	$ 317	$ 257	$ 60
Lighting					
Four 100-watt bulbs used 5 hours per day	Replace with fluourescent light.	$ 80	$ 59	$ 9	$ 50
Caulking					
Air leaks in 40% of door/window areas. Annual Heat Bill = $975 Annual Cooling Bill = $280	Re-caulk and weatherstrip around doors and windows. Add insulation around exhaust fans, etc.	$ 6	$ 1,255	$ 1,089	$ 166
Thermostat					
Maintain 72° setting during winter heating season.	a) Reduce thermostat to 62 during sleeping hours; 68° during waking hours.	$ 0	$ 846	$ 693	$ 153
Maintain 74° setting during summer cooling season	b) Raise thermostat to 78° during sleeping hours; 80° during waking hours, supplemented by electric fans.	$ 0	$ 243	$ 181	$ 62
Insulate Windows					
Single Pane Windows	Install plastic insulating film in in front of inside window panes (10 windows).	$ 20	$ 693	$ 579	$ 114
	TOTAL	**$ 140**			**$ 759**

Chapter Eight

Getting More for Your Real Estate Dollar

Is it a good time to buy a home?

It is a great time to buy a home, provided you buy for the right reasons. With interest rates at or near their lowest levels in more than a generation, the rationale for owning your primary residence could not be stronger. If you also consider the tax breaks associated with the mortgage interest deduction, it is hard to justify renting rather than owning your residence, particularly if you plan on living in the same area for the forseeable future.

However, much about the real estate business has changed. Twenty years ago, it was a forgone conclusion that home prices would appreciate 10-20% per year. Much of that rise was do to a once-in-a-lifetime demographic surge of Baby Boomers entering the housing markets for the first time. Today, supply and demand are more balanced and likely to continue that way. Thus, while in an earlier time it made sense to buy the biggest and most expensive house possible (because of rising property values and inflation), today it is wise to chose a residence that fits your lifestyle and that you can comfortably afford with no expectation of significant appreciation.

How much can I afford to pay for a home?

Lenders apply two rules in calculating the maximum price you can afford. According to these guidelines, your total monthly house payment, consisting of principle and interest on your loan, real estate taxes and insurance premiums, should not exceed 28% of your monthly income before taxes or 36% of your income when other long-term debts are included.

These are maximum limits, but we would encourage you to set your sights

Maximum Monthly Payment You Can Afford	Maximum Loan Amount ($)					
	(Interest Rate)*					
	6%	7%	8%	9%	10%	11%
$ 400	$ 66,700	$ 60,100	$ 54,500	$ 49,700	$ 45,600	$ 42,000
$ 600	100,074	90,200	81,800	74,600	68,400	63,000
$ 800	133,433	120,200	109,000	99,400	91,200	84,000
$ 1000	166,800	150,300	136,300	124,300	114,000	105,000
$ 1200	200,100	180,400	163,500	149,000	136,700	126,000
$ 1400	233,500	210,430	190,800	174,000	159,500	147,000
$ 1600	266,866	240,500	218,000	198,900	182,300	168,000
$ 1800	300,200	270,600	245,300	223,700	205,000	189,000
$ 2000	333,600	300,600	272,600	248,600	279,900	210,000

* Assumes 30-yr., fixed-rate loan

lower. Too many people buy the biggest house they can qualify for, without regard to other financial priorities. You will be better served buying a less expensive home and conserving your cash.

What if the home I presently own costs me more than I can realistically afford?

Consider selling. You simply cannot afford to overlook important savings objectives, such as a retirement plan, a college fund for your children or a cash reserve for unexpected emergencies. If you do not have enough money each month to fund these priorities and pay your monthly mortgage payment, you are spending too much on housing.

Besides my income, what other factors affect the price I can pay for a home?

Rising or falling interest rates can have a dramatic effect on the maximum loan for which you qualify. A change of two percentage points alters your purchasing power by $10-20,000 or more.

An even bigger factor is where you choose to live. Local market conditions have a profound impact on what your housing dollar will buy. In Houston, for example, the average home is priced at $100,000, while in the San Francisco Bay area, the median price is $330,000.

Is renting better than buying in some circumstances?

If you plan on moving in three years or less, renting may be the wiser choice

Median-Priced Single Family Home

Atlanta	$117,000
Baltimore	$123,000
Boston	$220,000
Chicago	$169,000
Cincinnati	$117,000
Cleveland	$125,000
Columbus	$123,000
Dallas	$122,000
Denver	$149,000
Detroit	$133,000
Houston	$100,000
Indianapolis	$110,000
Kansas City	$115,000
Los Angeles	$197,000
Louisville	$108,000
Miami	$123,000
Milwaukee	$133,000
Minneapolis	$131,000
Long Island	$194,000
Philadelphia	$138,000
Phoenix	$121,000
Pittsburgh	$94,000
Portland	$160,000
Rochester	$93,000
Salt Lake City	$133,000
San Diego	$215,000
San Francisco	$330,000
Seattle	$200,000
Tampa	$91,000
DC/MD/VA	$176,000

Source: National Association of Realtors, 1999 3rd Qtr. Survey

since the transaction costs involved in buying and selling a home may offset the mortgage interest deduction and intangible advantages of ownership. The only way to know for sure is to analyze the pros and cons of each alternative, assuming no price appreciation as well as modest gains of 2-3% per year.

How can I get the best deal when I buy a home?

The key is to make your search as organized and thorough as possible. Smart buyers have a keen understanding of the current market for homes and know the last price paid for each house in the neighborhoods they like. Sometimes, the information comes from real estate agents, but more often savy investors do their own legwork using county land records.

Market knowledge helps you recognize bargains and when to act on them. Finding bargains is another matter.

Where should I be searching?

No one approach works all the time, but by using several techniques, you can increase the likelihood that your search will produce results.

First, always use one or more real estate agents. They cost you nothing and give you access to computerized multiple-listing services identifying most homes for sale.

You should also contact major savings banks in your area for a list of their repossessed properties. Many of these homes are represented by real estate agents, but knowing that the property has been foreclosed is a tip-off that a lower offer may be accepted.

You can also use the internet, although your results will be spotty. No single internet source lists all of the homes in your area. In fact, real estate information on the world wide web borders on

the chaotic. There are literally thousands of real estate agents with their own internet addresses. The quality, depth and reliability of the information provided ranges from excellent to extremely poor. The problem is that without rummaging through all the sites, you can't tell the good ones from the bad. Several sites have tried to bring some order to the process and the situation is improving, although by no means ideal. These mega-sites allow you to search multiple data- bases for the community in which you are interested, saving you considerable time. These sites include one run by the **National Association of Realtors** (www.realtor.com), another called **Homescout** (www.homescout.com) and a third at www.homes.com. Logging on to the **International Real Estate Directory** (www.ired.com) allows you to identify sites run by individual agents in a particular community, but you will still need to spend time finding the good ones. Finally, you can try a site that promises listings of homes for sale by owner, the **Abele Owner's Network** (www.owners.com), but frankly the selections are so limited that you are better off reading the classifieds in your hometown paper for leads.

In fact, the weekend classifieds are still your best source for clues to motivated sellers anxious to deal. Words like "owner relocating," "owner financing" or "must sell" are hints of weakness that may spell opportunity.

Patience is critical if you want a really good deal. It is not unrealistic to assume it will take you three to five months to find the right property. For advice on the buying process, including many hints to help you make below-market deals, follow our step-by-step at the end of this chapter.

Are some months better than others for buying a home?

Yes. The best time to make a deal is in the slow selling seasons when buyers are scarce. The winter months of December, January and February are ideal, since properties look dreary and owners are edgy.

How can I find the lowest mortgage rates?

Don't rely exclusively on recommendations from real estate agents. Many agents have referral agreements with mortgage brokers who may be more interested in a commission than your best interests. You should always do your own independent investigation of the mortgage market, beginning with a quick scan of the rates offered by local mortgage companies. This survey is usually published in the Saturday or Sunday real estate section of most local newspapers.

In addition, we suggest that you use the internet. You can get a comprehensive overview of the real estate mortgage market through any number of sites including **Bank Rate Monitor** (www.bankrate.com), HSH Associates (www.hsh.com) and **Mortgage Market Information Services** ([www.interest. com](www.interest.com)). At the **HSH** and **Mortgage Market Information Services** sites, you can also do an immediate search of lenders that do loans in your area and their current offerings. You can also survey multiple lenders simultaneously through **Quicken Mortgage.com** ([www.quickenmort-gage.com](www.quickenmortgage.com)), **E-Loan** (www.eloan.com) and **Interloan.com** ([www.interloan. com](www.interloan.com)).

Be aware that the rates which are published on the internet and in newspapers are not comprehensive. Each lender offers many loan combinations which are not published but may be appropriate for your circumstances. Therefore, we recommend you use the internet and newspapers to screen your options, but follow-up with a phone call to the five or six most promising lenders. As you refine your search, keep in mind that interest rates are only part of the equation. Compare all the costs you must pay as part of the transaction including discount "points," application fees, appraisal charges, credits reports and private mortgage insurance. In many cases, excessive transaction charges can outweigh the advantages of a lower interest rate.

Should I choose a 30-year conventional loan or consider one of the various adjustable rate mortgages (ARMs)?

Adjustable rate mortgages (ARMS) became popular at a time of relatively high mortgage interest rates. Lenders hoped home buyers would be attracted by the lower initial interest rate of an ARM loan and the likelihood that prevailing interest rates would decline before the first interest rate adjustment took effect. ARMs are always a gamble. The borrower pays a below-market interest rate for a limited period of time, agreeing that the rate will be adjusted to market levels at a certain time in the future.

The determining factor in choosing between a fixed-rate mortgage and an ARM is your bet on the future. If you think rates will be lower in the years ahead than they are today, an ARM may be a good choice. On the other hand, if you believe future rates will be higher, an ARM is less appealing. Our general advice is to stick with conventional financing, particularly if you plan on living in your home for the foreseeable future. About the only exception is if you have a definite plan to sell your home within a specific time frame. If you planned to sell in five years, for example, an ARM loan with a 7-year adjustment period might make sense because you would never be exposed to the possibility of a higher rate.

When is the right time to refinance a mortgage?

You should always be prepared to refinance if you can significantly lower your mortgage payment and the costs associated with the refinancing can be recouped within a reasonable period of time. As a general rule, we recommend a hard look at refinancing options when the spread between market interest rates and your present mortgage is at least .5%. How much it will cost you to refinance then becomes the determining factor.

You should expect to recover those costs in less than five years and preferably much sooner. Do not refinance if you have plans to move in the foreseeable future.

We have prepared a worksheet at the end of this chapter to help you analyze refinancing options. If you prefer, you can also use the interactive mortgage calculators at www.interest.com, which can help you determine how long it will take you to recoup the costs of a particular refinancing opportunity.

How do bi-weekly or 15-year mortgages work and will they save me money?

With a **bi-weekly mortgage**, you make one-half of your mortgage payment every two weeks, instead of a single monthly payment. The net result is that you make 13 payments per year instead of the normal 12. The extra payment reduces the principal amount of your loan, which in turn saves you future interest expenses.

With a **15-year mortgage**, you pay off your loan in 15 years instead of the usual 30. Surprisingly, your monthly payment is only 25% higher than if you had a conventional mortgage. Again, you pay less interest so you save money.

Money Saved Compared to a Conventional Mortgage
($100,000 mortgage @10%)

Bi-weekly Mortgage		15-Year Mortgage
Total Savings		Total Savings
$ 45	After **1** year	$ 111
$ 1,267	After **5** years	$ 3,436
$ 6,148	After **10** years	$ 16,765
$ 16,987	After **15** years	$ 46,199
$ 30,623	After **20** years	$ 83,595
$ 57,609	After **25** years	$ 111,149
$ 68,959	After **30** years	$ 122,502

The problem with both these programs is that most people do not live in their homes long enough to justify the inconvenience and expense of the higher payments. As the chart below demonstrates, you must live in a home at least ten years before you realize significant savings. Time is therefore the key to deciding whether either plan is right for you.

In most cases, a much simpler alternative to the bi-weekly or 15-year mortgage is to make one or two extra payments on a conventional mortgage each year. You send these extra payments to your lender along with a cover letter, indicating that you wish the extra payment to be applied towards your outstanding loan balance (principal). Most mortgages allow you to make these unscheduled payments at any time without penalty, which means you have the flexibility of deciding when and how much to contribute.

For example, if you had a 30-year mortgage for $100,000 at 7.5% and made an extra $1,000 payment each year to reduce principal, you could reduce your loan term by 8.25 years and save $48,590 in interest charges. If you made a $2,000 payment each year, you would reduce the term 12.5 years and save more than $75,000 in interest costs.

To learn how supplemental payments can affect your mortgage, try out various scenarios using the financial calculators at the Omni Network web site (www.imfinc.com). If you do not have access to the internet, ask your lender to provide you with a written analysis of how a specific schedule of principal payments will affect the term of your loan and the amount of interest you will pay over the life of the mortgage.

Are home equity loans the best way to borrow extra cash?

Borrowing against the accumulated equity in your home is often your cheapest source for a personal loan, since the interest you pay is tax deductible. The biggest drawback is that your home serves as collateral for the loan. If you default on your payments, you could lose your house to your creditors.

It is best to avoid home equity loans, or any other type of personal loans, except in emergency situations. Loans are too often used to maintain a standard of living you simply can't afford. Borrow only if you must, but if you absolutely need the money, a home equity loan is preferable to credit cards, auto loans, student loans, etc.

How do I sell my home for the best price in the shortest time?

The three keys to a fast, profitable sale are the following:

- Setting a realistic price;
- Improving visual appeal; and
- Maximizing your home's exposure to qualified buyers.

Many unsuccessful sellers fail in all three categories.

Most important is a realistic price. Pricing a home should be a simple matter of comparing recent sales for comparable properties, yet many homeowners allow their emotions to interfere with common sense. Above-market prices scare away potential buyers, delaying a sale and increasing the likelihood of greater concessions after months of inactivity.

Cosmetic repairs are crucial if you seek top-dollar. Dirty walls, frayed carpet, cluttered closets, and a messy yard will turn off a large segment of potential buyers and result in low offers. Your home should be in "showroom" condition, sparkling clean and tastefully decorated.

Another overlooked step for a quick sale is effective marketing. Too many sellers are satisfied with a real estate agent who has the occasional open house or runs the infrequent newspaper ad. If buyers don't know your house is available, you will lose lots of opportunities. To sell your home faster than average, you've got to sell harder than your competition. Weekly open houses, flyers, and constant advertising are critical.

At the end of this chapter, you will find instructions that take you step-by-step through the sales process, including setting a competitive price, making your own assessment of needed improvements and designing a marketing plan with or without the help of a real estate agent.

You sound critical of real estate agents. Is it better to sell a home without an agent's help?

Real estate agents don't come cheap. Commissions to sell a home average 6%

of the sales price. For a $150,000 home, that's more than $9,000. Agents can be worth every penny if they are competent and experienced. Yet a recent survey by a respected consumer journal indicates that 1 out of 5 sellers are dissatisfied with their agent's work.

It is possible to sell a home without an agent's help. If you are thorough, organized and follow the directions in our step-by-step instructions, you should be able to do almost everything an agent can and save all of the agent's commission. The drawback is that if you try to sell your home without allowing agents to show your property to prospective buyers, you exclude a large portion of the potential market. Agents will avoid your house like the plague if you aren't paying a commission.

Buyers who work with agents are high-quality prospects you should not ignore, particularly in a soft market. Therefore, we recommend a compromise between selling a home yourself and relying exclusively on professional help. For a modest fee, a "do-it-yourself" brokerage service will provide you with forms, sale signs, lock boxes and access to the realtors' information network — the multiple listing service (MLS). You do all the legwork, but through the MLS, your home is also exposed to thousands of agents working with prospective buyers. If your home matches one of their client's search criteria, the agent will have no hesitation showing your home. If their client makes an offer you accept, you pay only half the regular commission (3%). On a $150,000 sale, that saves you more than $4,000.

Guide to
HOW MUCH HOUSE YOU CAN AFFORD

This worksheet will help you determine the maximum sales price you can afford for a new home. Three factors affect the amount:

Income:

Your monthly mortgage payment should not exceed 28% of your *pre-tax* income or 36% of your income when other long-term debts are taken into account.

Cash:

The cash you will need varies according to the terms you can negotiate with the seller, but in general, figure 5% or 10% for a downpayment and approximately 3–4% for loan points and miscellaneous closing costs.

Rates:

Monthly mortgage payments vary with interest rates. Higher rates *lower* affordability; lower rates *increase* it.

Example: $100,000 30-yr. fixed-rate mortgage

Interest Rate	Monthly Payment
6%	$599
7%	$685
8%	$733
9%	$804
10%	$877

Keep in mind that you are figuring your *maximum* affordability range. You would be prudent to buy *below* this amount, particularly if you are having a hard time meeting your current savings priorities.

If you do not wish to use this worksheet to determine your affordability range, you can do the same calculations over the internet at several sites. Try the mortgage calculators at **Mortgage Market Information Services** (www.interest.com) or at **HSH Associates** (www.hsh.com).

MAXIMUM SALES PRICE WORKSHEET

Step 1

Determine your available cash.

1. **How much money do you have for a downpayment and closing costs?** (Exclude money you have set aside for retirement, emergencies, etc.)

$_____$

2. **Are you also planning to use cash from the sale of your existing home?** If so, what is this amount after deducting commissions and other sales costs?

$_____$

3. **Will you be receiving assistance from a friend or relative?** If so, what is the amount?

source:_____ - $ _____

source: _____ - $ _____

4. **Can you expect any assistance from the Seller?** If so, what is this amount?

$_____$

5. **What is the total cash available for your home purchase?**

Total Cash = (1)+(2)+(3)+(4) $ _____

Step 2

Determine your income qualifications

1. **What is your current household income?**

$ _____

2. **Based on industry guidelines, you can qualify for a home mortgage if the total monthly payment does not exceed 28% of your monthly income before taxes. Based on these standards, what is the maximum payment you can afford?**

_____ x 0.28 = _____
HOUSEHOLD   MAXIMUM
INCOME   MONTHLY
                             PAYMENT

R
E
A
L

E
S
T
A
T
E

Step 3

Factor current interest rates

1. **What is the prevailing rate for 30-year fixed-rate mortgages?**
   Check Saturday's real estate section in your local newspaper for approximate rates or check the web:
   Bank Rate Monitor
   (www.bankrate.com)
   HSH Associates
   (www.hsh.com).

   _____%

2. **What is the maximum monthly payment you can afford, as determined in Step 2?**

   $_____

3. **Based on current rates, what is the maximum loan amount for which you qualify?**

   Use the rate chart to approximate your answer. For example, if today's interest rate is 8% and you can afford a monthly payment of $953, the maximum loan you can qualify for is $130,000.

   $ _____

   Author's note: To be completely accurate, you must also factor monthly real estate taxes and insurance premiums into your affordability range. However, for purposes of this exercise, we presume such payments will not be so high as to make dramatic differences in loan qualifications.

How Monthly Payment Is Affected by Changing Interest Rates

$ Loan Amount	6.5%	7%	7.5%	8%	8.5%	9%	9.5%	10%	10.5%	11%	11.5%
50,000	316	332	349	366	384	402	420	438	457	476	495
60,000	379	399	419	440	461	482	504	457	548	571	594
70,000	442	465	489	513	538	563	588	614	640	666	693
80,000	505	535	559	587	615	643	672	702	731	761	792
90,000	568	598	629	660	692	724	756	789	823	857	891
100,000	632	665	699	733	768	804	840	877	914	952	990
110,000	695	731	769	807	845	885	924	965	1106	1047	1089
120,000	758	798	839	880	922	965	1009	1053	1097	1142	1188
130,000	821	864	908	953	999	1046	1093	1140	1189	1238	1287
140,000	884	931	978	1027	1076	1126	1177	1228	1280	1333	1386
150,000	948	997	1048	1100	1153	1206	1261	1316	1372	1428	1485
160,000	1011	1064	1118	1174	1230	1287	1345	1404	1463	1523	1584
170,000	1074	1131	1188	1247	1307	1367	1429	1491	1555	1618	1683
180,000	1137	1197	1258	1320	1384	1448	1513	1579	1646	1714	1782
190,000	1200	1264	1328	1394	1460	1528	1597	1667	1738	1809	1881
200,000	1264	1330	1398	1467	1537	1609	1681	1755	1829	1904	1980
225,000	1422	1496	1573	1650	1730	1810	1891	1974	2058	2124	2228
250,000	1580	1663	1748	1843	1922	2011	2102	2193	2286	2380	2475
275,000	1738	1829	1922	2017	2114	2212	2312	2413	2515	2618	2723
300,000	1896	1995	2097	2201	2306	2413	2522	2632	2744	2856	2970
325,000	2054	2162	2272	2384	2498	2615	2732	2852	2972	3095	3218
350,000	2212	2328	2447	2568	2691	2816	2942	3071	3201	3333	3466

MAXIMUM SALES PRICE WORKSHEET

Step 4

Finalize your buying range:

1. **What is the maximum loan for which you qualify based on your income and current interest rates?** (See Step 3.)

$_____

2. **How much cash do you have available for a down payment and closing costs?** (See Step 1.)

$_____

3. **Do you have enough cash to complete the deal at the projected loan amount?** (Refer to the chart below to approximate your cash needs.)

Yes / No

4. **If you have sufficient cash to close the deal, add the price of your down payment (5% or 10%) to the loan for which you qualify, to determine your maximum buying range.**

Loan Amount	Estimated Cash Needed with 5% Downpayment	Estimated Cash Needed with 10% Downpayment
$ 75,000	$ 6,750	$ 10,500
$ 100,000	$ 9,000	$ 14,000
$ 125,000	$ 11,250	$ 17,500
$ 150,000	$ 13,500	$ 21,000
$ 175,000	$ 15,750	$ 24,500
$ 200,000	$ 18,000	$ 28,000
$ 225,000	$ 20,300	$ 31,500
$ 250,000	$ 22,500	$ 35,000
$ 300,000	$ 27,000	$ 42,000

5. **If you do not have enough cash to close the deal, you must reduce the maximum loan for which you qualify until you arrive at an amount for which you have both sufficient cash and income. Experiment with lower loan amounts until you reach a figure that works.**

Example: *If you qualify for a $100,000 loan and can afford a 10% cash down payment, your maximum buying range is $110,000 ($100,000 + $10,000).*

6. **What is your maximum buying range for a new home?**

$_____

7. **Your maximum range reflects standards set by lenders, but it is in your best interests to use less of your monthly income on housing expenses if possible. We recommend a buying range of between 20% and 23% of your monthly income. Repeat steps 2–4 using this lower percentage of income to determine your ideal buying range.**

$_____

MAXIMUM SALES PRICE WORKSHEET

Step 5

If housing prices in your area make affording a home difficult at any price, consider these four ways to increase your buying power:

1. **Shop for more creative financing.** Adjus-table-rate mortgages will reduce your monthly payments for the short-term, but you clearly risk higher payments should interest rates rise in the future. Many lenders also offer special 1% down or 0% down loans which carry higher interest rates than conventional mortgages. While these programs allow qualified borrowers to buy a property with little or no cash, we think it makes more sense to wait until you have the money for a down-payment before investing in real estate.

2. **Negotiate with the seller.** If cash is a problem, you can always try to get a second mortgage from the Seller, or ask for further concessions on the closing costs. Ask the Seller to pay your loan points, give you a 3-month grace period on payments, etc. Negotiate these terms before you sign a sales contract.

3. **Inquire about subsidized loans from FHA or the Veterans Administration.** For those who qualify, an FHA or VA loan can reduce your cash needs and monthly payments significantly. Contact a local lender for current eligibility rules.

4. **Look for state assistance.** If you have a low income, you may qualify for assistance from a state-sponsored program for first-time buyers. Eligibility standards vary, so call to see if you qualify.

State Housing Agencies for Low and Moderate Income Home Buyers' Assistance

Alabama	205 261-4310
Alaska	907 561-1900
Arizona	602 542-5321
Arkansas	501 682-5900
California	916 322-3991
Colorado	303 861-8962
Connecticut	203 721-9501
Delaware	302 736-4263
D.C.	202 628-0311
Florida	904 488-4197
Georgia	404 320-4840
Hawaii	808 848-3230
Idaho	208 336-0161
Illinois	312 836-5200
Indiana	317 232-7777
Iowa	515 242-4990
Kansas	913 296-3480
Kentucky	800 564-7630
Louisiana	504 925-3675
Maine	617 451-3480
Maryland	410 514-7000
Massachusetts	617 451-3480
Michigan	517 373-8370
Minnesota	612 286-7608
Mississippi	601 354-6062
Missouri	601 961-4514
Montana	406 444-3040
Nebraska	404 477-4406
Nevada	702 885-4258
New Hampshire	603 472-8623
New Jersey	609 890-8900
New Mexico	505 843-6880
New York	212 686-9700
N. Carolina	919 781-6115
N. Dakota	701 224-3434
Ohio	614 466-7970
Oklahoma	405 848-1144
Oregon	503 378-4343
Pennsylvania	717 780-3800
Rhode Island	401 751-5566
S. Carolina	803 734-8831
S. Dakota	605 773-3181
Tennessee	615 746-2400
Texas	512 474-2974
Utah	801 521-6950
Vermont	802 864-5743
Virginia	804 782-1986
Washington	206 464-7139
W. Virginia	304 345-6475
Wisconsin	608 266-7884
Wyoming	307 265-0603

Guide
SHOULD YOU RENT OR OWN?

Home ownership provides many bene-fits, including mortgage interest deduc-tions, predictable monthly payments and potential price appreciation. However, there are some circumstances when renting is better. The worksheet below is designed to weigh the financial costs and benefits of owning vs. renting, so you can make the right choice.

RENT OR OWN WORKSHEET

Step 1

How much do you estimate the new home will cost you?

(Choose one)

$75,000	$225,000
$100,000	$250,000
$150,000	$300,000
$175,000	$325,000
$200,000	$350,000

PURCHASE PRICE $_____

Step 2

Estimate the costs of buying the home.

Purchase Price	Transaction Costs
$ 75,000	$ 3,000
100,000	4,000
150,000	6,000
200,000	8,000
225,000	9,000
250,000	10,000
300,000	12,000
325,000	13,000
350,000	14,000

Assumes buyer pays 1.5 points to lender, 1% in up-front private mortgage insurance and 1.5% in miscellaneous closing costs.

TRANSACTION COST TO PURCHASE $_____

RENT OR OWN WORKSHEET

Step 3

If you purchased the home you desired, what would be your monthly payments for principal and interest, real estate taxes and insurance. Ask a real estate agent to prepare a precise calculation for the house you have identified, or use the chart below for an estimate.

MONTHLY PAYMENT $_____

Estimated Monthly Payment

Price of Home	Monthly Payment
$ 75,000	$ 527
100,000	729
125,000	911
150,000	1094
175,000	1361
200,000	1458
225,000	1640
250,000	1824
275,000	2006
300,000	2278

Assumes 90%, 30-year fixed-rate mortgage @ 7.5%, real estate taxes at $1 per $100 of assessed value and typical insurance rates. Actual monthly payments will vary according to local conditions and should be confirmed by seeking professional advice.

Step 4

Adjust your monthly payment to take into account the tax deductions to which you would be entitled. Ask a real estate agent to prepare a precise calculation for the house you have identified, or estimate the amount according to the instructions.

A. TOTAL MONTHLY PAYMENT
     (STEP 3) $_____

B. ESTIMATED FEDERAL TAX RATE
     15%   28%   31%   36%   _____%

C. TAX-ADJUSTED MONTHLY
     PAYMENT
     (TOTAL PAYMENT - TAX RATE) $ _____

Step 5

Estimate how long you would own the house.

(Choose one)

1 yr	3 yrs
5 yrs	7 yrs
9 yr.	10 yrs or more

Term of Occupancy   _____

RENT OR OWN WORKSHEET

Step 6

Determine your total tax-adjusted payments during your occupancy.

A. TOTAL MONTHS OF OCCUPANCY _____

B. TAX-ADJUSTED MONTHLY PAYMENT (STEP 4) $ _____

C. TOTAL TAX-ADJUSTED PAYMENTS DURING OCCUPANCY [(A) X (B)] $ _____

Step 7

Assuming normal inflation (5%), determine what the house will be worth when you sell.

PRICE AT RESALE $ _____

Price at Resale

Sale Price	1 yr	3 yr	5 yr	7 yr	9 yr	10 yr
$ 75,000	$ 79 K	$ 87 K	$ 96 K	$105 K	$116 K	$123 K
100,000	105 K	116 K	128 K	141 K	155 K	164 K
125,000	131 K	145 K	160 K	176 K	194 K	205 K
150,000	157 K	174 K	191 K	211 K	233 K	247 K
175,000	184 K	202 K	223 K	246 K	271 K	288 K
200,000	210 K	231 K	255 K	281 K	310 K	329 K
225,000	236 K	260 K	287 K	317 K	349 K	370 K
250,000	262 K	289 K	319 K	352 K	388 K	411 K
275,000	289 K	318 K	351 K	387 K	427 K	452 K
300,000	315 K	347 K	383 K	422 K	465 K	494 K

Step 8

Estimate your profit from the sale.

A. RE-SALE PRICE (STEP 7) $ _____

B. SALES COMMISSION (6% OF RE-SALE PRICE) _____ %

C. ORIGINAL PURCHASE PRICE (STEP 2) $ _____

D. TRANSACTION COSTS TO PURCHASE (STEP 3) $ _____

E. PROFIT FROM SALE [(A) - (B + C+ D)] $ _____

RENT OR OWN WORKSHEET

Step 9

Determine your actual occupancy expense by subtracting profits from tax-adjusted monthly payments.

A. TOTAL TAX-ADJUSTED
   PAYMENTS
   (STEP 6) $_____

B. PROFITS FROM RE-SALE
   (STEP 8) $_____

C. TOTAL OCCUPANCY
   EXPENSE [(A) - (B)] $_____

Step 10

Determine what would it cost you to rent a comparable home or apartment.
Consult a real estate agent or do your own research on local market conditions.

(CHOOSE ONE)
MONTHLY PAYMENTS

$400	$1,000
$500	$1,100
$600.	$1,200
$700.	$1,300
$800.	$1,400
$900.	$1,500

COMPARABLE MONTHLY
RENT PAYMENT $_____

Step 11

If you rent for an identical period, what are your total monthly payments, including projected increases of 5% per year?

Total Payments During Tenancy*						
Original Monthly Payments	1 yr	3 yr	5 yr	7 yr	9 yr	10 yr
$ 400 / mo.	$ 4,800	$ 15,100	$ 26,500	$ 39,000	$ 53,000	$ 60,400
500 / mo.	6,000	18,900	33,100	48,800	66,100	75,400
600 / mo.	7,200	22,700	39,800	58,600	79,400	90,681
700 / mo.	8,400	26,500	46,400	67,900	92,100	105,200
800 / mo.	9,600	30,300	53,100	78,200	105,900	120,900
900 / mo.	10,800	34,000	59,600	87,800	118,800	135,700
1,000 / mo.	12,000	37,800	66,300	97,600	132,000	150,800
1,100 / mo.	13,200	41,500	72,700	107,000	145,000	165,700
1,200 / mo.	14,400	45,400	79,600	117,300	159,000	181,600
1,300 / mo.	15,600	49,200	86,200	127,100	172,000	196,400
1,400 / mo.	16,800	53,000	92,800	136,700	185,000	211,323
1,500 / mo.	18,100	56,700	99,300	146,200	198,000	226,203

* Assumes rates increase 5% per year.

Total Rent Payments
During Occupancy $_____

Step 12

Purchasing a home requires an up-front down payment. If you rent, you could save this money and invest it in stocks, bonds or a money market account.

Assuming you invested in an index stock fund which returns an average of 8% per year, how much would the investment be worth at the end of your occupancy period?

Amount invested instead of used as a downpayment	Value at end of occupancy period			
	1 yr.	3 yrs.	5 yrs.	7 yrs.
$ 7,500	$630	$2,060	$3,660	$5,460
10,000	840	2,750	4,883	7,280
12,500	1,050	3,440	6,100	9,100
15,000	1,260	4,130	7,325	10,920
17,500	1,510	4,820	8,540	12,750
20,000	1,720	5,500	9,760	14,570
25,000	2,160	6,890	12,200	18,210
30,000	2,590	8,260	14,650	21,850

VALUE OF FUNDS INVESTED
INSTEAD OF USED FOR DOWN PAYMENT
$_____

Step 13

Determine your total occupancy costs if you rent?

A. TOTAL RENT PAYMENTS
(STEP 11) $_____

B. VALUE OF FUNDS INVESTED
INSTEAD OF USED FOR
DOWNPAYMENT $_____

C. OCCUPANCY COST
[(A) - (B)] $_____

Step 14

Compare total adjusted occupancy costs if you rent or buy?

A. TOTAL OCCUPANCY COSTS
IF YOU **BUY** (STEP 9) $_____

B. TOTAL OCCUPANCY COSTS
IF YOU **RENT** (STEP 13) $_____

Choose the best option.

REAL ESTATE

Guide to
BUYING YOUR NEXT HOUSE

This worksheet is the blueprint for your search and successful purchase of a new home. By following the step-by-step guidelines, you should be able to locate the best homes in your price range, negotiate the lowest price and set the stage for higher-than-average appreciation after you buy.

Before you begin, a word of advice. Many people sit back and let a real estate agent do all the work of finding the right home. Agents are an invaluable resource for buyers, but remember that they legally work for sellers and only get paid if you buy. An agent's goal is to sell you *any* home. Your goal is to find the *best* house at the *lowest* price.

You will be best served if you do as much of your own legwork as possible. The more knowledge you gain about your local real estate market, the more likely you will recognize bargains and know when to act on them. In the case of buying a home, hard work really does pay off.

BUYING YOUR NEXT HOUSE WORKSHEET

Locating Homes for Sale

Step 1

Refer to Part I of the Real Estate Savings System. What is your target price range for a new home? (Your target should be less than the maximum for which you qualify.)

TARGET PRICE $ _____

Step 2

Quickly scan the weekend real estate section in your local newspaper(s). In the areas you like, are homes selling in your price range? Make notes on several areas you may not have previously considered. Are homes in these neighborhoods priced so attractively that you should also consider them?

BUYING YOUR NEXT HOUSE WORKSHEET

AREA	*DESCRIPTION OF HOME*	*PRICE RANGE*
_____	_____	_____
_____	_____	_____
_____	_____	_____
_____	_____	_____
_____	_____	_____
_____	_____	_____
_____	_____	_____

Step 3

Visit at least two advertised "Open Houses" in each area you are considering. Do this for research, not with the expectation of finding your "dream" home.

Pay more attention to your drive than the actual house. You want general impressions of the area. How far is the drive from your current address? Do the neighborhoods look well-maintained?

Inside the houses, look at what your money buys. How many bedrooms? How large a yard? How many added features? Is there a garage? Again, you want general impressions you can compare to other areas you are scouting.

Many open houses are hosted by the real estate agent who listed the house for sale. They will undoubtedly be eager to work with you on finding other homes in the area. Take their business cards, but make no commitments to work with them. You want time to reflect on your own impressions of your tour before involving a salesperson.

R E A L   E S T A T E

Step 4

Rank the areas you surveyed in order of preference.

FIRST CHOICE: _____

SECOND CHOICE: _____

THIRD CHOICE: _____

BUYING YOUR NEXT HOUSE WORKSHEET

Step 5

Next weekend, take another driving tour, this time concentrating on the top areas on your list. During this second trip, you want to learn more about specific neighborhoods. How close are they to shopping? Which subdivisions look better than others? Keep notes on what you see, writing down the addresses of any homes for sale that look particularly appealing.

Area

Overall impressions of neighborhood

Neighborhoods you like

Neighborhoods you don't like

Step 6

In two weeks, contact a real estate agent who works in the neighborhood you've targeted. It's easy to find them. Simply refer to your list of homes for sale in Step 5, or the cards you saved from "open house" visits. You can also find good leads for agents who serve the neighborhoods you like by logging on to the *International Real Estate Directory* (www.ired.com), which allows you to identify sites run by individual agents in a particular community. When you call, be very specific in your request.

BUYING YOUR NEXT HOUSE WORKSHEET

Sample Dialogue:

❝ Hello. I am in the market for a new home and would like to arrange a time to tour some homes with you. Before we get together, I would like you to do a search of the Multiple Listing Service and identify at least 3-4 homes which meet my selection criteria. I would like to tour these homes at our first meeting. Here are my selection criteria.

Price: _____

Neighborhood(s): _____

Type of Property:
(i.e. single family house, condo,
townhouse, duplex, etc.) _____

Number of bedrooms: _____

Garage (Optional): _____

Age of Home: _____

Other Criteria: _____
_____
_____
_____

I am particularly interested in exceptionally good buying opportunities, such as a foreclosure, divorce sale, etc. Thank you very much. I look forward to meeting you. ❞

Why be so specific and demanding on the telephone? First, you don't want to waste time in an agent's office when you could be out looking at homes. Second, you want to politely but firmly communicate what you expect of any agent with whom you work.

Step 7

During your tour, keep careful notes on every home you look at, even if they don't appeal to you. You want a record you can refer back to for future reference.

Evaluating particular homes is a matter of personal taste. However, there are a few points you should keep in mind according to real estate pros:

- Homes on high ground are more desirable than homes in low lying areas.

- Corner lots are more desirable than interior lots.

- Homes in quiet settings are more desirable than homes on busy streets.

- The quality of neighborhood schools is important even if you do not have children (because of re-sale).

- 3-4 bedrooms are a better choice for re-sale than 1-2 bedroom homes.

- Unusually designed houses are often harder to sell than more traditional homes for the area.

- The highest-priced house in the neighborhood is generally not the best investment.

- Desirable features for re-sale include garages, basements, eat-in kitchens, fireplaces, family rooms and open floorplans.

- Less desirable features for re-sale include street parking, small kitchens, split-levels and dated fixtures.

- Peeling paint, faded carpet or other cosmetic problems depress prices but are easy to correct. They create buying opportunities that should be welcomed.

Continue to look at homes with agent(s) over several weekends until you feel reasonably confident of your understanding of price ranges and availability in your targeted areas. Even if you find one house in particular that you like, keep looking. You want to be totally informed about other options before writing an offer.

If you have access to the internet and want to satisfy yourself that you have researched *all* your options, try the search engines at the **National Association of Realtors** (www.realtor.com), **Homescout** (www.homescout.com) and (www.homes.com). You might also wish to search (www.owners.com) for homes which are not listed with real estate agents.

BUYING YOUR NEXT HOUSE WORKSHEET

Step 8

In addition to real estate agents, contact several large banks or savings & loans in your area and ask to speak with their "assets owned" or "repossession" department. Tell them you are interested in a list of their foreclosed properties which are for sale.

Foreclosed property usually sells at 70-90% of current market prices. If a house is located in your target area, it is definitely worth checking out.

Do not waste your time with auctions or courthouse sales. Unless you are a full-time investor, you are more likely to overpay for auctioned properties than find a great bargain.

Step 9

When you are ready to write an offer on any home, begin by determining an appropriate price.

BUYING YOUR NEXT HOUSE WORKSHEET

How to Determine an Offer Price

Step 1

List any sales in the neighborhood during the last 12 months. Ask your real estate agent to obtain as much information as possible from the **Multiple Listing Service** (MLS). In addition, personally visit the county tax office and inspect the assessment records for the street where the house is located. The tax records may indicate additional properties which sold without the help of real estate agents and will confirm the accuracy of the MLS sales data.

Recent Sales Comparables

	Property A	Property B	Property C	Property D
Address	_____	_____	_____	_____
Date Sold	_____	_____	_____	_____
Sale Price	_____	_____	_____	_____
Bedrooms	_____	_____	_____	_____
Baths	_____	_____	_____	_____
Amenities	_____	_____	_____	_____
Lot Size	_____	_____	_____	_____
Condition	_____	_____	_____	_____
General Impressions	_____	_____	_____	_____

Step 2

Of the properties you find in the MLS or tax records, which homes are most similar to the property you are considering?

What is the average sales price of these properties?

ADDRESS	DATE SOLD	SALES PRICE
_____	_____	$ _____
_____	_____	$ _____
_____	_____	$ _____
_____	_____	$ _____

Average Price $ _____

BUYING YOUR NEXT HOUSE WORKSHEET

Step 3

Is the home you are considering significantly different than the homes listed in Step 2 in terms of size, location, condition or amenities? If so, you will need to take these differences into account before determining an offer price.

A. *Average price range of comparable properties between these houses and the property* $ _____

B. *Differences between comparable properties and the house you are considering (try to quantify the difference in $$$)* $ _____

C. *Current market value of house you're considering (a+b) or (A-B)* $ _____

Step 4

The Adjusted Market Value is an appropriate negotiating limit for the house you wish to buy. Your opening bid should be 10% below this amount to leave room for negotiation.*

* Note. For foreclosed properties, deduct an extra 10% from your opening bid.

A. *Current market value* $ _____

B. *Opening bid: (A -10%)* $ _____

BUYING YOUR NEXT HOUSE WORKSHEET

How to Write an Offer

Step 1

Prepare a written offer with the help of the agent with whom you are working, or use an attorney if you are buying a home without an agent's assistance.

All offers should be made in writing. Oral agreements are not binding in real estate transactions. Important conditions to include:

❑ **Offer Price:** Opening bid.

❑ **Financing Contingency:** All offers should be subject to loan approval.

❑ **Down Payment:** As part of the financing contingency, state the maximum downpayment you wish to make [5%, 10%, 20%, etc.].

❑ **Inspection Contingency:** All offers should be subject to a thorough inspection by your representative within 7 days of your ratified contract.

❑ **Conveyance Clause:** List all appliances, lighting fixtures, window and wall coverings, as well as other items in the house which you want included in the deal.

❑ **Points:** Always ask the seller to pay 1 or 2 points towards the cost of your new mortgage.

❑ **Closing Costs:** Carefully recite Buyer's and Seller's obligations with respect to closing costs or escrow.

❑ **Settlement Date:** State a date for settlement and who the settlement agent will be. Give yourself plenty of time to arrange your financing (30-60 days).

❑ **Deposit:** Include with your offer a check for 1% of the sales price, to be held by the agent as good faith deposit in the event the Seller accepts your offer.

❑ **Expiration Date:** State a deadline for the Seller to accept your offer before it expires.

❑ **Refund Clause:** State that your deposit will be refunded in its entirety if your offer is not accepted by the Seller.

Step 2

During negotiations, be a shrewd strategist. If the Seller makes a counter-offer, avoid the temptation to split the difference between his response and your original offer. Only raise your bid slightly, forcing another move by the Seller.

Never prolong negotiations too long. Two counters are sufficient. If you cannot mutually agree on a price at or below the current market value, move on to another property.

BUYING YOUR NEXT HOUSE WORKSHEET

Closing the Sale

Step 1

Act quickly once you have a deal. Within three days of signing a contract, you or your realtor should do the following:

a. Contact a lender and schedule an appointment for a loan application;

b. Contact the settlement agent or escrow company and deliver a copy of the executed sales contract for their records; and

c. Contact a professional home inspector or arrange to inspect the property yourself.

Step 2

Keep in mind the following money-saving tips for settlement.

a. Ask if you can use the current owner's title insurance company. Many companies have a special rate for properties they have previously insured.

b. Never allow the lender to withhold more than two months of real estate taxes and insurance in an escrow account.

c. Always pay lender points with a separate check to be certain you can deduct them on your income taxes for the year of purchase.

BUYING YOUR NEXT HOUSE WORKSHEET

Notes On Properties

Address _____   Address _____

_____   _____

_____   _____

Agent/Phone _____   Agent/Phone _____

Asking Price _____   Asking Price _____

Approx. Sq. Ft. _____   Approx. Sq. Ft. _____

No. of Bedrooms _____   No. of Bedrooms _____

_____   _____

Baths _____   Baths _____

_____   _____

Year Built _____   Year Built _____

Garage _____   Garage _____

Basement _____   Basement _____

_____   _____

Lot Size _____   Lot Size _____

_____   _____

Amenities _____   Amenities _____

_____   _____

_____   _____

_____   _____

_____   _____

School District _____   School District _____

_____   _____

General _____   General _____

Comments _____   Comments _____

_____   _____

_____   _____

BUYING YOUR NEXT HOUSE WORKSHEET

Notes On Properties

Address _____	*Address* _____
_____	_____
_____	_____
Agent/Phone _____	*Agent/Phone* _____
Asking Price _____	*Asking Price* _____
Approx. Sq. Ft. _____	*Approx. Sq. Ft.* _____
No. of Bedrooms _____	*No. of Bedrooms* _____
_____	_____
Baths _____	*Baths* _____
_____	_____
Year Built _____	*Year Built* _____
Garage _____	*Garage* _____
Basement _____	*Basement* _____
_____	_____
Lot Size _____	*Lot Size* _____
_____	_____
Amenities _____	*Amenities* _____
_____	_____
_____	_____
_____	_____
_____	_____
School District _____	*School District* _____
_____	_____
General _____	*General* _____
Comments _____	*Comments* _____
_____	_____
_____	_____

REAL ESTATE

Guide to FINDING THE BEST HOME MORTGAGE

This worksheet will direct you through the maze of financing options for your new home. You will learn what criteria you should consider when choosing between fixed-rate and adjustable-rate mortgages, the advantages and disadvantages of bi-weekly or 15-year payment schedules and where to find loans with the lowest interest rates.

Mortgage Internet Resources

Financial Calculations

Mortgage Market Information Services
www.interest.com

Mortgage Net
www.mortgage-net.com

Omni Network
www.imfinc.com

Mortgage Rate Surveys

H.S.H. Associates
www.hsh.com

Mortgage Market Information Services
www.interest.com

Loan Applications

Quicken Mortgage
www.quickenmortgage.com

E-Loan
www.eloan.com

Interloan.com
www.interloan.com

Finding the best rate is critical since even small differences can have a major impact on your costs over the life of a loan. For example, adding just 1% to a $200,000 mortgage for 30 years at 8% fixed rate will cost you more than $12,000 in additional interest expenses over the life of the loan.

But interest rates are only part of the story. Equally important are the fees a lender charges to process a loan. In many instances, high closing costs will more than offset the advantages of a low-interest rate.

Note that if you or your spouse are a veteran of the armed forces, you may qualify for a Veterans Administration (VA) loan without a down payment. Contact the nearest regional office of the VA for a certificate of eligibility and more details. Even if you are not a veteran, if the purchase price of your new home is less than a maximum established by the Federal Housing Administration (FHA), you could possibly qualify for an FHA loan which only requires a 5% downpayment. FHA loan limits vary according to where you live. Any mortgage lender can provide you with more details.

FIND THE BEST HOME MORTGAGE WORKSHEET

Step 1

Call a local mortgage finance company or use the internet to survey lenders who do business in your area, keeping careful notes of your conversation(s) on the attached survey form.

Good internet web sites for this purpose include **Mortgage Market Information Services** (www.interest.com), **Mortgage Net** (www.mortgage-net.com), or **HSH Associates** (www.hsh.com). You can also survey a number of lenders at one time through mortgage matchmakers like **Quicken Mortgage.com** (www.quickenmortgage.com), **E-Loan** (www.eloan.com) and **Interloan.com** (www.interloan.com).

The internet sites allow you to compare and contrast different loan packages. You will be able to determine your precise monthly payment for principal and interest for any loan, as well as the total interest charges over the entire term.

If you do not have internet access, you can acquire the same information by speaking with a mortgage company representative by phone. In fact, it is a good idea to speak with a loan representative even if you obtain information from the internet, since you may learn about specific options which are not posted on the lender's web page.

Sample Dialogue:

66 *Hello. I am interested in buying a home located in _____ and I would like some preliminary information about your rates and loan options. The purchase price for the new home is $_____ and I am considering my downpayment options.*

Specifically, I would like to know about a 30-year fixed-rate loan, assuming a variety of different discount point* scenarios, including .5 points, 1 point, 1.5 points and 2 points.* For each option, I would like to know my cost for the discount, as well as my monthly payment for principal and interest. I would also like to know about your 15-year fixed-rate loan options. 99

*Note: *"Points" are pre-paid interest charges you pay in a lump sum when you close on a loan. A point is equal to 1% of the total loan amount. Lenders can tailor the points on any loan to your specifications. Therefore, it is possible to choose a loan with 0 points, 1 point, etc.*

REAL ESTATE

Points affect the interest rate of your loan. By choosing to pay more points, you can reduce your interest rate and monthly payment. Paying fewer points results in a higher rate and higher monthly payments.

As a rule, the addition of one point will lower the interest rate on a loan by .25%. For example, if a 1-point loan is 7.5%, a 2-point loan will usually be at 7.75 and a 0 point loan will be at 7.25%. However, you will need to check with every lender, since rates and terms do vary.

Unless the home seller has agreed to pay discount points on your behalf, follow the guidelines below to determine how many points you should pay:

- Pay 0 points if you will sell the house in less than 3 years and you need to conserve cash for a down payment.

- Pay 1 point if you will own your house 4-5 years and have the cash to pay for it. Pay 2 points if you will own your house six years or more.

- Pay more than 2 points if the seller agrees to pay for them.

Sample Dialogue:

> *I understand that if my down payment is less than 20 percent, I must pay private mortgage insurance (PMI) every month in addition to my regular payment for principal and interest. How much does this insurance cost? Do you have a program where I can avoid PMI by taking out two mortgages — a first trust for 80% of the loan and a second trust for 10%? If you have such a program, how does this plan compare to the PMI option? What will my monthly payments be for this second mortgage?*

Note: *Some lenders offer the option of avoiding mortgage insurance by in effect taking out two separate loans. This option is known as an 80-10-10 loan. In most cases, an 80-10-10 loan will cost less every month than a 90% loan with private mortgage insurance. You also get to deduct a larger percentage of your monthly payment on your income taxes with the 80-10-10 option. Private mortgage insurance premiums are not tax deductible.*

> *I would also like to know about a 3-year adjustable-rate loan, as well as a 7-year ARM and any others which you consider particularly attractive.*

Note: *Whether you choose an ARM loan depends on which direction you think interest rates are headed and how long you will own your home. Since the interest rates on an ARM loan can change, it is important to know when these changes might occur. Usually the adjustment period is expressed in years. For example, a 1-year adjustable rate, a 3-year adjustable rate, a 7-year adjustable rate, etc.*

FIND THE BEST HOME MORTGAGE WORKSHEET

The initial interest rate for an ARM loan is always lower than the rate for a 30-year fixed mortgage. However, since interest rates in the future may be higher than they are today, there is a risk that your future payments could be significantly higher than they would be if chose a 30-year fixed-rate mortgage.

We think ARM loans only make good sense if you plan on selling your home before the first adjustment. For example, if you are reasonably certain you will live in the house for 5 years, a 7-year ARM is a wise choice.

Sample Dialogue:

❝ *Finally, I would like to know your costs of closing the loan, including application fees, appraisals, credit reports and other charges.* ❞

Note: Pay special attention to closing costs. Many lenders will tease you with lower than average interest rates, but then overcharge you for closing expenses.

❝ *Thank you very much for the information. I am in the process of evaluating my options and will be back in touch as soon as I have made my decision on where to apply.* ❞

R E A L   E S T A T E

FIND THE BEST HOME MORTGAGE WORKSHEET

Loan Survey

	Lender	Lender	Lender
	Contact/Phone Number	Contact/Phone Number	Contact/ Phone Number

(a) Down payment

30-yr. fixed

	Rate	Point(s)	Payment	Rate	Point(s)	Payment	Rate	Point(s)	Payment
	Rate	Point(s)	Payment	Rate	Point(s)	Payment	Rate	Point(s)	Payment

15-yr. fixed

	Rate	Point(s)	Payment	Rate	Point(s)	Payment	Rate	Point(s)	Payment

(b) Mortgage insurance

or

	Monthly Premium	Monthly Premium	Monthly Premium

2nd trust in lieu of
PMI

	Rate	Point(s)	Payment	Rate	Point(s)	Payment	Rate	Point(s)	Payment

Total Monthly
Payment
[A + B]

(c) ARM Loan Option(s)
Initial rate

	Rate	Point(s)	Payment	Rate	Point(s)	Payment	Rate	Point(s)	Payment

Adjusted rate

	When	Max. Rate	When	Max. Rate	When	Max. Rate

(d) Closing Cost(s)

Application

Credit Report

Appraisal Fee

Title Report/
Insurance

Other Fees

Total Fees

FIND THE BEST HOME MORTGAGE WORKSHEET

Step 2

Compare each loan according to the following criteria:

A. Monthly payment

How much will you pay each month in principal and interest charges, as well as private mortgage insurance premiums, if any? If you are considering an ARM loan, consider payments based upon the initial interest rate as well as the maximum rate allowed following the adjustment.

to own the property? If you are considering a 15-year mortgage, how much do you save in interest charges over the life of the loan or until you plan to sell the property? Compare this amount to what you would pay in interest charges for a 30-year loan. Do the interest savings for a 15-year mortgage justify the higher monthly payment?

B. Interest charges

What is the total amount you will pay in interest charges over the life of the loan, or at least for as long as you plan

C. Closing costs

How much will the loan cost you up-front for discount points, application fees, appraisal costs and other charges?

	Lender #1	Lender #2	Lender #3
Loan term(s)	Rate Point(s)	Rate Point(s)	Rate Point(s)
Total monthly payment *[include 1st trust and PMI or 1st trust and 2nd trust]*			
Total interest charges *[for life of loan or until you plan to sell]*			
Total interest charges for 15-year loan option			
Total closing costs and points			

Step 3

Identify your best option.

Step 4

Call back the lender you identified as the best source for a loan, as well as your second and third choice.

Explain to each lender that after careful evaluation, you have narrowed you choices and that they are one of the finalists. Re-cap the deal they quoted to you and give them an opportunity to present a "best and final offer" within the next 24 hours. Most lenders will want to know what their competition is promising. Don't tell them – at least not yet. Explain that to be fair to all parties and save time, you do not want to negotiate separately with various lenders and would prefer a final bid.

Sample Dialogue:

" *Hello. I spoke with you previously about a loan. I've had the opportunity to survey many lenders and your deal was one of the best. I am particularly interested in a ____-yr. loan with ___ points. I have narrowed my choice to three lenders and I would like to clarify your deal before I make my application. Before I do that, I want to give you an opportunity to present a 'best and final' proposal for me to consider. I am doing this with the other two lenders as well, so to keep things fair, I don't want to discuss what the other lenders are offering at this time.* "

Step 5

Compare the "best and final" offers for the three lenders you've identified.

After you have chosen the best one, call the lender who was the next-best choice and explain that they were not the lowest bidder. Tell them exactly why another deal was better and give them another chance to beat it.

Sample Dialogue:

" *Hello, again. I want you to know that I got everyone's bids and that it looks like I am going to go with one of the other lenders. They were able to offer me a deal at the following terms.* [Explain terms]. *Because I've enjoyed talking with you, I will make you an offer. If you can significantly improve on the deal I've already been offered by the other lender, I am willing to give you the business, but I need to know right now.* "

Guide to
WHEN YOU SHOULD REFINANCE

Many people assume that refinancing an existing mortgage at lower interest rates will save money. Actually, the costs of refinancing often outweigh the savings of lower monthly payments, especially if you move within three years.

Does refinancing make sense for you? To find out, complete the worksheet below. You can also evaluate whether it makes sense to refinance using interactive calculators which can be found at several web sites, including *Mortgage Market Information Services* (www.interest.com), *Mortgage Net* (www.mortgage-net.com) or the *Omni Network* (www.imfinc.com).

WHEN TO REFINANCE WORKSHEET

Step 1

Determine what is the interest rate and current monthly payment for your mortgage.

Do not include real estate tax and insurance charges. Contact your lender if you are uncertain about your monthly payments for principal and interest.

INTEREST RATE _____

MONTHLY PAYMENT
(principal and interest) _____

WHEN TO REFINANCE WORKSHEET

Step 2

Contact your current lender and ask what terms they are offering to refinance a 30-year, fixed-rate mortgage, then complete the chart at right.

NEW INTEREST RATE: _____

NEW MONTHLY PAYMENT IF
YOU REFINANCE
(PRINCIPLE & INTEREST): _____

COSTS TO PROCESS LOAN:

Points _____

Application fee _____

Appraisal _____

Inspection _____

Title report _____

Credit report _____

Attorney's fees _____

Recording fees _____

Other charges _____

Total Charges _____

Step 3

Compare your current monthly payment to the new payment if you refinance.

A. CURRENT MONTHLY
PAYMENT _____

B. MONTHLY PAYMENT IF YOU
REFINANCE _____

MONTHLY SAVINGS (A less B) _____

WHEN TO REFINANCE WORKSHEET

Step 4

Determine your monthly savings
after considering tax consequences.

A. MONTHLY SAVINGS   _____

B. CURRENT FEDERAL INCOME
    TAX BRACKET
    (15%, 28%, 31%, 36%)   _____

C. CURRENT STATE TAX RATE   _____

D. COMBINED Federal / State
    TAX RATE (B+C)   _____

    AFTER-TAX SAVINGS
    [A - (A x D)]   _____

Step 5

Determine how many months it will
take for you to recoup the cost of
refinancing.

A. TOTAL REFINANCING
    CHARGES (See Step 2 .)   _____

B. MONTHLY SAVINGS
    (after taxes) (See Step 4.)   _____

    NUMBER OF MONTHS NEEDED
    TO RECOUP COSTS (A / B)   _____

Step 6

Determine how long do you plan to
live in your home.

_____ MONTHS

Step 7

Determine if you will live in the
property long enough to recoup the
costs of refinancing.

R
E
A
L

E
S
T
A
T
E

WHEN TO REFINANCE WORKSHEET

Step 8

Once you have decided whether refinancing makes sense, contact several additional lenders just as you might if you were applying for a new mortgage. (see: How to Find the Best Home Mortgage)

Sample Dialogue:

" Hello. I am interested in refinancing my mortgage and I would like some preliminary information about your current rates. I will need a loan for $_____ for my personal residence located in _____. I would like a rate quote for a 30-year, fixed-rate loan with _____ points. In addition to the rate, I would like to know my new monthly payments for principal and interest. I would also like to know your charges for a loan application, credit report, appraisal, title report, property inspection, recording fees, and any other relevant expenses. "

Mortgage Refinance Survey

Lender: _____ _____ _____ _____

Name of Contact: _____ _____ _____ _____

Phone: _____ _____ _____ _____

30-year fixed mortgage rate:
(0 points) _____ _____ _____ _____

New monthly payment

    Principal: _____ _____ _____ _____

    Interest: _____ _____ _____ _____

    Total Payment: _____ _____ _____ _____

Fees

    Points _____ _____ _____ _____

    Application fee _____ _____ _____ _____

    Credit report _____ _____ _____ _____

    Appraisal _____ _____ _____ _____

    Title report _____ _____ _____ _____

    Property inspection _____ _____ _____ _____

    Recording fee _____ _____ _____ _____

    Legal fees _____ _____ _____ _____

    Other charges _____ _____ _____ _____

    Total Fees _____ _____ _____ _____

REAL ESTATE

Guide to
HOW TO GET THE BEST DEAL ON A HOME EQUITY LOAN

Consumer debt is a significant problem for nearly two-thirds of all Americans. Borrowing money to fund an extravagant lifestyle is a bad idea, regardless of the terms. However, if you need a loan to fund your child's college education, to pay for much-needed home improvements, or to consolidate debts, consider a home equity loan your best option. Interest payments on home equity loans are tax deductible, which means your net costs are much lower than with a conventional loan. Assuming you are in the 28% tax bracket, for example, a home equity loan at a 10% interest rate actually costs you only 7.2% after taxes.

Be forewarned however, home equity loans are secured by the equity in your home. If you default, the lender can seize your house and sell it to satisfy your bad debt. You should therefore be certain you can handle the extra monthly payments, even if the unforeseen may happen, such as a major illness or unemployment.

This worksheet will help you determine your eligibility for a new home equity loan, as well as how to find the best terms for the lowest cost.

FINDING THE BEST HOME EQUITY LOAN WORKSHEET

Step 1

Determine your current equity in your home.

(A.) Estimate the price of your home if you sold it today: _____

(If you're not certain, call a local realtor and ask them for a free market assessment. Don't tell them you're applying for a home equity loan. Instead, say you're thinking about selling your home and that you want to know the current market value before making your decision.)

(B.) How much do you owe on your current mortgage(s)?
(Contact your lender for the current payoff amount.) _____

(C.) Total home equity _____
(A-B)

Step 2

Determine if your current equity is sufficient to qualify for a home equity loan.

As a general rule, most home equity lenders require that you have a minimum of 10% equity in your home. Note, however, that some lenders have loan plans at higher rates when equity levels are less than 10%. Contact specific lenders for details.

Step 3

Contact at least five local financial institutions, including at least two savings and loans, and any credit unions to which you belong.

LENDER	PHONE #
_____	_____
_____	_____
_____	_____
_____	_____
_____	_____

Step 4

Ask to speak with a lending officer for help in completing the detailed questionnaire below.

Sample Dialogue:

66 *Hello. I am interested in a home equity loan and I would like some preliminary information about your loan rates. According to my calculations, I have approximately $_____ of equity in my home. I estimate the current value of my home at $_____ and the current balance of my existing loan(s) at $_____.* 99

*Continue with **Lender Survey** on*

page 236.

R E A L E S T A T E

Lender Survey

Lender

What is the maximum amount I can borrow, assuming my information is accurate?

What is the current interest rate of your home equity loan?

Is this the normal interest rate, or is it a "teaser" rate that increases after a few months? If so, what is the regular rate?

How is the interest rate adjusted? (monthly, yearly, etc.)

Is there a limit to how high the rate can go?

What is the index against which rate increases (or decreases) are calculated?

What is the term of the loan?

What is the minimum monthly payment?

Can I pay off the loan at any time without penalty?

If the loan is in the form of a line of credit, how do I access the money? (check, credit card, etc.)

Do I pay an annual fee for the line-of-credit, and if so, how much?

What are the fees and/or points for processing my loan?

Do you have a loan program without fees or points?

Are there any restrictions on renting my home?

Step 5

Which lender offers the best home equity loan according to your survey?

BEST DEAL: _____

Guide to HOW TO SELL YOUR HOME WITH CONFIDENCE

This worksheet is a blueprint for selling your home. It will take you step-by-step through the process of establishing a realistic sales price, hiring a real estate agent (if you need one), marketing the property, negotiating a contract and closing the sale.

Selling a home is not difficult, but it does require constant commitment, particularly if you are in a slow real estate market. You must be willing to open your home to potential buyers, even when it seems there are none to be found. You must make sure the house is always clean and in perfect condition to encourage the best possible price. You must promote your home with more and better ads, brochures and signs than other properties for sale in your neighborhood. And you must repeat the entire process week-after-week until you are successful.

SELLING YOUR HOME WITH CONFIDENCE WORKSHEET

Step 1

Establish a realistic sales price.

A. Visit the county tax assessor's office and ask to see the assessment rolls for your neighborhood.* Tax records will show the most recent sales price for every home. Note the address and price for any homes sold in the last 12-18 months. You may obtain comparable information on recent sales from a realtor but the information may not be a thorough or accurate as what you will find doing a county land record search.

*Tax files are public records. Do not hesitate to ask a clerk for assistance if you are having problems locating the information you need. Done correctly, your research should take no more than 30 minutes.

Recent Sales in Your Neighborhood

ADDRESS	DATE SOLD	SALES PRICE	COMMENTS
_____	_____	_____	_____
_____	_____	_____	_____
_____	_____	_____	_____
_____	_____	_____	_____
_____	_____	_____	_____
_____	_____	_____	_____
_____	_____	_____	_____
_____	_____	_____	_____

B. Drive by the homes listed above and compare them to your own property.

Were any built by the same builder? Are the lot sizes similar? Do they look the same from the outside? Try to identify the homes which most closely resemble your own.

C. While you are in your car, also note any "For Sale" signs in the neighborhood.

Call the phone number on each sign to find out as much as you can about the property. If the call is to a real estate agent, resist the agent's attempt to meet with you.

Sample Dialogue:

Hello. I happened to be driving past the home on _____ Street, and noticed your sign. I was wondering if you could tell me the sales price and a little information about the size of the home.

Ask the appropriate questions to complete the chart below, then conclude the call as politely as possible.

Thank you. To be perfectly honest, I'm just gathering information right now. I appreciate your assistance and will be happy to call you when I am really serious about buying. Thanks again.

Current Properties For Sale in Your Neighborhood

Address

Phone

Asking Price

Bedrooms

Baths

Lot Size

Garage

Basement

Fireplace

Other Amenities

D. Which houses currently for sale are comparable to your own home?

ADDRESS

ASKING PRICE

E. Determine an appropriate sales price for your own home which is 5% higher than recent sales (Step B) and within the range of other properties currently for sale in your neighborhood (Step D).

Hint: A $100 or $1,000 reduction in price can have a big psychological impact. Always keep your asking price below well-recognized benchmarks. $149,900, for example, seems cheaper than $150,000 and attracts buyers searching the classifieds for homes under $150,000.

YOUR ASKING PRICE $ _____

R E A L   E S T A T E

Step 2

Select a real estate agent.
Regardless of whether you use them, always interview several real estate agents about selling your home. Their insights will reinforce or challenge your own conclusions about the current real estate market, confirm an appropriate asking price, and suggest ways to make your home more appealing.

A. Identify at least three agents to contact. Rely on references from friends or contact real estate offices prominently located near your home. If you don't have a particular agent in mind, ask to speak with the managing agent. Ask them to recommend an experienced, full-time agent who is one of the biggest producers in the office.

B. Call each agent and invite them to your home for an interview.

Sample Dialogue:

" *Hello. I am thinking about selling my home, located at . Your services come highly recommended and I would like to meet you at my home to get better acquainted. Before our meeting, I would like you to do some preliminary research about recent sales. I would also like to hear your specific marketing suggestions and an appropriate asking price for my property.* "

C. Gauge each agent's competency by listening carefully to what they say, and don't say, during your meeting.

Prospective Real Estate Agents

REAL ESTATE COMPANY	RECOMMENDED AGENT	PHONE	DATE OF APPT.	TIME

Agent Survey

	#1	#2	#3
Agent:			
How insightful are they about your home's strongest and weakest selling points?			
What suggestions do they offer to increase buyer appeal?			
How knowledgeable are they about your neighborhood?			
Is their price recommendation supported by recent market comparables?			
How aggressive is their marketing plan?			
(a) How many open houses will they hold? (You want at least two per month.)			
(b) Will they support the listing with ads in local newspapers at *their* expense?			
(c) When will they place your home in the realtor's Multiple Listing Service?			
(d) Will they conduct an open house for other real estate agents to introduce them to your home?			
What is their commission?			

D. Choose the most competent agent you've interviewed if you still want to use a realtor. Insist on a supplement to their standard listing agreement which states:

✔ Specific dates on which they will conduct open houses during the listing period (at least two per month);

✔ Specific dates for advertising, as well as where the ads will be placed;

✔ A clause specifying your right as Seller to approve all advertising and listing copy in advance,

✔ Acceptable rules regarding use of lock box, prior notice before house tours, etc.; and

✔ The right to cancel the listing in 60 days at your option.

R E A L

E S T A T E

Step 3

Consider selling without an agent.
Many people correctly conclude that real estate agents are, in many cases, overpaid for their work. Conducting open houses, qualifying potential buyers, negotiating terms and closing a sale are time consuming but not very difficult. The fact is, there is no reason you can't do the job yourself.

Advance preparation is key. Before advertising your property, you should accumulate all the materials you will need for the sales process.
Remember that you are competing with real estate agents trying to sell their own listings. You must be every bit as thorough and professional if you hope to attract a buyer. Following the suggestions below should help.

1. **Determine an appropriate asking price.**
   Many do-it-yourself homesellers overprice their properties, discouraging inquiries. Price your home slightly below comparable homes for sale in order to encourage buyer traffic. Usually, a $500 to $1,500 discount is sufficient.

REVISED SALES PRICE $ _____

2. **Organize yourself on paper.**

   a. Prepare a type-written summary of comparable sales in your neighborhood, including address, date sold and sales price. (Prospective buyers will want proof your home is fairly priced.)

   b. Ask a lawyer for a standard sales contract you can use when some one wants to write an offer.

   c. Contact a local mortgage broker. In return for distributing his/her business card at your open house, ask them to prepare a chart summarizing typical monthly payments for a house in your price range. Their examples should include a 30-year fixed-rate mortgage and a 1-year ARM, assuming both a 5% and a 10% downpayment. Also ask them to estimate the minimum income necessary to qualify for each loan.

   d. Prepare a type-written brochure describing your home. Include sales price, year built, your day and evening phone numbers, room dimensions, lot size, current taxes, average utility bill and the location of local schools and shopping centers.

   e. Prepare a sign-in sheet to register prospective buyers who tour your home by appointment or during open houses.

3. **Invest in quality signs.**
   Go to a professional sign store and order custom "For Sale" signs which include your day and evening phone numbers. Also order several "Open House" signs with appropriate directional arrows to guide home shoppers from the main road or highway directly to your door. Signs account for 50% of buyer traffic. Do not skimp on quality or quantity.

4. **Put your home in prime sales condition.**

> ## ✔ Home Checkup
>
> ### Repair or Replace
> ( ) Stained or Ripped Carpet
> ( ) Damaged Brick or Siding
> ( ) Dated Appliances and Bathroom Fixtures
> ( ) Lights that do not work
> ( ) Dead Plants or Damaged Lawn
>
> ### Thoroughly Clean
> ( ) Windows (inside or out)
> ( ) Floors
> ( ) Furniture (wax)
> ( ) Oven
> ( ) Bathroom Sinks, Tubs, Toilets
> ( ) Refrigerator
> ( ) Closets
> ( ) Garage
> ( ) Driveway (remove oil stain)
>
> ### Paint
> ( ) Interior / Exterior as necessary
>   (use neutral colors if repainting)

5. **Conduct an open house every Sunday, from noon to 5 pm.**
   Open houses expose your home to buyers too shy to pick up the phone and make an appointment. Make it easy for them to stop by under more casual circumstances. During open houses, make sure all rooms are clean and free of clutter. Lights should be turned on in every room and all personal articles (i.e., combs, tooth brushes, clothes) should be put away. Hide any valuables such as cash and jewelry.

6. **Advertise every weekend.**
   Without the agent's network working on your behalf, you must promote your property as often as possible.

Special note: As mentioned earlier in this chapter, there is a compromise between hiring an agent and selling a property yourself. "Help-You-Sell' services provide you with sales signs, forms and contracts, and access to the realtors' computer network, usually for $300 or less. If you sell the home yourself, you save a 6% sales commission. If a real estate agent delivers a buyer with an offer which is acceptable, you pay only a partial commission (3%). Help-You-Sell services can be found in the Yellow Pages under "Real Estate."

REAL ESTATE

Step 4

Negotiate successfully.
Most sales are won or lost during the negotiation. You will usually prevail in this process if you prepare your strategy in advance and follow several rules:

Decide the minimum price you will accept before negotiations start. Do not wait until the heat of battle to decide your bottom line.

Never respond to an offer without knowing a buyer's qualifications.
Insist on a summary of income, liabilities and cash for a down payment before you start talking price.

Negotiate exclusively in writing. All offers and counter-offers must be in writing to be legally binding.

Don't reject low bids without making a counter-offer. Some buyers will always start with a low-ball offer, hoping you are desperate. Consider it part of the negotiating process instead of an insult.

Don't counter a bid in proportional increments. Avoid the initial temptation to split the difference between your asking price and the Buyer's offer. Lower your price in smaller increments than the buyer raises his/her offer.

Remember to include these points in the negotiation:

(a) **Termination Date.** Insist that the contract will expire in 45 days if the Buyer has not secured financing.

(b) **Inspection Waiver.** If the Buyer makes his offer contingent on a home inspection, make certain the contingency expires within 7 days after the sales contract is executed.

(c) **Sale Contingency.** Try to avoid deals contingent on a Buyer selling another home. If you must accept such a deal, insist on a 24-hour "kick-out" clause -- if you receive another offer, the first buyer has 24 hours to remove the contingency or you are free to sell to the second party.

(d) **Points.** It is strategically better to lower your price than to pay points — buyers usually focus on price more than other terms.

(e) **Closing Costs.** Buyer and Seller should each pay for their respective closing costs.

(f) **Settlement Date.** Make certain any date is compatible with your move to another location.

Step 5

Tips for settlement or escrow.
Most of the settlement work is done by the buyer and his/her representatives. Nevertheless, you should stay in close contact to be certain everything proceeds on schedule and to intervene if there are any problems.

✔ Settlement Checklist

( ) 1 day after contract is signed :
Contact settlement attorney or escrow agent and make sure they have a copy of the sales contract.

( ) 3 days after contract is signed :
Contact mortgage company to make sure buyer has made an application.

( ) 2 weeks after contract is signed :
Re-contact mortgage company to inquire about the loan status.

( ) 3 weeks after contract is signed :
Contact settlement attorney or agent to make sure appraisal and title report have been ordered. Also inquire about an exact time and date for settlement.

( ) 1 week before closing :
Contact mortgage company to make sure buyer has been approved for loan.

( ) 1 day before closing :
Contact settlement attorney to make sure loan proceeds have been received.

10-20

Special note *if you have an FHA Mortgage:*
FHA guidelines allow lenders to charge you an entire month's worth of interest, even if you sell your home at the beginning of the month. To avoid additional charges, try to schedule settlement as late in the month as possible.

FHA mortgage holders may also be entitled to a refund of insurance premiums after a home is sold. To find out if you qualify, write:

> *HUD-DSB*
> *P.O. Box 23699*
> *Washington, D.C. 20026-3699*

REAL ESTATE

HERE'S THE PROOF

For most people, a home is the biggest purchase of a lifetime. Choosing the right property, negotiating a competitive price and finding the lowest-priced financing options can have a dramatic impact on your finances. Consider the following examples:

Suggestion: Shop carefully for a mortgage, even when the difference in interest rates between lenders is only $1/4$ of a percent.

Scenario: *You buy a house with a $230,000, 30-year fixed-rate mortgage. By shopping diligently for a loan, you find a lender that is offering an interest rate which is 1/4% lower than the competition (7.25% vs. 7.5%). You live in the property for 12 years.*

	@ 7.25%	@ 7.5%
Total Interest Paid	$ 184,927	$ 191,899
Total Savings	**$6,972**	

Suggestion: Never refinance if you plan to move before you can recoup the transaction costs of the new loan.

Scenario: *Your present mortgage for $125,000 is at 8.5%. You consider refinancing at 7.75%, knowing you will be selling your home in two years.*

	Current Loan @ 8.5%	New Loan @ 7.75%
Monthly Payment	$ 961	$ 895
24 Month Savings	$1,893	
Refinancing Costs*	($ 3,125)	
Total savings by not Refinancing	**$ 1,232**	

* *Refinancing costs include 1.5 points and 1% in fees and expenses.*

Suggestion: List your property with a home-selling service and do the legwork yourself, instead of hiring a real estate agent to sell your home.

Suggestion: Pay points separately at closing so you can deduct them on your Federal Income Tax.

Sale Price $225,000		
	Do-It-Yourself	*Hire a Realtor*
Listing Agent	**Ntl. Homeowner's Services** **Falls Church, VA**	**Long & Foster Realtors** **Fairfax, VA**
Buyer's Agent	**Shannon & Luchs Alexandra, VA**	**Shannon & Luchs Alexandra, VA**
Listing Fee	*$300*	*0*
Total Commission Paid	*$6,750*	*$13,500*
Total Savings	*$6,450*	

$175,000 Loan with 1.5 points		
	Points Paid Separately	*Points Not Paid Separately*
Amount Paid @ Closing	*$2,625*	*$2,625*
Income Tax Deduction (28% Federal Tax Bracket)	*$2,625*	*0*
Total Savings	*$735*	

Chapter Nine

Lower Your Costs for Banking and Financial Services

Why is it getting more expensive to bank?

Competition among banks has been eroded by mergers and consolidations. There are many fewer banks today than five years ago and those that remain are larger and more impersonal. In fact, the largest 1% of all banks now control 65% of all funds on deposit in the U.S. The survivors in the bank merger war have found it relatively easy to increase the fees they charge their customers. Simply put, banks are charging more because they can get away with it. It is not uncommon for a bank to charge $30 or more for a returned check, $15 per month for failing to maintain a minimum monthly balance and as much as $2 for using an out-of-network ATM machine. And that same bank that gleefully charges you for any petty infraction also gets away with paying miserly interest on your funds on deposit. At a time when the prime rate is 5.5%, for example, some banks are paying only 2.5% interest to their checking account depositors. Other banks pay no interest at all, which means you pay *them* for the privilege of holding on to your money.

Bankers argue that high fees and low interest rates are necessary to cover increasing costs. But this is only partly true. The real reason is that checking accounts no longer generate as much in the way of other kinds of profitable business. In the old days, the bank that maintained your checking account was also the bank that issued your credit card, sold you a mortgage and financed your car purchase. Even if they didn't make a lot of money on your checking, they could count on making up the difference and then some through these other transactions. Today, firms that specialize in credit cards or car loans have siphoned away much of this business. And even if your bank still offers these services, profit margins are much thinner. Faced with these new realities, banks are no longer willing to subsidize checking accounts.

What can I do to lower my costs?

Join a credit union if you can. A credit union is a non-profit cooperative owned and controlled by depositors. Credit unions generally pay better rates for funds on deposit, charge lower fees for most services and are a better source for many loans. Annoying fees are also kept to a minimum, since a credit union is primarily concerned with servicing its members, not generating the largest profit.

By law, credit unions must restrict membership to people who share a common bond. In many cases, this connection is employment, although credit unions can be organized by any group. There are credit unions for government workers, employees of a particular company, trade group or other entity and even credit unions for members of certain professional organizations. Check with the personnel department where you work or the phone book for credit unions in your area that you might be eligible to join.

If enrolling in a credit union is not an option, you can still do certain things to minimize the high cost of banking. First, choose the type of bank which is likely to give you the best value for the services you need. If all you require is a place to deposit a few checks and an account to pay your bills every month, you will probably benefit by choosing a small, locally-owned and operated bank in your neighborhood. According to a study by the Washington DC-based U.S. Public Interest Research Group, a customer at a small bank is likely to pay $190.33 in annual account fees compared to $218.27 for a customer at a larger institution. However, these are just averages. Each bank has its own fee structure, so it pays to shop carefully. And while small banks are less likely to charge exorbitant fees for a bounced check, there are certain cases where bigger is better. Larger banks typically offer better deals to customers willing to keep a minimum balance in excess of $1,000. They also maintain a more extensive network of ATMs, so you are less likely to use a machine outside your bank's network and incur extra fees. The perfect combination, of course, is a large bank that still feels like a local one, but they are nearly an endangered species.

If you are proficient on a computer and don't mind an even less personal relationship, you may want to consider an *internet* bank that conducts all of its business electronically and by mail. **Security First Network Bank** (www. sfnb.com) offers free checking, 20 free electronic bill payments and 10 free ATM withdrawals every month for customers who maintain a $1,000 minimum balance.

How can I find the best rates on bank CDs and money-market accounts?

Go online with **Bank Rate Monitor** (www.bankrate.com) or **IBC Financial Data Services** (www.ibcdata.com). At either site, you can do a search for the highest-yielding bank deposit accounts. Remember that since all bank CDs and money-market accounts are federally insured up to $100,000, it makes no difference whether you open an account around the corner or halfway across the country. If there is a significant difference between the rates offered by local banks and what you can find searching the web data base, it makes sense to open an account at the more distant institution by mail.

On the other hand, you may wish to consider the desirability of keeping your funds on deposit at a bank altogether. While it is true that only bank deposits are federally insured (up to

$100,000), there are many alternatives which offer higher yields for negligible risk including money market *mutual funds*. In such accounts, money on deposit is invested in short-term notes and securities which usually mature in seven days or less. You buy shares in the fund, which maintains a constant share price of $1. The only fluctuation is the amount of interest you earn, which is adjusted daily. Interest rates are usually .5% to 1.5% *higher* than bank money market accounts and are an excellent alternative for liquid assets you may need at any moment.

There are three types of money market mutual funds. *General funds* invest in short-term government and corporate securities. *U.S. Treasury funds*, as the name implies, invest exclusively in treasury bonds. *Municipal funds* invest in short-term local government obligations which are exempt from federal income taxes. These funds are preferable if you are in a high tax bracket since the after-tax yield is considerably higher than your net return on a taxable fund. Some municipal money market funds are further limited to bonds issued by a single state. These single-state funds are exempt from both federal *and* state taxes for residents who live in that state.

To find the highest-yielding money-market mutual funds, check Monday's issue of **Barrons** magazine or the Thursday edition of **The Wall St. Journal.** Alternatively, you can use the survey at **IBC Financial Data** (www.ibcdata.com) which lists current yields and historical returns. If you don't have time for research, consider the following funds which have above-average historical performance.

Recommended Money Market Funds

General Funds
Vanguard Prime
800-662-7447

MM Schwab Value Advantage
800-435-4000

U.S. Treasury Funds
Dreyfus Basic U.S. Govt.
800-223-9846

Spartan Treasury MM
800-544-8888

Municipal Bond Funds
Strong Municipal
800-368-3863

Vanguard Tax-Exempt
800-835-1510

How do I find the best deal on a credit card?

The only "good deal" is to pay off your entire balance every month to avoid interest charges. Unfortunately, most people do the exact opposite. According to a 1998 study by a leading consumer organization, the average credit card holder in the U.S. carries a $4,000 balance and pays approximately $720 every year in interest.

You would think that with interest rates

at historical lows, consumers would rebel at credit card companies charging 18% on credit card balances. Yet most people simply shrug their shoulders and make a token payment every month.

If you are serious about reducing expenses and saving for your future, you simply must pay off your credit card balances. If that process is likely to take more than a few months, consider these options:

First, consider transferring your current balance to a new card that charges less interest. You can find these cards by checking the weekly surveys produced by **Bank Rate Monitor** (www. bankrate.com). While the deals are always changing, there is always a stable of lenders interested in your business at rates that are often half of what many companies charge. On the day we checked, here were just a few of the examples:

Huntington National Bank
800-480-2265
7.75% annual percentage rate on outstanding balances

Bank One
800-346-5538
3.9% annual percentage rate on outstanding balances for the first 6 months; 9.99% thereafter.

First Chicago
800-766-4623
3.9% annual percentage rate on outstanding balances for the first 6 months; 9.99% thereafter.

You may find that there are limits to how much of your old balance the new credit card company will allow you to transfer. If that is the case, you may want to consider a more dramatic solution.

One option is to take out a home equity loan that consolidates all of your outstanding debts. Rates are often 60% less than what your credit card company is charging, plus your interest payments are tax deductible. The only downside is that your debt is guaranteed by the equity in your home. If you default, your home could wind up in foreclosure.

What about rebate cards?

If you charge a lot over the course of a year *and* you pay off your balance every month, a rebate card can be a good deal. There are plenty of choices.

You can select from cards which rebate cash, credits for gas or discounts on the purchase of a new car, as well as frequent flyer miles. Remember, though, that most rebate cards charge a hefty annual fee of between $50 and $100.

If you do not ring up a lot of charges every year, the rebates probably won't offset the higher annual fee. For example, if you only charge $400 per month, your annual rebate amounts to less than $50. Rebate cards also charge some of the highest interest rates on unpaid balances.

Rebate Cards

Cards that rebate cash

Chevy Chase
800-334-2378
Cash Rewards Visa
1% cash rebate

Discover Card
800-347-26837
1% cash rebate

Optima Card
800-467-8462
2% cash rebate

Cards that rebate gas discounts

Amoco
800-858-3299
3% rebate on gas purchases

Exxon
800-554-6914
3% rebate on gas purchases

Shell
800-373-3427
5% rebate on gas purchases

Cards that rebate airline miles

American Airlines Citibank Aadvantage
800-950-5114
1 mile for every dollar charged

United Airlines Mileage First Card
800-537-7783
1 mile for every dollar charged

Cards that rebate car discounts

Citibank Drivers Advantage
800-967-8500
2% rebate on any new car purchased or leased

General Motors
800-947-1000
5% rebate on any GM lease or purchase

Are there any advantage to "Gold" or "Platinum" cards?

No. They are mostly marketing gimmicks to build up your ego. Some people justify the higher annual fee because the card offers travel insurance or a puny discount on car rentals, but that's a stretch. The fact is that it's just a piece of plastic.

How should I choose a stockbroker?

The internet has revolutionized the stock market in ways you should not ignore. Today, anyone with a modem and a computer has access to data that a few years ago was exclusively in the hands of top Wall Street analysts. Of course, it's what you do with the information that counts.

Making well-informed investment decisions is much more important than what you pay for a stock trade. Of course, if you are comfortable making your own choices, there is no reason you shouldn't make your purchases through a discount broker. On the other hand, if you need the knowledge and expertise of a professional, paying a fee to an advisor or higher commissions to a stock broker is perfectly acceptable. In other words, there is no right way to buy and sell stocks or mutual funds.

If you are the do-it-yourself type, chances are you already use a discount broker. However, in recent years, the discount business has morphed into three hybrids:

• Full service firms that offer web trades, state-of-the-art research, branch offices and 24-hour customer service;

• Discount brokerages that offer internet-only service; and

• Bargain brokers who charge rock-bottom prices but offer little in the way of service or amenities.

Expect to pay $25 to $30 from a full service discount broker, such as **Schwab** (www.schwab.com) or **Fidelity** (www.fidelity.com), $15 from internet-only discounters like **E-Trade** (www-etrade.com) or **Waterhouse Securities** (www.waterhouse.com) and less than $9 from low-cost leaders such as **Datek** (www.datek.com) or **Ameritrade** (www.Ameritrade.com). Again, there is no *right* choice, but we prefer the larger, full-service firms. Particularly if you only make a few trades every year, the superior service and reliability of a **Schwab** or **Fidelity** is worth the premium. The smaller firms have suffered frequent service glitches and system-wide crashes that could prevent you from accessing your account when timing is critical. Unless you trade frequently (3-4 trades per month), the commission charge should be a secondary consideration.

That's also true when seeking out professional help. Whether you use a traditional broker affiliated with a major firm such as **Merrill Lynch**, **AG Edwards** or **Morgan Stanley-Dean Witter**, or a fee-only financial advisor that manages your investment portfolio for an annual fee, the quality and profitability of the advice you receive should be the prime consideration. Expect to pay around $175 for most trades with a major broker, although customers with large accounts can often negotiate lower rates. Fee advisors typically charge 1% or 2% per year for the funds they manage.

Can I avoid some of the headaches and costs by choosing mutual funds instead of individual stocks?

Unfortunately, choosing from among more than 6,000 mutual funds is nearly as confusing as picking individual stocks. Sure, it's the fund manager that makes the decisions on which stocks to buy and sell, but how good is the manager?

The fact is that it is extremely hard for any fund manager to consistently outperform the stock market as a whole. That's because while at certain times a particular stock-picking philosophy may be superior, over long periods the law of averages prevails. Picking winners every time is no easier on Wall Street than it is in Las Vegas.

Recent studies have demonstrated that at least during the bull market of the 1990's, funds which invest in *all* stocks that comprise a market index, such as the **S&P 500**, have outperformed the vast majority of funds which are actively managed. As always, there is debate about whether index funds will continue to outperform actively managed funds in the years ahead. However, if the pace of investment in index funds is any indication, the trend is likely to continue. The largest mutual fund company in America, **Vanguard Funds** (www.vanguard.com) got that way pioneering the index fund formula.

Whether or not you buy index funds, you should follow the advice of many mutual fund experts and avoid any fund which charges you a fee or "load" when you buy or sell shares. *Load* funds, by contrast, impose fees up to 5% of the cost of your investment. Most *load* funds are sold by commissioned stock brokers or by fund managers who claim superior stock-picking skills. In truth, most of these funds fail to beat market averages and under-perform *no-load* funds after taking into account the extra fees.

You can buy *no-load* funds directly through fund companies who sell them, or through a discount broker like **Charles Schwab**, through its "*one source*" service. Keep in mind that "no-load" refers only to sales charges. *All* mutual funds charge management and marketing expenses which are deducted from the daily share price. A typical fund will charge between 1% and 3% per year.

Top Performing Mutual Funds (1994-1998)

Large Company Growth

	Avg. Return per year
Vanguard Growth Index	27.79 %
Wilshire Target Large Co. Growth	26.74 %
Fidelity Dividend Growth	26.53 %
Vanguard U.S. Growth	26.16 %
Dreyfus Appreciation	24.61 %
T. Rowe Price Blue Chip Growth	23.89 %

Small Company Growth

Baron Asset	19.86 %
Safeco Growth	19.00 %
Schroder U.S. Smaller Companies	17.00 %
Wasatch Growth	16.83 %
FAM Value	16.00 %

Balanced Funds

Invesco Balanced	19.33 %
Janus Balanced	18.60 %
Vanguard Wellington	16.24 %
Invesco Total Return	16.20 %
Gabelli Westwood Balanced Return	16.17 %

International Funds

	Avg. Return per year
Janus Worldwide	19.34 %
BT Investment International Equity	15.77 %
UMB Scout Worldwide	14.53 %
Harbor International Growth	14.14 %
Fidelity Diversified International	13.24 %

Taxable Bond Funds

Fremond Bond	8.02 %
Harbor Bond	7.60 %
Dodge & Cox Income	7.54 %
Vanguard GNMA	7.43 %
Lexington GNMA	7.29 %

Tax-Free Bond Funds

SIT Tax-Free	6.71 %
Vanguard Intermediate Term TE	5.59 %
T. Rowe Price Tax-Free	5.38 %
American Century-Benham Int. Term	5.16 %
Vanguard Limited Term	4.55 %

If I am doing research on particular stocks or mutual funds, where do you suggest I look for information?

If you open an account with **Charles Schwab** (www.schwab.com), **Fidelity Investments** (www.fidelity.com), **E-Trade** (www.etrade.com) or other discount brokerage firms, you will automatically gain access to the firm's on-line research services that provide earnings estimates, analyst opinions, stock charts, breaking news and other vital data on demand.

You can also get valuable information, even without opening a brokerage account, by logging on to any number of financial web sites.

Best Financial Websites

Microsoft MoneyCentral
www.msn.com

The Motley Fool
www.motleyfool.com

Raging Bull
www.ragingbull.com

Yahoo! Finance
www.yahoo.com

Zacks
www.zacks.com

Big Charts
www.bigcharts.com

Smart Money
www.smartmoney.com

Bloomberg
www.bloomberg.com

CNNfn
www.cnnfn.com

Morningstar
www.morningstar.com

CBS MarketWatch
www.cbs.marketwatch.com

Standard & Poor's
www.personalwealth.com

Street Eye
www.streeteye.com

The Street.com
www.thestreet.com

Guide to CHOOSING STOCKS AND MUTUAL FUNDS

Discount Brokers

Charles Schwab
800-225-8570
www.schwab.com

E-Trade
888-772-3477
www.etrade.com

Fidelity Investments
800-544-6666
www.fidelity.com

Waterhouse Securities
800-933-0555
www.waterhouse.com

Ameritrade
800-669-3900
www.ameritrade.com

Datek Online
800-823-2835
www.datek.com

Online Research and Analysis

Microsoft Investor
www.msn.com

Motley Fool
www.fool.com

Raging Bull
www.ragingbull.com

Bloomberg
www.bloomberg.com

CBS Market Watch
www.cbs.market-watch.com

Smart Money
www.smartmoney.com

Big Charts
www.bigcharts.com

Mutual Fund Families

Aim
800-347-1919
www.aimfunds.com

Alliance
800-221-5672
www.alliancecapital.com

American Century
800-345-2021
www.americancentury.com

Berger
800-333-1001
www.bergerfunds.com

Brandywine
800-338-1579
www.brandywine.com

Calvert
800-368-2748
www.calvertgroup.com

Dreyfus
00-782-66208
www.dreyfus.com

Eaton Vance
800-225-6265
www.eatonvance.com

Evergreen
800-235-0064
www.evergreen-funds.com

Fidelity
800-544-8888
www.fidelity.com

First Investors
800-423-4026
www.firstinvestors.com

Founders
800-525-2440
www.founders.com

Mutual Fund Families

Franklin Templeton
800-342-5236
www.franklintemple-ton.com

Gabelli
800-422-3554
www.gabelli.com

John Hancock
800-225-5291
www.johnhancock.com

IDS
800-328-8300
www.americanex-press.com

Invesco
800-525-8085
www.invesco.com

Janus
800-525-898
www.janusfunds.com

Kauffman Funds
800-261-0555
www.kauffman.com

Kemper
800-621-1148
www.kemper.com

MFS
800-522-4202
www.mfs.com

Lord Abbett
800-821-5129
www.lordabbett.com

Managers
800-835-3879
www.managersfunds.com

Montgomery
800-243-4361
www.montgomery-funds.com

Neuberger Berman
800-877-9700
www.nbfunds.com

Oberweiss
800-245-7311
www.owfunds.com

Oppenheimer
800-525-7048
www.oppenheimer-funds.com

Pilgrim
800-334-3444
www.pilgrimfunds.com

Pimco
800-927-4648
www.pimco.com

Pioneer
800-225-6292
www.pioneerfunds.com

Putnam
800-225-1581
www.putnaminv.com

Scudder
800-225-2470
www.scudder.com

Sit Funds
800-332-5580
www.sitfunds.com

State Street
800-882-0052
www.statestreet.com

Stein Roe
800-368-3863
www.steinroe.com

T. Rowe Price
800-638-5660
www.troweprice.com

Vanguard
800-662-7447
www.vanguard.com

Warburg-Pincus
800-888-6878
www.warburg.com

Wells Fargo
800-237-8472
www.wellsfargo.com

Zweig
800-272-2700
www.zweig.com

In order for you to reach your financial goals, your investments must grow over a period of years at a rate that is significantly higher than inflation. Optimally, real growth (after deducting the affects of inflation) should be in the range of 5% to 7%.

Historically, only the stock market has provided these kinds of returns. Even taking into account the market disruptions caused by the Great Depression, World War II and the oil embargo of the mid-1970's, stocks have returned, on average, better than 10% per year.

While there is no guarantee of future performance, the record over time is convincing that stocks will outperform other investments.

Investors have a choice of purchasing shares of individual companies or by owning shares of a mutual fund that holds a diversified portfolio of securities.

An investor who buys stocks directly enjoys the advantages and inherent risks of picking the companies to own one at a time. Choose the right companies and you can get rich quickly, since your investments are concentrated rather than diversified. This was certainly true for early buyers of *Microsoft*, *AOL*, *Cisco Systems* and other stellar performers.

But how can you be sure that you will be picking winners rather than losers?

Many investors prefer someone else do the stock picking. In this case, the investor chooses which mutual fund to buy, but then it is up to the mutual fund manager to make day-to-day decisions about which stocks to own. True, the investor is faced with fewer choices, but picking the best mutual fund can be just as daunting as selecting the right stocks.

There are more than 6,000 mutual funds to choose from and the distinctions between funds and their investment objectives are harder than ever to discern, so whether you buy stocks yourself or depend on a mutual fund manager, the burden of choosing the right investments and monitoring performance still falls into your lap. You've got decide which stocks or which mutual funds to buy, how long to hold them and when, if ever, to sell. Your decisions are critical to your financial future. Fortunately, you no longer need to rely on a commissioned salesman (stock broker) to make your decisions, nor do you need to spend hours in the public library pouring over investment literature. Everything you need to make informed decisions is available to you, free, on the internet. In fact, there is so much information available that you run a greater risk of being overwhelmed by data than by the lack of it.

We've tried to simplify the process to some degree through the step-by-step instructions outlined below.

Step 1

Determine your objective.

Whether you have a lump sum to invest, or figure on making regular contributions to a retirement program, you need a *plan* before you start throwing your money around.

What kind of time horizon do you have? Are you investing for the short term or the long haul? And what kind of risks are you prepared to accept along the way?

If your goal is a secure retirement, there are a number of web sites that can help you identify precisely how much you should be setting aside every month to reach your ultimate objective. The programs allow you to plug in different assumptions regarding your age at retirement, the affects of inflation and changing investment yields.

One of the first, and as far as we are concerned, still the best planning tools is the **Quicken** financial planner (www.quicken.com.) There are also retirement planning tutorials at **Microsoft Money Central** (www.msn.com), **Charles**

Schwab (www.schwab .com) and **Fidelity Investments** (www.fidelity .com). All of the programs will take you an average of ten minutes to complete, but when you are finished, you should have a clear understanding of how much you will ultimately need to reach your retirement objective, broken down into monthly installments beginning immediately.

If you want a quick estimate of what your savings objectives should be, without resorting to more elaborate web guides, you can refer to the charts below.

Based upon your annual income needs at retirement, excluding Social Security, what are your total savings requirements?

Retirement Savings Objective : _____

Annual Income Requirement	Total Savings Required If You Retire At...		
	Age 65	**Age 60**	**Age 55**
$ 10,000	$ 176,000	$ 189,000	$ 217,000
20,000	352,000	396,000	434,000
30,000	528,000	594,000	651,000
40,000	704,000	792,000	868,000
50,000	880,000	990,000	1,085,000
60,000	1,057,000	1,188,000	1,302,000
70,000	1,233,000	1,387,000	1,519,000
80,000	1,409,000	1,585,000	1,736,000
90,000	1,585,000	1,783,000	1,953,000

FINANCE

Assuming no other savings, how much must you invest each month to realize your savings objective by the time you reach retirement?

Monthly Investment Required : _____

Savings Required	Monthly Savings Needed* (years to retirement)						
	35 yrs.	30 yrs.	25 yrs.	20 yrs.	15 yrs.	10 yrs.	5 yrs.
$ 100,000	108	175	225	308	450	733	1,566
200,000	216	350	450	616	900	1,466	3,133
300,000	325	525	675	925	1,350	2,200	4,700
400,000	433	700	900	1,233	1,800	2,933	6,266
500,000	541	875	1,125	1,541	2,250	3,666	7,833
600,000	650	1,050	1,350	1,850	2,700	4,400	9,333
700,000	758	1,225	1,575	2,158	3,150	5,133	10,916
800,000	866	1,400	1,800	2,466	3,600	5,866	12,500
900,000	975	1,575	2,025	2,775	4,050	6,600	14,166
1,000,000	1,083	1,750	2,250	3,083	4,500	7,333	15,666

* assumes 4% growth after inflation

Note: If your savings requirement is not listed, extrapolate the results. For example, if you require $2,000,000 at retirement in 35 years, double the answer found for $1,000,000 (i.e., $1,083 x 2).

Step 2

Open an investment account(s).

If you are investing for the long haul, service and reliability are far more important considerations than the cost per trade. While there may be lower-priced alternatives, **Charles Schwab** (www.schwab.com) and **Fidelity Investments** (www.fidelity.com) offer the best combination of on-line research, moderately-priced transaction costs and customer support. If you plan on doing lots of trading (several trades per month), it may pay to use a discount broker such as **TD Waterhouse** (www.waterhouse, .com) or **Ameritrade** (www.ameri-trade.com), that charges less than $10 per trade. However, be forewarned that customer service is not nearly as good from these sources.

Step 3

Maximize retirement investments whenever possible.

Once you have identified a monthly savings goal, you must decide how to structure your monthly deposits. The federal government exempts certain categories of retirement savings from income tax until you begin making scheduled withdrawals. Examples of these accounts include IRAs, Roth IRAs and 401 (k) plans, as well as Keogh plans for the self-employed. Contributions to all tax-deferred retirement plans are limited and tied to eligibility rules. However, your goal should always be to maximize your tax-deferred contributions whenever possible.

Taxable* vs. Tax-Deferred Investment Yields
(investing $2,000 per year @ 10%)

Years	Value of Taxable Account	Value of Tax-Deferred Account
30	$ 120,694	$ 357,000
25	84,761	213,300
20	57,603	124,124
15	37,077	68,731
10	21,565	34,337
5	9,841	12,981

Note: While you may be limited in the amount you can contribute to tax-deferred accounts, you should always make up any deficiencies with monthly contributions to *taxable* accounts. It is likely you will need both taxable and tax-deferred accounts to reach your financial objectives.

Step 4

Decide on an investment mix.

Theories abound regarding how best to allocate your investments. Generally, the more time you have before you will need to cash out, the larger the percentage of funds you can allocate to stocks and stock mutual funds. Most experts consider a mix of 80% stocks and 20% fixed income (i.e., CD's, money market accounts, bonds) to be for aggressive investors with a long time horizon. A mix of 70% stocks and 30% fixed income is probably most common. Conservative investors who might need to redeem their investments in 3-5 years or less might wish to consider a mix closer to 50% stocks and stock mutual funds and 50% fixed income.

Step 5

Decide on general areas for investment.

Stocks
If you are going to buy individual stocks, consider owning shares of leading companies in industries that are likely to experience above-average growth in the years ahead. Balance your portfolio with a mix of companies in predictable sectors of the economy that are also likely to prosper, while avoiding industries with growth rates that are slower than average.

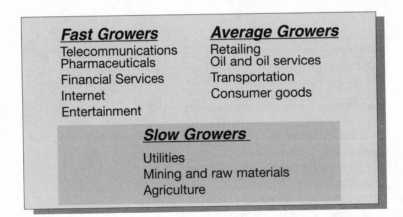

Fast Growers
Telecommunications
Pharmaceuticals
Financial Services
Internet
Entertainment

Average Growers
Retailing
Oil and oil services
Transportation
Consumer goods

Slow Growers
Utilities
Mining and raw materials
Agriculture

Mutual Funds

If you choose to invest in mutual funds, you will need to decide among more than a dozen fund types, each with a slightly different investment strategy and risk profile. No one category is best in all markets, or for all investors. What is more, the distinctions between fund types have blurred in recent years as fund managers have felt compelled to pursue whichever strategy is likely to produce the highest return in the short term. You should research any fund in detail, but certain adjectives should give you a clue as to the fund's share price volatility and risk level.

Aggressive Funds	Moderate-Risk Funds	Lower-Risk Funds
Aggressive Growth	Growth and Income	Value
Growth	Balanced	Income
Emerging Market	International Equity	Dogs of the Dow
Small Cap	S & P 500 Index	Total Return
Emerging Growth	Bond	Large Cap
Micro Cap	Mid Cap	
High Yield Bond		
Nasdaq Index		

Step 6

Screen for specific investment ideas.

Stocks

Before investing in particular stocks, do as much research as possible on the best candidates. There is no limit to the sources for investment ideas. Think about leading companies in the industries identified in Step 5. You generally can't go too wrong with the largest and most profitable company in a given sector.

Sites like *Microsoft's MoneyCentral* (www.msn.com) feature daily online articles that contain investment ideas. Other sites of this nature include *Yahoo! Finance* (www.yahoo.com), the *Motley Fool* (www.fool.com) and *CBS MarketWatch* (www.cbs.marketwatch .com).

You can also use stock screening software at sites like *Morningstar* (www. morningstar.com) *Schwab* (www. schwab.com) and *Fidelity Investments* (www.fidelity.com). These screening programs allow you to search the data base of all stocks, sorted by various factors including return on investment, earnings growth and debt ratios.

Once you have a number of stocks that look promising, you can begin the process of serious evaluation.

Using the analytical tools available on *Microsoft's MoneyCentral Investor* or

FINANCE

your online broker, take a close look at the company's investment fundamentals.

Price / Earnings Ratio

Divide the current share price by the latest earnings per share, both for the current year and based on projections of next year's earnings. P/E ratios vary over time and by industry. Generally, fast growing companies enjoy higher P/E multiples than their slower growing counterparts. It is impossible to generalize about whether a particular company is over-valued or undervalued based on the P/E ratio, but as a general rule, you should be attracted to companies with P/E ratios no higher than the projected rate of profit growth over the coming year. In other words, if profits at company "x" will grow 25% next year, it is not unreasonable to assume a P/E ratio of 25 represents "fair" value. Be forewarned that companies in the high tech arena often trade at P/E multiples which are much higher than stocks in slower growing industries. It is not unusual to see companies in particularly hot segments of the high tech field trading at multiples of 50 to 200 times earnings. These higher multiples must be considered in the context of projected profit growth over the next several years.

Profits

When evaluating stock investments, past profit performance is less important than future earnings expectations. As a rule, choose from companies with annual profit growth rates which are expected to rise at least 15 to 20% over the coming year. Higher growth rates are even better.

Chart Pattern

Stocks generally follow certain time-tested patterns concerning rising and falling share prices. As a rule, stocks rise or fall until they reach certain points of resistance. If you understand these resistance patterns, you generally will have a good idea whether over the short term, a stock is likely to go up in value or decline. Obviously, it is best to buy stocks that are building momentum to the upside – i.e., higher highs and higher lows. Stocks which are losing momentum – i.e., lower highs and lower lows are typically less attractive. Most brokerage web sites have charting capabilities. Pay particular attention to a stock's chart pattern plotted against its 10-day and 200-day moving averages. When the price of a stock breaks through the moving average, either to the upside or the downside, the trend is likely to continue (up or down) at an accelerated rate.

Ratings

Most stocks are rated for safety and growth potential by leading investment analysts. One of the most widely followed ratings sources is the *Value Line Investment Survey* (www.value line.com) The *Value Line Investment Survey* provides weekly analysis on more than 1,700 leading stocks in 92 industries. Each stock gets a separate rating for timeliness (the best time to buy or sell) and safety (risk that the stock will rise or fall in value).

Rating Categories

#1	*Best*
#2	*Better than average*
#3	*Average*
#4	*Below average*
#5	*Poor*

Most public libraries subscribe to the **Value Line**. You can subscribe yourself, but it is relatively expensive. A 1-year subscription to the Investment Survey, which covers 1,600 of the most widely held stocks, costs $575/yr. An expanded edition covering 6,000 securities will cost you $995. 10-week trial subscriptions are also available at reduced fees.

Another source of information and ratings of various stocks is **Standard & Poors** (www.personalwealth.com). The **S&P Stock Guide** assigns stocks ratings in the following categories:

A +   *Highest Recommendation*
A   *High Recommendation*
A-   *Above-average Recommendation*
B+   *Average Recommendation*
B-   *Below-Average Recommendation*
B-   *Poor Recommendation*
C   *Lowest Recommendation*

An online subscription to the **S&P Stock Guide** is $9.95 per month. However, why pay for the reports when you can get them for free simply by opening an account at discount broker **Charles Schwab** (www.schwab.com).

Final Analysis

If you want a final and thorough compilation and analysis of all the available data on a particular stock, log on to the **Microsoft Money Central Investor** web site (www.msn.com). Choose "stocks" and then enter the stock symbol for the company you are considering. Then choose "research wizard." **Money Central Investor** provides a concise report that answers the key questions you need to make an investment decision:

Fundamentals: What business is the company in? Is the business sound and growing?

Price History: What have investors been willing to pay in the past for the stock?

Price Target: How much are investors likely to pay for the stock in the future?

Catalysts: What catalysts will change investor perceptions of the stock in the future?

Comparison: How does the stock compare to others in its industry?

Mutual Funds

Sorting through the more than 6,000 mutual funds for the top performers used to be an exhausting chore, but most brokerage web sites allow you to screen funds based on investment objectives, appreciation potential and risk.

Once you have decided on what type of fund you wish to choose from (i.e., aggressive growth, balanced, international, etc.,), selecting from the best in the category is relatively straightforward.

By far, the most popular site for analyzing mutual funds is at **Morningstar** (www.morningstar.com). For years, the company has tracked the investment performance of all mutual funds, assigning each fund a rating of one to five stars. The ratings are now available on their web site for free.

Morningstar's ratings within a given category are based upon a numerical analysis of a mutual fund's price performance and volatility. Each fund is assigned a score, which is then plotted against other funds in the category.

5 Stars ★★★★★
Top 10% of funds in category

4 Stars ★★★★
Higher 70—90% of funds in category

3 Stars ★★★
Middle 30—70 % of funds in category

2 Stars ★★
Lower 10—30% of funds in category

1 Star ★
Lowest 10% of funds in category

Another screening tool can be found at **MSN MoneyCentral Investor** (www.msn.com), which incorporates **Morningstar** data, along with other information under the "mutual funds research wizard" heading. As in the case of stocks, the MSN research wizard gives a thorough analysis of a fund in layman's terms which answers the key questions you need to make an informed choice.

Category: *What is the aim of the fund? What securities does it buy?*

Price History: *How well has the fund performed over time?*

Management: *Who runs the fund and how often does management change?*

Risk: *How much volatility has the fund exposed investors to?*

Comparison: *How does the fund compare to others in its category?*

As a general rule, you should be choosing no-load funds – funds you can buy without paying commissions. You can buy the shares directly through the mutual fund company, or alternatively through a participating discount broker such as **Schwab**, **Fidelity** or **E-Trade.**

Also, be certain that you look at the performance of the mutual fund over an extended period of time. Today's high flyer may be tomorrow's loser. Look for funds that have above average returns in good times and bad. The one exception would be sector funds, which specialize in a particular group of stocks or industries. A fund that invests exclusively in financial services stocks, for example, can be expected to do better than average when interest rates are falling, and below average when they are rising. Industry-specific mutual funds should be bought and sold with shorter time frames involved and the intention to sell when market conditions change.

Finally, consider funds which invest in an index of stocks, such as the **S&P 500**, the **Nasdaq 100** or the **Russell 2000.** These funds own *all* of the stocks in the index, meaning that the decisions of a mutual fund manager are nearly eliminated. The theory is that a mutual fund manager is just as prone to making wrong choices as right ones. By owning the entire index, you eliminate the possibility of wrong bets relative to the market as a whole. Studies indicate that index funds generally outperform the vast majority of actively-managed funds. However, it is also true that the small minority of actively-managed funds that do beat the market averages usually do so by a wide margin.

Chapter Ten
Eat Out For Less

How can I save money in restaurants?

Believe it or not, there is a strategic way to order in any restaurant to maximize your eating pleasure while minimizing the cost. The key is understanding menu pricing and how restaurants use psychology to inflate your bill. Long ago, restauranteurs discovered that customers worry about the price of entrees but rarely focus on the extras. That's why in nine out of ten establishments, alcoholic beverages, appetizers and desserts are *overpriced*. You can cut your tab at least 40% and still enjoy the best food the restaurant has to offer by limiting your order to the main entrée. Ask for ice water with a wedge of lemon and pass on the dessert and coffee.

But that's not all you can do. When you go out, choose restaurants where you generally get the best value for your money. Ethnic restaurants are often your best choice, especially establishments that serve Mexican, Chinese, Italian, Vietnamese or Thai food.

If there's a very special (and expensive) place you've always wanted to try, you can enjoy the great food and ambiance for about half the price simply by visiting at lunch rather than dinner. Lunch patrons are notoriously more value-conscious than their dinner counterparts. A restaurant with an overpriced lunch menu couldn't attract enough customers, so prices are always significantly less at the noon hour.

Finally, don't be afraid to share. About eight years ago, fast-food restaurants began to "super-size" their portions. The theory was that customers would pay more for larger servings, which proved to be true. More recently, the trend has spread to sit-down eateries in a BIG way. A single entrée in many restaurants is now more than enough to satisfy *two* hungry eaters. The logical response is to share a single order with your dining companion. Don't be shy or embarrassed to ask for an extra plate. If you need an excuse to avoid feeling embarrassed, tell the waiter you're just not feeling hungry.

I like a glass of wine at dinner. Are you saying I should give it up to save money?

We're talking about choices, not hard and fast rules. If you want wine, try ordering a glass, or a carafe of the house wine instead of an expensive bottle.

Do the same rules apply at fast-food restaurants?

Yes. The big profit margins are on soft drinks, french fries and over-sized sandwiches. That's why a company like **McDonald's** constantly promotes low-priced cheeseburgers, but never mentions the cost for a Coke and large fries. Stick to the basics and you will beat the franchises at their own game. Choose a regular hamburger instead of the triple combo, and again don't hesitate to order a glass of ice water. If it's pizza you crave, stay away from the extra toppings which can often double the price of your order.

What's the best way to find a good restaurant?

Word of mouth is much better than relying on restaurant reviews. Many publications favor eateries that are also major advertisers. You never know whether the glowing praise is because the restaurant's food is so good or because of the full-page layout they bought last month. Stick to recommendations from friends or objective sources you can trust.

Restaurant Values in Major Cities Accross the U.S.

Atlanta
A Slocum's Tavern
C Honto
I DePalma's
S Stringer's Fish Camp
F Chef's Cafe
M San Jose
O Harold's BBQ

Baltimore
A Alonso's Bay Cafe
C Thai
I Trattoria Petrucci
S Fisherman's Warf
F Cafe Normandie
M Tio Pepe's
O Haussner's

Boston
A Bartley's Burgers
C Chau Chow
I Lucia's Ristorante
S Legal Seafood
F Oliver's
M Rudy's Cafe
O Galleria Umberto

Chicago
A Glady's Luncheonette
C Formosa
I Trattoria Convito
S Harry G's Crabhouse
F Jean Claude
M Frontera Grill
O Home Run Inn (Pizza)

Cincinnati
A Cafe at the Palm Court
C Ben Thai
I Germanos
O Rockwood Pottery

Cleveland
A Cooker Bar & Grill
C Paul's Siam Cuisine
I Amici's
M Lopez y Gonzalez
O Sterle's Slovenian
      Country House

Dallas / Ft. Worth
A Celebration
C Tong's House
F Le Madeleine
M La Calle Doce
O Sonny Bryan's BBQ
O Gennie's Bishop Grill

Denver
A Rocky Mountain Diner
C Imperial Chinese
I Pasta, Pasta, Pasta
F European Cafe (Boulder)
M La Cueva

Houston
A Taste of Texas
C Shanghai River
I Buca di Bacco
S Pappadeaux Seafood
      Kitchen
F Treebeards
M Pappasito's Cantina
O Luby's Cafeteria

Los Angeles
A Philippe the Original
C Yang Chow
I Cafe Petito
S Fish Company
F Barsac Brasserie
M La Parrilla
O Authentic Cafe

New Orleans
A Camellia Grill
C Five Happiness
I Pie in the Sky
S Casamentos
F L'Economie
M Taqueria Corona
O Mother's

New York City
A Thompkins Park
C Wong Kee
I Cuccina di Pesce
S Jane St. Seafood
F Paris Commune
M Pedro Paramo
O Pig Heaven

Philadelphia
A The Commisary
C Sang Kee Peking Duck
I Mr. Martino's Trattoria
I Flying Fish
F Le Petit Cafe
M Tequila's
O Reading Terminal Mkt.

San Francisco
A Stars' Cafe
C House of Nanking
I Cafe Riggio
S Swans Oyster Depot
F Cafe Claude
M Casa Aguila
O Cafe @ Chez Panisse

Seattle
A Scott's 205th St. Grill
C House of Hong
I Il Paesano
S Sailfish Grill
F Cafe de Paris
M Casa U Betcha
O Rhododendron Cafe

St. Louis
A Blue Water Grill
C Mai Lee (Vietnamese)
I Little Sicily
S Sliders
M Pueblo Nuevo
O Phil's BBQ

Washington, D.C.
A Houston's
C Hunan Number One
I Cafe Petito
S Market Inn
F Le Bistro Francais
M Austin Grill
O Dungrats (Thai)

American **C**hinese/Asian **I**talian **S**eafood **F**rench **M**exican **O**ut-of-the-Ordinary

Crowds are also a good indicator. If a place always seems busy, chances are something good is happening inside. One excellent source of restaurant ideas is the **ZAGAT Restaurant Survey** www.zagat.com (1-800-333-3421), which rates dining establishments in all price ranges in dozens of U.S. cities. The **ZAGAT** reviews are unbiased compilations of reader comments which are surprisingly candid!

You can develop your own dining guide using the enclosed "Favorite Restaurants" log. Use it to make note of recommendations from friends, favorable newspaper reviews and your own personal experiences. It's a great source of ideas when you want to try someplace new.

Also, try any of the restaurants in our lisings of great restaurant values in major cities across the U.S.A. They are hometown favorites which offer some of the best values for your dining dollar, according to surveys of frequent restaurant customers and newspaper critics.

What's an appropriate tip?

Waiters and waitresses work hard for their money. A standard tip is 15% of your bill, no more or less. Unfortunately, many people over-tip because they make mathematical errors. You can eliminate this problem if you follow this easy formula:

Step 1

Move the decimal point on your final bill one place to the left.

> **Example: Final Tab = $ 28.50**
> **Move decimal point: $ 2.85**

Step 2

Add 50% to your total in step 1.

Example: $ 2.85 + $ 1.43 = $ 4.28

Correct Tip = $4.28

EAT OUT FOR LESS
15% TIP GUIDE

TAB	TIP	TAB	TIP	TAB	TIP	TAB	TIP
		21.00	3.15	41.00	6.15	71.00	10.65
		22.00	3.30	42.00	6.30	72.00	10.80
		23.00	3.45	43.00	6.45	73.00	10.95
4.00	.60	24.00	3.60	44.00	6.60	74.00	11.10
5.00	.75	25.00	3.75	45.00	6.75	75.00	11.25
6.00	.90	26.00	3.90	46.00	6.90	76.00	11.40
7.00	1.05	27.00	4.05	47.00	7.05	77.00	11.55
8.00	1.20	28.00	4.20	48.00	7.20	78.00	11.70
9.00	1.35	29.00	4.35	49.00	2.35	79.00	11.85
10.00	1.50	30.00	4.50	50.00	7.50	80.00	12.00
11.00	1.65	31.00	4.65	51.00	7.65	81.00	12.15
12.00	1.80	32.00	4.80	52.00	7.80	82.00	12.30
13.00	1.95	33.00	4.95	53.00	7.95	83.00	12.45
14.00	2.10	34.00	5.10	54.00	8.10	84.00	12.60
15.00	2.25	35.00	5.25	55.00	8.25	85.00	12.75
16.00	2.40	36.00	5.40	56.00	8.40	86.00	12.90
17.00	2.55	37.00	5.55	57.00	8.55	87.00	13.05
18.00	2.70	38.00	5.70	58.00	8.70	88.00	13.20
19.00	2.85	39.00	5.85	59.00	8.85	89.00	13.35
20.00	3.00	40.00	6.00	60.00	9.00	90.00	13.50
				61.00	9.15	91.00	13.65
				62.00	9.30	92.00	13.80
				63.00	9.45	93.00	13.95
				64.00	9.60	94.00	14.10
				65.00	9.75	95.00	14.25
				66.00	9.90	96.00	14.40
				67.00	10.05	97.00	14.55
				68.00	10.20	98.00	14.70
				69.00	10.35	99.00	14.85
				70.00	10.50	100.00	15.00

FOLD · FOLD

EAT OUT FOR LESS
15% TIP GUIDE

TAB	TIP	TAB	TIP	TAB	TIP	TAB	TIP
		21.00	3.15	41.00	6.15	71.00	10.65
		22.00	3.30	42.00	6.30	72.00	10.80
		23.00	3.45	43.00	6.45	73.00	10.95
4.00	.60	24.00	3.60	44.00	6.60	74.00	11.10
5.00	.75	25.00	3.75	45.00	6.75	75.00	11.25
6.00	.90	26.00	3.90	46.00	6.90	76.00	11.40
7.00	1.05	27.00	4.05	47.00	7.05	77.00	11.55
8.00	1.20	28.00	4.20	48.00	7.20	78.00	11.70
9.00	1.35	29.00	4.35	49.00	2.35	79.00	11.85
10.00	1.50	30.00	4.50	50.00	7.50	80.00	12.00
11.00	1.65	31.00	4.65	51.00	7.65	81.00	12.15
12.00	1.80	32.00	4.80	52.00	7.80	82.00	12.30
13.00	1.95	33.00	4.95	53.00	7.95	83.00	12.45
14.00	2.10	34.00	5.10	54.00	8.10	84.00	12.60
15.00	2.25	35.00	5.25	55.00	8.25	85.00	12.75
16.00	2.40	36.00	5.40	56.00	8.40	86.00	12.90
17.00	2.55	37.00	5.55	57.00	8.55	87.00	13.05
18.00	2.70	38.00	5.70	58.00	8.70	88.00	13.20
19.00	2.85	39.00	5.85	59.00	8.85	89.00	13.35
20.00	3.00	40.00	6.00	60.00	9.00	90.00	13.50
				61.00	9.15	91.00	13.65
				62.00	9.30	92.00	13.80
				63.00	9.45	93.00	13.95
				64.00	9.60	94.00	14.10
				65.00	9.75	95.00	14.25
				66.00	9.90	96.00	14.40
				67.00	10.05	97.00	14.55
				68.00	10.20	98.00	14.70
				69.00	10.35	99.00	14.85
				70.00	10.50	100.00	15.00

FOLD · FOLD

Guide to
EAT OUT FOR LESS

Use this worksheet to keep track of your favorite restaurants and those recommended by your friends.

EAT OUT FOR LESS WORKSHEET

Favorite Restaurants

American

Restaurant _____

Location _____

Phone/Reservations _____

Prices _____

Recommended Dish _____

_____

Comments _____

_____

Who Says It's Good _____

Restaurant _____

Location _____

Phone/Reservations _____

Prices _____

Recommended Dish _____

_____

Comments _____

_____

Who Says It's Good _____

Asian

Restaurant _____

Location _____

Phone/Reservations _____

Prices _____

Recommended Dish _____

_____

Comments _____

_____

Who Says It's Good _____

Restaurant _____

Location _____

Phone/Reservations _____

Prices _____

Recommended Dish _____

_____

Comments _____

_____

Who Says It's Good _____

EAT OUT FOR LESS WORKSHEET

Continental

Restaurant _____   Restaurant _____

Location _____   Location _____

Phone/Reservations _____   Phone/Reservations _____

Prices _____   Prices _____

Recommended Dish _____   Recommended Dish _____

_____   _____

Comments _____   Comments _____

_____   _____

Who Says It's Good _____   Who Says It's Good _____

French

Restaurant _____   Restaurant _____

Location _____   Location _____

Phone/Reservations _____   Phone/Reservations _____

Prices _____   Prices _____

Recommended Dish _____   Recommended Dish _____

_____   _____

Comments _____   Comments _____

_____   _____

Who Says It's Good _____   Who Says It's Good _____

Italian

Restaurant _____   Restaurant _____

Location _____   Location _____

Phone/Reservations _____   Phone/Reservations _____

Prices _____   Prices _____

Recommended Dish _____   Recommended Dish _____

_____   _____

Comments _____   Comments _____

_____   _____

Who Says It's Good _____   Who Says It's Good _____

EAT OUT FOR LESS WORKSHEET

Mexican

Restaurant _____

Location _____

Phone/Reservations _____

Prices _____

Recommended Dish _____

_____

Comments _____

_____

Who Says It's Good _____

Restaurant _____

Location _____

Phone/Reservations _____

Prices _____

Recommended Dish _____

_____

Comments _____

_____

Who Says It's Good _____

Sea Food

Restaurant _____

Location _____

Phone/Reservations _____

Prices _____

Recommended Dish _____

_____

Comments _____

_____

Who Says It's Good _____

Restaurant _____

Location _____

Phone/Reservations _____

Prices _____

Recommended Dish _____

_____

Comments _____

_____

Who Says It's Good _____

Thai

Restaurant _____

Location _____

Phone/Reservations _____

Prices _____

Recommended Dish _____

_____

Comments _____

_____

Who Says It's Good _____

Restaurant _____

Location _____

Phone/Reservations _____

Prices _____

Recommended Dish _____

_____

Comments _____

_____

Who Says It's Good _____

EAT OUT FOR LESS WORKSHEET

Special Occasion

Restaurant _____

Location _____

Phone/Reservations _____

Prices _____

Recommended Dish _____

_____

Comments _____

_____

Who Says It's Good _____

Restaurant _____

Location _____

Phone/Reservations _____

Prices _____

Recommended Dish _____

_____

Comments _____

_____

Who Says It's Good _____

Breakfast / Brunch

Restaurant _____

Location _____

Phone/Reservations _____

Prices _____

Recommended Dish _____

_____

Comments _____

_____

Who Says It's Good _____

Restaurant _____

Location _____

Phone/Reservations _____

Prices _____

Recommended Dish _____

_____

Comments _____

_____

Who Says It's Good _____

Lunch / Sandwich

Restaurant _____

Location _____

Phone/Reservations _____

Prices _____

Recommended Dish _____

_____

Comments _____

_____

Who Says It's Good _____

Restaurant _____

Location _____

Phone/Reservations _____

Prices _____

Recommended Dish _____

_____

Comments _____

_____

Who Says It's Good _____

EAT OUT FOR LESS WORKSHEET

Miscellaneous

Restaurant _____

Location _____

Phone/Reservations _____

Prices _____

Recommended Dish _____

_____

Comments _____

_____

Who Says It's Good _____

Restaurant _____

Location _____

Phone/Reservations _____

Prices _____

Recommended Dish _____

_____

Comments _____

_____

Who Says It's Good _____

Restaurant _____

Location _____

Phone/Reservations _____

Prices _____

Recommended Dish _____

_____

Comments _____

_____

Who Says It's Good _____

Restaurant _____

Location _____

Phone/Reservations _____

Prices _____

Recommended Dish _____

_____

Comments _____

_____

Who Says It's Good _____

Restaurant _____

Location _____

Phone/Reservations _____

Prices _____

Recommended Dish _____

_____

Comments _____

_____

Who Says It's Good _____

Restaurant _____

Location _____

Phone/Reservations _____

Prices _____

Recommended Dish _____

_____

Comments _____

_____

Who Says It's Good _____

When it come to eating out, modest changes in your ordering habits can mean big savings on your final bill. As the examples below illustrate, you can cut your tabs 30%–40% while still enjoying the dining experience.

Suggestion: **Skip the fries and soft drinks when ordering at a fast food restaurant.**

Example: Wendy's

Regular Order	*Eat Out for Less*
2 1/4 lb single hamburgers	2 1/4 lb single hamburgers
2 large fries	2 large waters w/ lemon
2 large sodas	
Total: $7.66	**Total: $3.70**
	Savings: $3.96

Suggestion: **Order basic burgers not deluxe versions with extra toppings and cheese.**

Example: McDonald's

Regular Order	*Eat Out for Less*
2 Big Macs	4 Cheeseburgers
Total: $3.78	**Total: $2.76**
	Savings: $1.02

Suggestion: **Avoid appetizers, alcohol and desserts at sit-down restaurants. Confine your order to entrees and a beverage and make dessert at home.**

Example: Silver Diner, Reston, Va.

Lunch for Two

Regular Order	*Eat Out for Less*
Chicken wing appetizer $4.95	Grilled chicken sandwich $5.95
Corn Soup appetizer $3.95	Chicken Caesar salad $6.95
Grilled chicken sandwhich $4.95	2 ice water w/ lemon $0.00
Chicken Ceasar salad $4.95	
2 white wines.. $7.50	
2 Ice cream sundaes $6.90	
Tip $5.43	Tip $1.93
Total: $38.63	**Total: $14.83**
	Savings: $23.80

Chapter Eleven

Quality Health Care at a Reasonable Cost

Why should I be concerned with money when my health is at stake?

Unfortunately, health care is a business. Doctors, hospitals and insurance companies have made it that way so you have no choice but to approach every transaction with the same skepticism that you use when contracting for any other product or service. Obviously, your goal isn't the cheapest treatment or the lowest price, but the best care you can find to meet your medical needs. Finding it isn't always easy.

To a large degree, the health care system has turned adversarial. Insurance companies and employers are so preoccupied with keeping costs down that the sacred relationship between doctor and patient has been badly compromised. Insurers are now gatekeepers who often decide when you get treatment, which drugs you're prescribed, what your doctor will be paid and how much comes out of your pocket.

Insurance companies are not the only ones to blame, however. Doctors and hospitals were responsible for annual double-digit increases in the cost of services throughout the 1980's and early 1990's. Greed, it seems, is universal.

All of this means that in an arena in which you are emotionally vulnerable and probably least prepared to make informed judgments, you have no choice but to assert yourself and become your own advocate.

How can I question a doctor or an insurance company if I'm not a medical expert?

Just because you can't make specific medical judgments doesn't mean you should give a free pass to a doctor or an insurance claims specialist. You can do plenty to assure that you're receiving the best available care.

The first step is choosing the best primary-care physician you can find. In today's health care system, primary doctors are critical. They are your main point of contact with the entire medical establishment. If your primary doctor is overworked, lazy or poorly informed, you face considerable risk that a serious medical condition could be overlooked or improperly treated. Great doctors don't charge more than average ones, so take time to find one with a solid reputation in the community, strong recommendations from other doctors, training from a top medical school and board certification in his or her specialty.

Of course, a great doctor is not necessarily free to practice medicine the way they know best. Most doctors are continually monitored by insurance companies for "care utilization." If your doctor orders what the insurance company considers unnecessary tests, prescribes costly medications or recommends therapies which conflict with standard protocols, he or she could be dropped by the plan. In the final analysis, doctors are forced to work according to the insurance company's rules, even when those rules are not in your best interests.

That's why you should go to any doctor's office prepared to ask lots of questions. When you ask questions, you make it harder for a physician to hide behind rules and protocols and force him or her to relate to you as a human being as well as a patient. Questions force a doctor to slow down and take time with you, even if he or she would prefer moving on to the five other people waiting in examining rooms. Make no mistake, you have a right and a need to know what your lab results mean, the pros and cons of various drug therapies, when various tests are appropriate and the names of top specialists when you need them. Too many patients are shy and timid at precisely the time a more aggressive approach is essential. If you do not speak up when you feel you are not getting adequate attention, who will?

In some cases, you need to go beyond asking questions of your primary-care physician and assert yourself further. For instance, you should insist on seeking a second opinion from another doctor any time you are told you will need surgery or that your diagnosis is life threatening. Likewise, if your doctor cannot determine what is wrong with you after at least three visits or if he or she attributes your problem to "nerves" when you know better, it is best to seek the advice of another expert.

How do I know the right questions to ask?

The internet has helped to level the playing field between patients and their doctors since the public now has access to state-of-the-art information until recently only available in leading medical school libraries. There are sites on every disease or medical condition, as well as specialized databases which you can search for information highly specific to your symptoms. You can find out information on experimental treatments and new drug trials, the latest on potential side effects of various prescriptions, at what age routine tests should be incorporated into your wellness exam, connections to support groups and advocacy organizations, as well as the opportunity to pose questions to leading experts.

This chapter includes a chart listing a wealth of health internet resources. At the **American Medical Association** site (www.ama-assn.org), you can check the credentials of any doctor in the United States. **Healthfinder** (www.healthfinder.org) helps you navigate through all of the medical sites linked to the federal government, including the *National Institute of Health (NIH)*, the *National Cancer Institute (NCI)* and the *Food & Drug Administration (FDA)*. You can check on women's health issues at *OBGYN Net* (www.obgyn.net), heart matters at the *American Heart Association's* site (www.american-heart.org), cancer specifics at *Onco-link* (www.oncolink.upenn.edu.) and information on hard-to-diagnose conditions at the *National Organization of Rare Disorders* (www.steptn.com/nord) to name but a few. Most medical sites tend to offer links and suggestion to other web addresses that can also help you in your search for information.

Doing your own research makes increasing sense. According to a recent study by the *U.S. Government's General Accounting Office (GAO)*, 60% of all rectal cancers in the U.S., 50% of testicular cancer cases as well as 18% of the cases of Hodgkins disease and 20% of non-Hodgkins lymphoma are not treated using best practices. *Consumer Reports* concluded that a high percentage of hospitals and health plans do not routinely prescribe "beta blockers" even though these drugs can dramatically reduce the risk of death during a heart attack. In another study, the National Cancer Institute estimates than 175,000 lives could be saved or extended each year if patients received the most effective treatments available.

Like it or not, you are the first, last and best line of defense against improper, inadequate or incompetent treatment.

What should I do if my insurance company denies my claim or refuses to cover treatment that I need?

Read your insurance policy carefully to make certain you have a reasonable case. Don't expect to be covered for something that is clearly excluded in your plan. By the same token, recognize that most policy provisions are subject to interpretation, particularly if it can be argued that a given drug test or treatment is medically necessary or constitutes the best practice of medicine.

Your doctor can be an important ally. If he or she strongly believes that a particular treatment or test is needed, you have a good chance to appeal your insurance company's decision. Begin by contacting the company on your own. Encourage your doctor to do the same. Bypass the insurance company's first line of defense, the "friendly" operators who normally take your calls. Instead, ask to speak with someone in the department that handles medical case management. You want to find out exactly what the process is for filing an appeal and how long it will take. While you are on the phone, ask for a written explanation which describes why your treatment or claim has been denied. Follow-up the verbal request with a written letter and begin keeping a detailed journal of all your contacts with the insurance company. Document everything!

While the appeal is in process, ask your doctor to refer you to an out-of-network physician in order to obtain a second opinion about your situation. You may have to pay for this evaluation out of your own pocket, but if your condition is serious enough, the cost is well worth it. The "second opinion" can corroborate your case that treatment is medically necessary. Do not explain that you are in a dispute with your insurance company, but do ask this second doctor if he or she would be willing to bill you at the same rate they would charge the insurance companies with whom he or she does business.

Once you have a letter from your doctor, a second opinion from an out-of-network physician and a letter from your insurance company explaining the reason your claim has been denied, contact your state department of insurance and inquire about what rights you may have. Florida, for example, has a special appeals board that hears disputes between patients and insurance providers. You should also notify the benefits manager at work about your situation. In many cases, employers can intervene on behalf of employees when they feel the insurance company is wrongfully interpreting the company's group policy. In short, do everything you can to complain, politely cajole and otherwise be a "squeaky wheel" that won't take "no" for an answer. Keep in mind, though, that while it is smart to be aggressive, acting nasty and confrontational with insurance company employees usually makes them even more stubborn.

Finally, remember that your first priority should always be your health. If the appeals to your insurance company fail and your doctor still feels you need a particular test, drug or procedure, pay for it yourself. Then go talk to a lawyer.

What if the insurance company tells me my claim exceeds "usual and customary" charges? Do I have any recourse?

It depends on the type of insurance policy. Some plans restrict you to a certain list of doctors and hospitals that negotiate discounted fees directly with the insurance company. If you are a member of such a plan, you pay a modest co-pay charge for each visit to the doctor plus a percentage of fees until you satisfy an annual deductible. As long as you remain in the network, there should not be any added charges which exceed usual and customary rates. On the other hand, if your plan does not have an in-network benefit, you could easily find yourself in the middle of a billing dispute.

Faced with such a problem, do the following:

1. Talk to your doctor.

He or she may be willing to reduce their charges or contact the insurance company to appeal. In some cases, a doctor may have used an improper billing code that can easily be corrected.

2. Find out from an impartial source whether the insurance company's position is reasonable.

You can find out by consulting a little-known service available on the internet operated by a medical software company, *Intellimed International* (www.mecqa.com). *Intellimed* operates a database that tracks the national average for reasonable and customary charges for virtually any medical procedure. Simply enter the procedure and Intellimed can tell you what your doctor should be charging and what your insurance company should be paying.

3. Appeal to your insurance company.

Ask to speak with the department that processes claims reimbursements and inquire about appeal procedures. Before you call, make certain your doctor has used the appropriate billing code and that you have researched customary charges at the *Intellimed* web site.

If I have health insurance through work and I lose my job, will I be able to find affordable coverage on my own?

Federal law guarantees that if you work for a company with twenty or more employees, you can maintain your group health insurance for up to eighteen months following job termination. The "catch" is that you have to pay 102% of the monthly group insurance premium you and your company had previously paid on your behalf. You will find that paying the company's share of your premium will add considerably to your overall cost. In some cases, buying an individual policy with less generous benefits may be a better alternative to maintaining your company plan.

If I buy my own health insurance, what type of plan do you recommend?

Your three basic options are:

Fee-for-Service Plans, which allow you to choose your own doctors and hospitals;

Preferred Provider Plans, which allow you to choose from a list of participating doctors and hospitals in your area; and

Health Maintenance Organizations (HMO's), which offer complete coverage by staff physicians at HMO facilities.

Each option has pros and cons. Fee-for-Service Plans offer you the most freedom in choosing doctors and specialists as the need arises. The downside is that you are reimbursed for "usual and customary" charges which may not reflect your actual bills. Fee for service plans are generally the most expensive health insurance option.

By contrast, an HMO gives you few if any choices in doctors or hospitals in exchange for the certainty that your monthly premium covers all your medical expenses. Some people like the trade-off. Others don't.

The middle ground is occupied by Preferred Provider Plans – groups of participating doctors and hospitals that agree to follow the insurance company's rules and practices while remaining independent contractors. You get more choice than you would from an

HMO but fewer options than if you go with a Fee-for-Service plan.

Surveys indicate that most people are happy with the plans they choose, but this is probably because they have used the health care system sporadically and have not experienced a major illness. Quality-of-care studies also fail to quantify major differences between HMO's, PPO's and Fee-for-Service plans.

I've had a difficult time finding an insurer that will cover me because of a pre-existing condition or poor health. Is there anything I can do?

If you've been covered by a group plan at work, or have been purchasing extended coverage over the last 18 months since leaving your job, you enjoy some protection under the Health Insurance Portability and Accountability Act. Under the law, if you purchase coverage in a group plan and have not let your coverage lapse for more than 63 days, an insurance company cannot deny coverage nor impose pre-existing condition exclusions for more than 12 months for any condition diagnosed or treated in the preceeding 6 months. The law is primarily intended to help people who change jobs from losing insurance coverage from their new employer.

If you do not have group coverage from work, finding health insurance with a pre-existing medical condition will be harder but you still have options, depending on where you live.

In at least 13 states, Blue Cross/Blue Shield programs will insure you regard-less of your health if you apply during certain times of the year. These "open enrollment" periods may be limited to only a few weeks each year so it is important to check with the local program for details. If a Blue Cross program is not an option, you may be in luck if you live in a state which operates a high-risk insurance pool. These state administered plans presently operate in 25 states and insure more than 100,000 individuals with preexisting conditions. In most states, premiums in the risk pool are 25 to 50 percent higher than for comparable policies a healthy person can buy.

States With Open Enrollment for Blue Cross / Blue Shield	States Sponsoring High-Risk Insurance Pools	States Without Programs for the Hard-to-Insure
Alabama	Alaska	Arizona
Hawaii	Arkansas	Idaho
Maryland	California	Kansas
Michigan	Colorado	Kentucky
New Hampshire	Connecticut	Ohio
New Jersey	Delaware	South Dakota
New York	Florida	West Virginia
North Carolina	Iowa	
Pennsylvania	Illinois	
Rhode Island	Indiana	
Vermont	Kansas	
Virginia	Louisiana	
D.C.	Massachusetts	
	Minnesota	
	Mississippi	
	Missouri	
	Montana	
	Nebraska	
	Nevada	
	North Dakota	
	New Mexico	
	Oregon	
	Oklahoma	
	South Carolina	
	Tennessee	
	Utah	
	Washington	
	Wisconsin	
	Wyoming	

I'm self-employed. What are my best options for low-cost health insurance?

If you belong to a trade association or professional organization, it may offer a group plan which may be superior to individual coverage. However, it is far more likely that the plan is not any better than what you can find on your own. Contact a local insurance agent who specializes in the health care market and ask him to describe the various plans that are available in your area. Forget about using the internet, since it is extremely important to find a program which is rated highly in your particular area.

What about Medicare?

If you are over 65, Medicare covers a certain percentage of hospital care, doctor bills and outpatient services. The program is divided into parts A and B. Under part A, which you generally receive free-of-charge, you are covered for hospital stays up to 90 days after meeting certain deductibles. Part B, which costs approximately $45 per month, covers up to 80% of eligible costs for doctor visits, office exams, lab tests, emergency care and prescriptions.

Even though Medicare covers a large percentage of health care costs, there are major gaps in coverage which can only be covered by supplementary Medigap insurance and these gaps are growing as the government scales back benefits.

What's not covered by Medicare

• Hospital stays over 90 days;

• $760 deductible for each hospital stay and $190 per day for days 61-90;

• Private rooms;

• $96 per day for skilled nursing care for days 21-100 and all costs thereafter;

• $100 annual deductible for doctor visits;

• 20% of doctor visits and lab tests, plus all charges in excess of Medicare-approved amounts;

• Healthcare outside the U.S.; and

• Prescriptions

To make it easier for consumers to comparison shop for Medigap insurance, all states (except Minnesota, Massachusetts and Wisconsin) limit the number of different policies that can be sold to no more than 10 standard plans which are identical from one insurer to the next. Each has a letter designation ranging from "A" through "J." Because insurers are not permitted to change the combination of benefits or the letter designations of any of the plans, they compete exclusively on service, reliability and price. A step-by-step worksheet at the end of this chapter can help you select the best plan for your needs.

How can I save on prescriptions?

First, make certain that you need the medicine. It is common for doctors to prescribe antibiotics and pain medications as a precaution, even though they may not be medically necessary. Question your doctor thoroughly about whether you truly need a prescription.

If you do, then follow-up with these requests:

- Ask for free samples, if any are available;

- Request a generic version of the drug, if possible; and

- Request pills in double doses (if you will be taking them over an extended period), which you can then cut in half to save money.

When you leave the doctor's office, do not be shy about comparison shopping among competing pharmacies, unless your insurance company limits your options. Prices can vary dramatically from one drug store to the next. In fact, a particular store may be cheaper for one medication but more expensive for another. Also check prices at several of these mail-order discount pharmacies.

Discount Prescriptions Via the Internet

Rx Universe
www.rxuniverse.com

Online Drugstore
www.onlinedrugstore.com

Cyber Pharmacy
www.cyberpharmacy.com

JD Pharmacy
www.jdpharmacy.com

What about non-prescription, over-the-counter medicines?

Many OTC products treat so-called "self limiting" conditions such as colds or stomach pains which will improve with or without treatment. However, if you want to save money on over-the-counter medications to relieve symptoms, keep in mind four key points:

- **Always buy the generic version containing the same active ingredient as name-brand medications.**

Generic or store brands containing the same active ingredients as nationally advertised products are usually 40-60% cheaper and are equally effective. You can easily compare products simply by reading the label to identify the active ingredient of competing brands.

Discount Prescriptions By Mail

Action Mail Order	☎ 1-800-452-1976
Health Care Services	☎ 1-800-758-0555
Medi-Mail	☎ 1-800-331-1458
AARP Pharmacy*	☎ 1-800-456-2226
Contact Lens Express	☎ 1-800-422-5367

* you do not need to be a member of AARP to take advantage of this service

- **Choose larger sizes of products you use frequently.**

The unit prices of most over-the-counter medications are usually cheaper in larger quantities. Buy larger sizes of pain medications, antacids, allergy drugs and hand creams or lotions.

- **Avoid multi-symptom cold medications, choosing products that treat specific symptoms instead.**

Multi-symptom products contain drugs you may not need. These drug combinations can also work against each other and prevent you from feeling better. Most doctors recommend treating specific problems with specific drugs for safer, more effective relief.

Stuffy Nose
Decongestant tablets or sprays containing pseudoephedrine including **Dimetapp, Drixoral, Sudafed, Triminic, Afrin, Dristan** *and* **Neosyne-phrine** *or generic brands.*

Runny Nose
Do not treat. A runny nose is part of the body's healing process and helps you get better faster.

Dry Cough
Products containing Dextro-methorpham, including **Benylin, Drixoral, Pertussin, Robitusson,** *or generic brands.*

Loose Cough
Products containing guaifenesin, including **Robitusson** *or generic brands.*

Sore Throat
Generic versions of pain relievers containing aspirin (adults only), ibuprofin, acetaminophen or naproxin.

- **Shop discount drug stores rather than full-service supermarkets.**

Supermarkets typically have higher prices on drugs because most of their marketing is focused on lower food prices. Discount drug stores generally buy in larger volume and often have a better selection of generic products.

Do home remedies really work?

Some do. Many medical conditions are self-limiting. You will get better regardless of the treatment. Home remedies are no worse than many over-the-counter medicines. In addition, many foods contain medicinal properties that can provide effective treatment of certain conditions. Always consult a physician if symptoms persist.

Home Remedies that Work

Bee Sting (non-allergic)	Raw Onion, Baking Soda
Canker Sore	Wet tea bag (to reduce pain and inflamation)
Cholesterol (lowering of)	Niacin or Psyllium (i.e., Metamusul)
Cold Symptoms	Chicken Soup
Constipation	Wheat Bran
Heart Attack (lessen risk of)	Aspirin*
Heartburn	Bananas or Chamomile Tea
Hemorrhoids	Vaseline
High Blood Pressure	Celery, Bananas
Mosquito Bite	Paste of Lemon Juice, Corn Starch and Witch Hazel
Motion Sickness	Ginger Root
Muscle Strains	Ice Pack, Aspirin
Urinary Infection (recurrence of)	Cranberry Juice

* Note: Always consult a physician before treating serious medical conditions or if symptoms persist. The use of aspirin to help prevent heart attack or Niacin to reduce cholesterol may cause serious side effects. Also consult a doctor before beginning such a program. Celery and bananas have been shown to provide some relief from mild forms of high blood pressure, but should not be used as a substitute for prescribed medicine. Again, consult a doctor.

Guide to CHOOSING THE BEST DOCTORS

Not all doctors and medical facilities are created equal. Just as some teachers are better than others and certain restaurants serve better food, medical centers and the people who work in them vary greatly in skill and expertise. Most patients are so intimidated by the medical profession that they simply assume that the person treating them knows what they are doing. In fact, by taking more initiative to find the very best doctors and hospitals, you can have a major impact on the quality of care you receive.

CHOOSE THE BEST DOCTOR WORKSHEET

Step 1

Select the right doctor.

Finding the right doctor is as much art as it is science. There are no published rating guides and the information that is available tends to be so general as to be almost useless. Unless your doctor has been convicted of fraud, you won't find out much by calling the local medical society. Therefore, you have to be somewhat of a detective in order to get a good sense of who the best doctors in your community are likely to be.

There are several factors you should consider in your choice of doctors that are knowable. These include a doctor's reputation in the community, his or her education, age and experience, personality and office policies.

To gather information on these various factors, proceed as follows.

Read your insurance policy.

Does your plan restrict you to certain physicians who practice in your area? If you belong to a Preferred Provider Network, chances are your insurance company publishes a list of doctors who are members of the plan. You will obviously have to limit your choice to these doctors. However, remember that you can choose among any of the doctors listed. Chances are you will find a physician with better experience in credentials closer to the largest, best-known hospital in your area. In other words, don't limit your choice to doctors who simply have an office in your neighborhood.

If you belong to a fee-for-service insurance plan, your choice of doctors is not nearly as limited. You will have a greater list of candidates, to be sure, but with more numbers comes the possibility of more confusion.

CHOOSE THE BEST DOCTOR WORKSHEET

Develop a preliminary list of doctors.

If you are working from a list of approved doctors within your health network, you will want to do some preliminary screening. You can do this based on several criteria. Ideally, you want a male or female doctor age 35-45, who attended a top medical school and is board certified in a particular speciality, such as internal medicine, pediatrics (for children) or family medicine.

Doctors in middle age generally have the best combination of up-to-date training and experience. Younger physicians, because they have been practicing for fewer years, are often lacking the "seasoning" which comes from seeing a large number of patients over an extended length of time. Older doctors obviously have the most experience, but they may not be as current in their training.

One gauge of whether a doctor is up-to-date in their knowledge of the latest developments in their field is whether they have been board-certified. To obtain certification, a doctor must complete rigorous post-graduate education requirements and pass competency exams. Not all doctors are board-certified, but the better ones usually are.

Another indicator of the quality of a doctor's education is which medical school he or she attended. The best medical schools typically turn out the better doctors since admission requirements are tougher and the curriculum more challenging. *U.S. News & World Report* publishes an annual guide to the top medical schools which you can access on their web site (www.usnews.com). There are also several other services which rank these facilities, but the following institutions are judeged as some of the best.

Top Medical Schools

Harvard	Washington Univ. (Mo.)
Yale	Univ. of Rochester
Stanford	NYU
Michigan	Univ. of N. Carolina
Northwestern	Univ. of Penn.
Tulane	Columbia
Vanderbilt	Cornell
Tufts	Duke
Johns Hopkins	Univ. of Minnesota
U. C. San Francisco	Univ. of Virginia
Univ. of Chicago	Georgetown
UCLA	

You can check out a doctor's credentials and education by either contacting his or her office, reviewing a synopsis prepared by your insurer, or by using the "Doctor Finder" locator at the *American Medical Association's* reference site (www.ama-assn.org).

CHOOSE THE BEST DOCTOR WORKSHEET

Seek recommendations from area hospitals or doctors.

Call the largest, best-known hospital in your area, preferably a facility affiliated with a major university medical school. Ask for the Hospital Administrator's office and then proceed with the dialogue below:

Sample Dialogue:

❝ Hello. I am relatively new to the area and I am looking for a recommendation for one of the best doctors in the area as my primary physician. I was wondering if you could tell me the names of several doctors affiliated with the hospital who are particularly well known and respected? I prefer a board-certified internist with at least five years of experience with the hospital. Incidentally, which doctor do you use? ❞

If you know someone in your community who is a doctor, ask them who they would choose as their primary physician, or who they might recommend to a friend.

Contact the doctor offices on your preliminary list.

Sample Dialogue:

❝ Hello. I am looking for a primary physician and I received Dr. _____'s name as a recommendation. If you don't mind, I was wondering if you could answer a few questions for me about the doctor's practice? ❞

CHOOSE THE BEST DOCTOR WORKSHEET

Phone Survey

Obtain the following Information for each doctor...

	Dr. #1	Dr. #2	Dr.#3

1. **Is your office accepting patients?**

2. **How does your office handle after-hours emergencies?** *(You don't want a doctor you can't reach when it's important.)*

3. **Is the doctor available for a phone consultation if I have a medical question?** *(Taking patient phone calls is a good indication of a doctor's personal style and willingness to communicate with his or her patients.)*

4. **What happens If my insurance company says the doctor's bill exceeds usual and customary charges?**

   Will your office intervene on my behalf?

5. **Is the doctor board-certified?**

   If so, in what specialities? (Board certification tells you the doctor has successfully completed additional course work and rigorous examinations in that specialty.)

6. **Does the doctor maintain evening or weekend hours?** *(Convenient hours are important if you find it difficult to leave work during the day.)*

Choose the best doctor.

Choose the best doctor based on your research. If you have more specific questions, call back and ask for a brief appointment to meet the doctor. A good family doctor should always be willing to meet you briefly for a short introduction.

CHOOSE THE BEST DOCTOR WORKSHEET

Step 2

Maximize the relationship with your doctor.

Once you find a good family doctor, your key to high-quality, value-oriented care is to ask plenty of questions during office visits. If your doctor does not patiently answer your questions, you need to find a new doctor.

Questions to ask your doctor...

Before any test

1. What will this test tell you?

2. Is it absolutely necessary?

3. Are there any risks associated with the test?

Before getting a prescription

1. Is the prescription the drug of choice for my condition?

2. Could I treat my condition conservatively, without drugs?

3. What are the side-effects?

4. Do you have any samples in the office?

5. Is their a generic version that might be less expensive?

6. Does it make sense to prescribe a larger dose? I wouldn't mind cutting the pill in half to cut down on the cost.

If you need surgery

1. What are the risks if I elect not to have surgery?

2. What are the risks if I do have the surgery?

3. Can my condition be treated conservatively with medication?

4. Before I say "yes," I would like to get a second opinion. Will you send copies of my records to whomever I choose?

5. Can I have my choice of surgery dates and hospitals? I would like to go to the best hospital in the area and prefer to avoid Mondays and Fridays.*

*(**Note:** According to statistics, a larger number of medical errors occur during periods of fatigue and stress, particularly at the start of the week and at the end.)

CHOOSE THE BEST DOCTOR WORKSHEET

Step 3

Choose the best hospital.
All hospitals are not created equal. There are big differences in the quality of care you receive at some hospitals versus others. Studies show that you face a greater risk of complications, infections and even death if you choose the wrong facility.

Medical centers affiliated with major universities are almost always your best hospital option.

These facilities are the first to receive the latest state-of-the-art technology. They also have the highest doctor/patient ratios and because they are teaching facilities, there is constant quality control and peer review.

American Medical Association (AMA) -approved community hospitals are the next best alternative. You can find out whether a hospital is AMA-approved simply by calling the hospital's office administrator.

Top-Rated Hospitals

Alabama	Birmingham Medical Center (University of Alabama)	**New York**	Mt. Sinai Hospital (NYC)
California	San Francisco Med. Cntr. (University of Cal., Berkely)		NYU Medical Cntr. (NYC)
	Stanford University Med. Cntr.		Columbia Presbyterian (NYC)
	Cedars Sinai Med. Cntr. (LA)		Cornell Med. Cntr. (NYC)
	UCLA Medical Center (LA)		Strong Mem. (Rochester)
Colorado	University of Colorado Health Science Center	**N. Carolina**	Duke Hospital (Durham)
		Ohio	Cleveland Clinic
			University Hosp. (Cleveland)

Pennsylvania Univ. of Penn. Med. Cntr. (Phildelphia)
Univ. of Pittsburgh Med. Cntr.

Texas Baylor Med. Cntr. (Houston)
SW Medical Cntr. (Dallas) (University of Texas)
Methodist Hospital (Houston)

Tennessee Vanderbilt Med. Cntr. (Nash.)

Washington University Hosp. (Seattle)

Connecticut Yale-New Haven Med. Cntr. / Hartford Hospital

Florida Jackson Mem. Hospital (Miami)

Georgia Emory University (Atlanta)

Illinois Michael Reese Hosp. (Chicago) / St. Lukes Hospital (Chicago) / University of Chicago Med. Cntr. / Northwestern Mem. Hosp. (Chicago)

Maryland Johns Hopkins (Baltimore)

Massachusetts Mass. General (Boston) / Brigham & Women's (Boston)

Michigan Henry Ford Med. Cntr. (Detroit) / University Hospital (Ann Arbor)

Minnesota University of Minnesota Med. Cntr. (Minneapolis) / Mayo Clinic (Rochester)

The Best Specialty Clinics in the U.S.

Cancer	Memorial Sloan Kettering Cancer Ctr.	NY, NY	☎ 212-639-2000
	Anderson Tumor Institute	Houston	☎ 713-792-2121
Heart	Miami Heart Institute	Miami	☎ 305-672-1111
	Cleveland Clinic	Cleveland	☎ 800-223-2273
Diabetes	Joslin Diabetes Clinic	Boston	☎ 617-732-2400
Eye	Mass. Eye & Ear Infirmiary	Boston	☎ 617-523-7900
	Jules Stein Eye Institute	L.A.	☎ 213-825-5000
	Wills Eye Hospital	Philadelphia	☎ 305-326-6000
	Scei Eye Institute	Miami	☎ 215-662-8100
Ear	Shea Clinic	Memphis	☎ 901-761-9720
Stroke	Patricia Neal Stroke Center	Knoxville	☎ 615-541-1167
Kidney	Lahey Clinic	Boston	☎ 617-237-5100
Alergies/ Immun.	Scripps Clinic	La Jolla	☎ 619-455-9100

CHOOSE THE BEST DOCTOR WORKSHEET

"For-profit" hospitals are often the least desirable choice. They are generally not as well staffed or equipped and the pressure to earn a profit can affect the quality of care.

Interestingly, Health Maintenance Organization (HMO) hospitals generally enjoy a good reputation. You are much less likely to be subjected to unnecessary treatment, tests or surgery, which is often your greatest risk whenever you are in a hospital.

Bigger hospitals are better. The larger the hospital, the more doctors, nurses, equipment and expertise. Five-hundred bed facilities are ideal.

U.S. News & World Report does an excellent job of rating hospitals throughout the United States. Try their interactive web site (www.usnews.com) which allows you to search for the best facilities in your area.

Guide to CHOOSING THE BEST HEALTH PLAN

Sixty-five percent of all Americans are insured under job-related health plans. If you are not insured at work, or if you have the option of choosing among several employer-subsidized plans, this worksheet will help you choose the best policy at the lowest price.

CHOOSE THE BEST HEALTH PLAN WORKSHEET

Step 1

Choose the best type of policy.

There are three types of medical insurance. Traditional fee-based plans like **Blue Cross/Blue Shield,** health maintenance organization (HMO) plans such as **Kaiser Permanente,** or preferred provider programs sponsored by insurers and affiliated doctors and hospitals.

No type of policy is best for everyone. The right policy for you depends upon your age and current health, your financial situation and the insurance needs of other family members. Monthly insurance premiums are an important consideration, but so is the amount you must pay for each doctor visit.

Fee Plans

Visit any doctor or hospital you choose.

Pay an annual deductible before receiving benefits.

Pay 20% of most doctor visits (co-payment).

No charge for customary costs of hospitalization, surgery or emergency care (exceptions apply).

HMOs

Visit only HMO doctors and hospitals.

Receive benefits immediately (no deductable).

No charge for doctors visits or minimal charge.

No charge for hospitalization, surgery or emergency care (no exceptions).

Preferred Provider Plans (PPO)

Visit doctors and hospitals who participate in the plan.

Pay an annual deductible before receiving benefits.

Minimal charge for doctor visits ($5-10/visit).

No charge for hospitalization, surgery or emergency care (exceptions apply).

CHOOSE THE BEST HEALTH PLAN WORKSHEET

Step 2

Locate the coverage you want.

Fee Service or PPO Plans

Look under "Insurance" in the Phone Directory and identify at least two independent agents who advertise as health insurance specialists. Also note the phone numbers for the local Blue *Cross/Blue Shield* plan in your area.

HMO Plans

Look under "Health Maintenance Organiza-tions" in the Phone Directory and identify at least two HMOs with facilities near your home or office.

INDEPENDENT AGENT   PHONE

_____   _____

_____   _____

BLUE CROSS/BLUE SHIELD   PHONE

_____   _____

HMO   PHONE

_____   _____

_____   _____

_____   _____

H
E
A
L
T
H

C
A
R
E

What Type of Insurance Is Best?

Young & Single
Fee Plan

Reason:
Fee plans have the lowest monthly premiums, making them the best choice for healthy young adults. Co-payments are not a significant factor since doctor visits are infrequent.

Just Married
Fee Plan or PPO

Reason:
Few visits to the doctor make fee plans the least expensive alternative. PPOs are recommended if you're planning a family since you will protect yourself against the high cost of maternity care while retaining the right to choose your doctor.

Young Family
HMO

Reason:
Kids require routine medical care quite often. With HMOs you'll avoid the costly 20% co-payments for doctor visits and check-ups.

Couples without Kids
Fee Plan

Reason:
Without kids, doctors visits will be less frequent, so a fee plan will cost you less overall. Fee plans also give you freedom of choice when you do need a doctor.

Mature Family
(children 14 or older)
HMO or PPO

Reason:
Adolescent children need more routine medical care than their parents, making HMOs the least costly plan overall. PPOs offer the same benefits while increasing your choice of doctors.

Older & Single
(ages 45-65)
Fee Plan

Reason:
As you get older, the chances of developing a serious illness increase. Fee plans allow you to seek out the best medical experts available. Co-payments may be high, but without children you can afford to devote a higher percentage of income to health care.

Retired Couple
(ages 65+)
HMO or Medicare-Subsidized Plan

Reason:
HMOs protect seniors on fixed income from unexpected medical bills with a single monthly premium and no paperwork. Newer, Medicare-subsidized plans, such as Secure Horizons, have no monthly fees and charge just $5 per doctor visit.

CHOOSE THE BEST HEALTH PLAN WORKSHEET

Step 3

Compare policies.
Use this dialogue and comparison chart when shopping for health insurance.

Sample Dialogue:

" Hello. I'm looking for a health insurance policy for myself (and my family). I would like to receive a price quote on the best plan(s) you have available. My age and medical history (and my family's) are as follows (state names, ages, whether any family members smoke, and any existing medical problems). I'd like to compare the features of several policies so I would appreciate it if you could describe the plans based on some questions I ask you. If you need a few minutes to get a price quote(s), I'd be happy to hold or you can call me back. "

Comparison Chart

		PLAN A	PLAN B	PLAN C	PLAN D	HMO
1	Name of Company				Blue Cross Blue Shield	
2	How much will the plan pay for the following:					
	In-office Doctor Visits	%	%	%	%	%
	Routine Physicals or Preventive Care	%	%	%	%	%
	Hospitalization	%	%	%	%	%
	Surgery	%	%	%	%	%
	Emergency Care	%	%	%	%	%
	Maternity Care	%	%	%	%	%
	Dental Care		%		%	%
	Mental Health Care	%	%	%	%	%
	Rehabilitation Therapy	%	%	%	%	%
	Prescriptions	%	%	%	%	%

3 Are there specific types of care which are not covered at all or at reduced costs?

Yes No	Yes No	Yes No	Yes No	Yes No
Exclusions	Exclusions	Exclusions	Exclusions	Exclusions
_____	_____	_____	_____	_____
_____	_____	_____	_____	_____
_____	_____	_____	_____	_____

4 Can coverage be terminated if the health status of any family member changes?

Yes No	Yes No	Yes No	Yes No	Yes No

5 Will my rates change if the health status of any family member changes?

Yes No	Yes No	Yes No	Yes No	Yes No

6 May I chose my own doctors?

Yes No	Yes No	Yes No	Yes No	**No**

7 Are there several deductible options available? What are they and to how many family members do the deductibles apply?

Annual Deductible Options	How many per family	Annual Deductible Options	How many per family	Annual Deductible Options	How many per family	Annual Deductible Options	How many per family	**No Deductible**
_____	1	_____	1	_____	1	_____	1	
_____	2	_____	2	_____	2	_____	2	
_____	3	_____	3	_____	3	_____	3	
_____	4	_____	4	_____	4	_____	4	
_____	Circle one	_____	Circle one	_____	Circle one	_____	Circle one	

8 What is my maximum co-payment per year?

Maximum Co-payment		Maximum Co-payment		Maximum Co-payment		Maximum Co-payment		**No Co-Payment**
_____	Per Person	_____	Per Person	_____	Per Person	_____	Per Person	
_____	Per Family	_____	Per Family	_____	Per Family	_____	Per Family	

9 Is there a maximum limit on benefits? If so, what is the amount?

Yes No	Yes No	Yes No	Yes No	Yes No
Amount	Amount	Amount	Amount	Amount
_____	_____	_____	_____	_____

10 Depending on the deductible I choose, how much is the monthly insurance premium?

Annual Deductible	Monthly Premium	Annual Deductible	Monthly Premium	Annual Deductible	Monthly Premium	Annual Deductible	Monthly Premium	Annual Deductible	Monthly Premium
_____	_____	_____	_____	_____	_____	_____	_____	_____	_____
_____	_____	_____	_____	_____	_____	_____	_____	_____	_____
_____	_____	_____	_____	_____	_____	_____	_____	_____	_____
_____	_____	_____	_____	_____	_____	_____	_____	_____	_____

HEALTH CARE

CHOOSE THE BEST HEALTH PLAN WORKSHEET

Step 4

Evaluate competing insurance plans.

Answering the following questions will help you sort through your insurance options and choose the policy that's best for your circumstances.

a. In the event of a serious health emergency, how much could you pay out of your pocket for medical care? (Circle one)

Less than $500	$500- $1,000	$1,000- $2,000	$2,000- $3,000	$3,000- $4,000	$4,000- $5,000

b. How often does your family require medical care?

More than once a month	Once per month	Once every 3 months	Once every 6 months	Once every year	Almost never

c. Do you anticipate any medical problems in the foreseeable future or a worsening of present conditions?

_____

_____

d. Is a future pregnancy likely?

Yes   No

e. Which insurance plan outlined in step 3 offers the most comprehensive protection for the type(s) of care your family may need in the foreseeable future?

_____

f. Which combination of deductible and maximum co-payment results in the lowest monthly premium?

Max. co-payment	Annual deductible	Monthly premium

g. Is the annual deductible more than you can afford?

Yes   No

h. Do you expect a high frequency of doctor visits throughout the next year?

Yes   No

If so, will co-payments noticeably increase your cost of medical care? (Especially for young families who visit doctors frequently.)

Yes   No

i. Which plan meets your anticipated health care needs for the foreseeable future?

_____

Guide to
CHOOSING THE BEST MEDIGAP INSURANCE

If you are 65 or older, you are entitled to medical benefits under the federally sponsored Medicare program. Unfortunately, there are huge gaps in Medicare protection which can cost you plenty if you suffer a serious illness. Therefore, you should probably acquire a supplemental policy that protects you against prolonged hospitalization costs and other charges which exceed Medicare's maximum allowances.

This worksheet will guide you through the steps necessary to find the best supplemental policies.

BEST MEDIGAP INSURANCE WORKSHEET

Step 1

If you are 65 or older, contact your nearest Social Security office to register for Medicare benefits if you have not already done so.

*For the office nearest you, contact the Social Security Hotline: **800-772-1213***

Step 2

Learn how the Medicare plan works before you shop for a supplemental policy.

See chart on page 302.

BEST MEDIGAP INSURANCE WORKSHEET

Medicare Benefits Explained

	Hospitalization Part "A"	Doctors Visits (Optional) Part "B"
Cost	FREE	$45 per month
What's Covered	Hospital room Intensive care General nursing Hospital rehab. services Lab work & x-rays	Office Exams and Treatment Ambulance Service Emergency care Lab tests and x-rays Medical equipment prescribed for home use
What's Not Covered	Doctor's fees Private hospital room Nursing home or custodial care	Prescriptions, Physicals, Eye or Dental care, Immunizations
Deductible	$760 per hospitalization of 60 days (Return visits within 60 days are considered one hospitalization.)	$100 per year
What You Pay After Deductible	1-60 days in hospital: $0 60-90 days in hospital: $190/day 90-150 days in hospital: $380/day 150+ days in hospital:100% of charges	20% of allowable charges plus 100% of non-allowable charges (Many doctors' charges exceed Medicare allowances)

Step 3

Add a Medigap policy that fits your needs.

When describing the benefits of each of the Medigap plans, insurance companies must use the same format, language and definitions. They also are required to use a uniform chart and outline of coverage to summarize the benefits. These requirements are intended to make it easier for you to compare policies. As you shop for a Medigap policy, keep in mind that each company's products are alike, so they are competing on service, reliability and price. Prices vary significantly so shop multiple sources!

Medicare supplement insurance can be sold in only 10 standard plans. This chart shows the benefits included in each plan. Every company must make available plan "A." Some plans may not be available in your state. Basic benefits, which apply to all plans, include an additional 365 days of hospitalization after Medicare benefits end and the 20% co-insurance deductible for doctor visits, tests and other approved treatments.

Medigap policies can also be sold as "Medicare SELECT" plans. The only difference between Medicare SELECT and stan-

BEST MEDIGAP INSURANCE WORKSHEET

dard Medigap insurance is that each insurer has specific hospitals, and in some cases specific doctors, that you must use, except in an emergency, in order to be eligible for full benefits. Medicare SELECT policies generally have lower premiums because of this requirement.

You may also opt to purchase Medigap coverage through an HMO or health network. Each plan has its own network of hospitals, skilled nursing facilities, home health agencies, doctors and other professionals. Depending on how the plan is organized, services are usually provided at one or more centrally located health care facilities or in the private practice offices of the doctors and other health care professionals that are part of the plan.

Standard Medigap Policies

PLAN	A	B	C	D	E	F	G	H	I	J
Basic Benefit	✔	✔	✔	✔	✔	✔	✔	✔	✔	✔
Skilled Nursing Co-insurance			✔	✔	✔	✔	✔	✔	✔	✔
Part "A" Deductible		✔	✔	✔	✔	✔	✔	✔	✔	✔
Part "B" Deductible			✔			✔				✔
Excess Part "B" Charges						✔	✔		✔	✔
Foreign Travel Emergency			✔	✔	✔	✔	✔	✔	✔	✔
At Home Recovery				✔			✔		✔	✔
Basic Drug Benefit ($1,250 limit)								✔	✔	✔
Preventive Care					✔					✔

BEST MEDIGAP INSURANCE WORKSHEET

Step 4

Contact an independent insurance agent who specializes in health insurance benefits.

Also look in the phone book for HMO plans in your area. Tell the agent what kind of Medigap policy you want and ask him for price quotes from competing carriers. Also ask him about the reputations of the companies for quality care and service. You will probably want a plan that already includes your current doctor(s) in its network. Beware of attained age policies that are less expensive in early years but become much more expensive as you get older. Issue-age or community-rated plans are preferable.

Step 5

Make your choice

Based on your survey, decide which insurance provider to choose for your medigap policy. Make certain you always compare policies in the same letter-grade category.

BEST MEDIGAP INSURANCE WORKSHEET

Medical Information Resources

Doctors Guide to the Internet
www.pslgroup.com
Best site for medical links of all kinds

Healthfinder
www.healthfinder.gov
Gateway for U.S. gov't. health resources

Medline
www.nlm.nih.gov
National Health Institute Library of Medicine

Mayo Clinic
www.mayo.ivi.com
General reference site to top medical clinic in U.S.

Health A to Z
www.healthatoz.com
General health search engine

American Medical Association
www.ama-assn.org
Check on background of any doctor in the U.S.

Medicine Net
www.medicinenet.com
Commercial site on drugs & medicines

Rx List
www.rxlist.com
Information about pharmaceuticals

Medical Matrix
www.slackinc.com/matrix
Annotated health links for professionals

Info Med
http://infomed.yale.edu
Link to Yale Medical School library

Alternative Medicine Link
www.pittedu~cbw/altm.html
Links to non-traditional medical treatment

Homeopathic Information
www.hotwired.com/drweil
Harvard expert on alternative thearapies

Dr. Koop
www.drkoop.com
General medical site with links, forums, etc.

Special Services

Shriner's Hospital Referral
www.shrinershq.org
813-281-0300
Free care to children needing burn/orthop. services

Hospital Free Care
www.institute-dc.org
800-638-0742
Free services to qualified under Hill/Burton Act

Free Prescription Drugs
www.ims-l.com~freerx
573-778-1118
Free prescriptions for qualified patients in need

Free Prescription Drugs
www.phrma.org/patient
Directory of programs for subsidized prescriptions

Child Air Support
www.childtransport.org
888-296-1217
Free air travel to children needing medical care

Organ Transplant
www.unos.org
888-894-6361
Information on organ donor/recipient programs

BEST MEDIGAP INSURANCE WORKSHEET

Special Services continued

Living Bank
www.livingbank.org
Organ Transplant information

Doctor Help Line
www.allexperts.com/
medical/index.shtml
Doctors who answer your questions online

Med Help Line
www.medhelp.org
Ask your question. Dr. responds by e-mail

Specific Diseases

AIDS

Aids National Info Clearinghouse
www.cdcnpin.org
800-458-5231

Experimental Treatment Program
www.actis.org
800-874-2572

Allergies

Ntl. Institute for Allergies
www.niaid.hih.gov

Am. College of Allergy & Immunology
http://allergy.mcg.edu/

ALS

ALS Foundation
www.als.org
800-782-4747

Alzheimer's Disease

Alzheimer Page
www.biostat.wvstl.edu
/alzheimer

National Alzheimer's Assn.
www.alz.org
800-272-3900

Arthritis

National Arthritis Foundation
www.arthritis.org
800-283-7800

Asthma

Asthma Information Line
www.aaai.org
800-822-2762

National Asthma Center
www.njrc.org
800-222-5864

Birth Defects

National Easter Seals Society
www.easter-seals.org
800-221-6827

Blindness

National Eye Care Project
www.eyenet.org
800-222-3937

Breast Cancer

Breast Cancer Info Links
http://homeatt.net/~kis
safrog/links.html

Cancer

National Cancer Institute
http://cancernet.nci.ni
h.gov/use
800-422-6237

American Cancer Society
www.cancer.org
800-227-2345

BEST MEDIGAP INSURANCE WORKSHEET

Specific Diseases

Onco-Link
www.oncolink.upenn.edu/

Crohn's Disease
Ntl. Crohn's & Colitis Found.
www.ccfa.com
800-932-2423

Cystic Fibrosis
Cystic Fibrosis Foundation
www.cff.org
800-344-4823

Depression
Mental Health Net
www.cmhc.com

National Depressive Assn.
www.ndmda.org
800-826-3632

Depression Link
www.psycom.net/depression.central.html

Diabetes
American Diabetes Assoc.
www.diabetes.org
800-582-8323

Diabetes Research Institute
www.drinet.org

Juvenile Diabetes Foundation
www.jdfcure.com
800-533-2873

Downs Syndrome
National Downs Syndrome Society
www.ndss.org
800-221-4602

Endometriosis
National Endometriosis Association
www.endometriosisassn.org
800-992-3636

Epilepsy
The Epilepsy Foundation
www.efa.org
800-332-1000

Eye Disease
Eye Disease Web Link
http://webeye.ophth.uiowa.edu/dept/websites/eyeres.htm

Glaucoma
Glaucoma Research Foundation
www.glaucoma.org
800-826-6693

Gynecological Disorders
OB-GYN Net
www.obgyn.net

Headache
National Headache Foundation
www.headaches.org
800-523-8858

Heart Disease
American Heart Association
www.amhrt.org
800-242-8721

Heart Info Network
www.heartinfo.org

American College of Cardiology
www.acc.org

Kidney Disease
National Kidney Foundation
www.kidney.org
800-622-9010

NIH Institute on Kidney Disease
www.niddk.nih.gov
301-496-3583

Lupus
Lupus Web Links
www.hamline.edu/lupus

BEST MEDIGAP INSURANCE WORKSHEET

Specific Diseases

Lung Disease
American Lung Association
www.lungusa.org
800-586-4872

Multiple Sclerosis
National M.S. Society
www.nmss.org
800-624-8236

Intl. M.S. Support Foundation
www.msnews.org

Osteoporosis
National Osteoporosis Foundation
www.osteo.org
800-624-2663

Parkinson's Disease
Am. Parkinson's Disease Assoc.
www.apdaparkinson.com
800-223-2732

National Parkinson's Foundation
www.parkinson.org
800-327-4545

Prostate Cancer
Prostate Cancer Homepage
www.cancer.med.umich.edu/prostean/prost-can.html

Rare Diseases
Ntl. Org. for Rare Disorders
www.pcnet.com/~orphan
800-447-6673

Sexually Transmitted Diseases
STI Healthcare Network
www.sti.healthcare.org.uk

Spinal Cord Injuries
Spinal Cord Resource Center
www.goes.com
800-962-8629

Stroke
National Stroke Association
www.stroke.org
800-787-6537

HERE'S THE PROOF

Estimates vary, but according to several widely respected consumer organizations, as many as 50% of the surgical procedures and drugs prescribed by American doctors may be unnecessary.

Such a statistic is difficult to prove, but we think this chapter can help you become a more informed and aggressive advocate for your own health. Even though we can't quantify the benefits of this approach, there are other suggestions in this chapter that will help you get better value for your health care dollar

Suggestion: Lower your monthly health health insurance premiums by raising your deductibles.

Example: We obtained rate quotes on a major medical/hospitalization policy for a 35-year-old man (non-smoker) living in the suburban Washington, D.C. area. A policy offered by Washington National Insurance Company was typical. By raising the annual deductible from $250 to $1,000, we lowered the premiums by $781 per year. Even in a bad year when medical bills exceed $1,000, the higher deductible policy still saves you money.

Note: If your annual medical expenses are less than $1,000, you obviously save money with higher deductibles, but you still save money even if your medical bills are much higher. For example, with $2,500 in medical bills, your total out-of-pocket expense for insurance premiums, deductibles and 20% co-payment are $3,590 under the low-deductible policy, but only $3,108 with the high-deductible plan, a $482 savings.

Suggestion: Shop carefully among competing pharmacies for the price on prescription drugs.

Example: We surveyed prices at dozens of pharmacies in Bethesda and Silver Spring, Maryland, looking for the best deals on a number of popular prescription medicines. In the most outrageous example, the highest-priced source was more than twice as expensive as the low price leader.

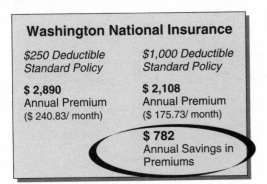

Washington National Insurance

$250 Deductible Standard Policy	$1,000 Deductible Standard Policy
$ 2,890 Annual Premium ($ 240.83/ month)	**$ 2,108** Annual Premium ($ 175.73/ month)
	$ 782 Annual Savings in Premiums

HERE'S THE PROOF

Suggestion: Buy generic versions of over-the-counter pain medications (i.e., aspirin, acetaminophen, ibuprofen) instead of more expensive name brands of the same drugs.

Shelf Prices @ CVS Pharmacy
Herndon, VA

	Quantity	Dosage	Price	Savings
ASPIRIN				
Generic CVS Aspirin	200 tablets	325 mg	$ 2.47	$ 7.40
Bayer Aspirin	200 tablets	325 mg	$ 9.87	
ACETAMINOPHEN				
Generic CVS Acetaminophen	30 tablets	500 mg	$ .97	$ 3.12
Tylenol Acetaminophen	30 tablets	500 mg	$ 4.09	
IBUPROFEN				
Generic CVS Ibuprofen	165 tablets	200 mg	$ 6.97	$ 4.52
Advil Ibuprofen	165 tablets	200 mg	$ 11.49	

Chapter Twelve

Home Electronics, Computers and Major Appliances

How do I find the lowest prices on electronics and computer equipment?

Before you worry about price, think about *value*. All too often, shoppers rush to buy a camera, TV, stereo or computer without doing their homework. They don't know which manfacturers build the most reliable equipment or which features are the best gauge of quality and performance. Instead, they jump at anything on sale because of the low price, or they pay a premium for top-of-the-line equipment with lots of "bells and whistles" they will rarely use.

To make sure you select a product with the best combination of price, features and reliability, start by reviewing the buying guides available at your local library, such as those published by ***Consumer Reports*** www.consumereports.com or ***Consumers' Digest*** www.consumers digest.com. You can also try ***CompareNet***, www.comparenet.com. These sources will give you specific advice on particular product categories, manufacturers and model numbers. For more general information, consult the buying instruction guide at the end of this chapter.

Only after you have identified the best models and manufacturers should you then focus on finding sources with the lowest prices.

Where do I begin my search?

Start by getting a price from a local retailer like ***Circuit City***, ***Best Buy*** or ***Comp U.S.A.*** Then use the sources contained in our buying instruction guide. We've identified a number of unconventional sources where you are likely to find some of the lowest prices on virtually every category of appliance, home electronics and computer equipment. In most cases, these sources can be contacted by phone or via the internet. Once you've compared these discount sources with retailers in your area, you should have no trouble finding the best deal.

How useful is the internet in finding the lowest price?

As we said, many of the best discount sources can be contacted by telephone.

However, there is no question that the web can make your search easier and more efficient provided you know what you're doing. Just because you can type a model number into a search engine doesn't mean you're going to locate a bargain. You must know which sites are likely to yield the best results for a given product category. Otherwise, you can literally waste hours searching among thousands of sites that promise bargains but rarely deliver.

The net is also better for locating bargains in certain categories more than others. It's particularly good for computer equipment and software, which stands to reason since computer experts were the original internet pioneers. You can buy computer stuff through cyberspace auctions, you can use internet shopping agents to search dozens of vendors for the lowest prices or you can contact some manufacturers directly. Outside the computer category, the performance of the internet is more sporadic in locating bargains. This is particuliarly true for large appliances, TV equipment and stereos.

Tell me about internet shopping agents. Can they really help me to find the best deals?

Shopping agents, often referred to as "BOTS", are specialized internet search engines that will allow you to compare prices among vendors for a particular product. Simply enter the manufacturer and model you're looking for and the BOT will search its database and report back the results identifying the lowest-priced sources.

Because BOTS only search for prices on the internet, and because computers and computer equipment are the products most often sold online, it stands to reason that BOTS are most effective for comparing prices on computer products. They are far less effective for home electronics, cameras and other equipment, where it is recommended that you contact discount sources directly.

From a merchant or manufacturer's perspective, shopping BOTS have a frightening potential since they give consumers power to find the lowest prices with very little effort. Not surprisingly, bigger internet players have stepped in to rob the BOTS of some of their early potential. Recently, companies like *America Online*, *Amazon.Com*, *Yahoo!* and *Excite@Home* have acquired independent BOT services which have been reconfigured to conduct narrow searches among vendors who pay to be listed on the BOT service. Rather than true shopping robots that scan the entire internet, these watered-down services are really glorified advertising directories. To offset this problem, we recommended that any time you conduct a price search on the internet, you survey at least three BOTS to assure that you are getting a representative vendor sample.

Some of the highest-rated BOTS include *C-Net* (www.shopper.com), *Killer App Express* (www.killerapp.com) and *Price Scan* (www.pricescan.com).

What about internet auctions. How do they work?

Imagine you were sitting in the audience of a major auction house. Items would be presented for your consideration and you could bid on anything that sparked your interest. An internet auction works the same way except all the action is in cyberspace. Say someone wants to sell a computer monitor. For a modest fee (usually $10 or 5% of the sales price) they post a description of the item on the auction web site, along with a suggested opening price and a deadline for accepting bids. Prospective buyers submit bids via e-mail, which in turn are posted on the web site for everyone to see. When the bidding is closed, the successful bidder is notified to forward a payment either directly to the seller or to the auction house which acts as an escrow agent. The seller, in turn, ships the item to the bidder. As soon as the bidder inspects the item and accepts delivery, the payment is released to the seller.

Aren't auctions time-consuming?

They certainly aren't as easy as walking into a store and handing over your Visa card. First, you have to determine whether an item is for sale on a given auction site. Then you must devote time to submitting your offer and revising it as the auction proceeds, possibly over a period of days or weeks. Finally, you must arrange for payment, be present for delivery and deal with the hassles of a return shipment if the product is not acceptable. Because of the potential headaches, auctions are only worth the extra effort when the bargains are

truly exceptional. To improve your chances of success at an auction, keep the following rules in mind:

Do your homework.
Research the quality and reliability of a particular brand, as well the item's fair market value or retail price before submitting an offer. If you're not saving at least 40%, don't bother.

Bid early.
Most auctions give priority based on the first time you place a bid. If someone else bids more, you just need to match their price to come out on top.

Bid low.
You can always raise your offer if the bidding requires it, always keeping in mind that the final price you pay should be at least 40% better than what you would pay from conventional sources.

Check out the vendor.
At many auction sites, you can look up information about the reliability of the seller you are dealing with. If you can't find any information, you can also search for the vendor's name in various internet news groups where comments might be posted. Conduct your search using the **Deja News** search engine (www. dejanews.com). If you still can not find any information, do not hesitate to contact a seller by phone to set your mind at ease.

Use a credit card, pay C.O.D. or request an escrow transaction.
You can get a full refund from your credit card company, even if the vendor refuses to cooperate, in the case of fraud or other deception. In no event should you ever pre-pay with cash or check. Escrow services, such as **I-Escrow**

(www.iescrow.com) and **Trade-Direct** (www.trade-direct.com), are neutral third parties that assure both the buyer and seller are protected.

What are the best auction sites?

E-Bay (www.ebay.com) and **Amazon. com** (www.amazon.com) have the largest sites, but you might also check out **Web Auction** (www.webauction.com), **UBid** (www.ubid.com), **Price Watch** (www.pricewatch.com) and **On Sale** (www.onsale.com).

You can locate auction sites that are likely to carry a certain category of products by logging on to the **Internet Auction List** (www.internetauction-list.com). You can even be more specific by using **BidFind** (www.vsn.com), a site which allows you to search more than 100 auction sites simultaneously for the item you are trying to locate.

What if I don't have access to the internet?

Obviously, you can't participate in an internet auction or use a shopping BOT without online access. Nevertheless, many discount sources can be contacted directly by phone.. In fact, getting answers from a real person can often be more efficient than surfing through reams of data, particularly if you know precisely what you're trying to find.

Will I always do better from a discount source or internet vendor than I will from my local retailer?

It is rare that a local retailer can beat the prices from the sources we've iden-

tified, but it is not uncommon for a local merchant to come close to these discount prices, particularly on selected items. We always suggest that you contact at least one merchant in your area in addition to the vendors listed in the book. If can find a local price which is comparable to the internet/mail order source, buy the item locally.

Some additional factors to consider:
- **Sales Tax**
  If you buy over the phone or via the internet from an out-of-state source, you are not generally charged sales tax. The added savings can be significant, particularly for expensive electronic components and computer equipment.

- **Delivery Charges**
  Always factor shipping charges into the cost of any item that will be delivered to you. In some cases, the added costs can offset a lower sales price, tipping your decision in favor of a local merchant.

- **Repairs**
  It is always easier to return an item to a local merchant if something goes wrong immediately after you buy it. However a manufacturer's warranty, which is your only protection after 30 days, is honored by local repair shops regardless of where you purchased the equipment.

Is it fair to get advice from a local salesperson and then buy from somebody else?

That's a personal decision, but in our view there is nothing wrong with visiting local stores as part of your effort to learn everything you can about your buying options. Keep in mind that advice from a salesman may or may not be accurate. You are better off doing your research from unbiased sources like **Consumer Reports** or **Consumers Digest.**

Should I buy an extended warranty?

No. Extended warranties are high-profit add-ons which are generally not worth the premium. In fact, some vendors sell at rock-bottom prices hoping to make up the difference with an over-priced warranty. If a component does not fail during the normal warranty period, chances are it will work for years without a breakdown. Perhaps the only extended service plan that may be worth buying is the one that promises free technical support for your computer purchase. Unless you are a computer expert, fixing inevitable hardware and software glitches on your own can be time-consuming and frustrating. Under these circumstances, being able to contact an expert 24 hours-a-day is well worth the additional expense.

What's the best tip for saving money on major appliances?

Forget "bells" and "whistles." Manufacturers add digital displays, more cycles, extra compartments or other extras to justify higher prices and bigger profits. Standard models typically do the same job without the hype for a lot less money. For example, a famous-maker washer with standard controls and regular wash cycles cost $345 at a major retail chain. Adding digital displays and a fancy nameplate raises the price of the "deluxe" model to $629, even though the two versions have identical motors and interior components.

How do I tell the difference between an extra feature that adds value and a gimmick?

Common sense is your best guide. Remember that the basic technology that drives washing machines, clothes dryers, refrigerators, ovens and disposals has not changed in 50 years. In almost every case, cheaper models are as good or nearly as good as their more expensive cousins. Here's a specific list of features that are not worth the extra money:

Superfluous Features

Dishwashers

- Digital controls
- Second spray unit
- Designer colors

Clothes Dryers

- Digital controls
- 3 or more dry cycles
- Pot scrubber cycle

Clothes Washers

- Digital controls
- Enhanced agitator
- Designer colors

Microwaves

- Browning elements
- Turntables
- Temperature probes

Refrigerators

- Multi-zone temperature controls
- Designer colors
- Special compartments

Where can I get the best deals on major appliances?

Usually the best source for major appliances are discount retailers like **K-Mart,**

Walmart, **Wards**, **Circuit City** or **Best Buy**. Wait for clearance sales and compare prices at several stores before buying. Mail-order or web vendors rarely can offer the best prices because of the high cost of shipping and installation.

Are utility costs an important consideration in selecting appliances?

Yes, in some cases. The annual electric bill for a 19 cubic ft. refrigerator can be as low as $157 or as high as $215, depending on the brand you choose. Since the useful life of a refrigerator is 15 years or longer, the savings you can realize from choosing an energy-efficient model is much more than the difference in price. Differences in electrical usage for dishwashers, clothes washers, dryers and microwave ovens is less significant.

Comparing Operating Costs for Refrigerators

	1 year	5 years	10 years	20 years
Most-efficient model	$157	$785	$1,570	$3,140
Least-efficient model	$215	$1,075	$2,150	$4,300
TOTAL SAVINGS	$58	$290	$580	$1,160

How do I know whether to repair or replace an appliance?

Most major appliances are incredibly durable. In fact, there are relatively few moving parts that can break. In most cases, replacing a burned-out motor or malfunctioning switch means that you can expect years of additional service from your machine. However, a large percentage of appliances are replaced, not because they wear out or break down, but because they no longer look fashionable. How many avocado-green refrigerators have you seen lately?

Guide to BUYING STEREO EQUIPMENT, TV's, VCR's, CAMERAS AND HOME ELECTRONICS

Recommended Discount Sources

For Stereos, TVs and Electronics

Wholesale Connection
800-226-2800
www.wholesale
connection.com

Sound City
800-542-7283
www.soundcity.com

Webtronics
800-444-6300
www.sammans.com

Consumer Direct Warehouse
800-789-4260
www.consumer-direct.com

Electronics Zone
800-327-5815
www.800.com

For Cameras

Camera World
800-222-1557
www.cameraworld.com

Focus Camera
800-221-0828
www.focuscamera.com

Cambridge Camera
800-221-2253
www.cambridgeny.com

Wall St. Camera
800-221-4090
www.wallstreetcamera.
com

Best Stop Digital Camera
800-339-8357
www.beststopdigital.com

47th St. Photo
212-398-6812
www.47stphoto.com

HOME ELECTRONICS

✔ BUYING TIPS

For All Electronics

✔ **Don't fall in love with engineering.**

One of the biggest scams in home electronics is to seduce shoppers with impressive-sounding engineering specifications. Manufacturers will boast that their products have more amps, more watts and more power than the competition in order to support a higher price tag. The fact is that in most cases, the slight gain in performance is rarely worth the extra cost. Stick with mid-range performance for the best value. Chances are you'll never notice the difference.

✔ **Forget the extras.**

Electronics manufacturers make their biggest profits when they add extra features (bells & whistles) to their standard machines. Unless you really need the super-slow motion on your camcorder or the dual-screen TV, opt for a model without the frills.

Equipment Ratings

Consumer Reports
www.consumereports.com

Consumers Digest
www.consumersdigest.com

Compare Net
www.compare.net

Stereo Equipment

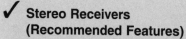

✔ **Stereo Receivers (Recommended Features)**
- 50-60 watts per channel (normal systems)
- 60-100 watts per channel (surround sound systems)
- Sensitivity rating of 12.0dBf or less Distortion of less than .1% THD

Avoid over-powered receivers unless you are planning on an elaborate surround-sound system. Quality among all the major manufacturers is generally good.

✔ BUYING TIPS

✔ **CD Players**
(Recommended Features)
- Multi-disc carousel loading

Shop for the best deal. Sound quality is excellent, regardless of the manufacturer or price.

✔ **Cassette Decks**
(Recommended Features)
- 2 recording heads
- 2 or 3 drive motors
- Dolby C or Dolby S (best) noise-reduction system

Unless you already have an extensive tape collection, why bother with a cassette machine? CD systems are far superior. If you want a cassette machine to dub music tapes, choose a mid-priced system, since performance is noticeably worse in cheaper models.

✔ **Speakers**
(Recommended Features)
- none

Forget about "frequency response" and other technical specifications. Speakers with identical specs can sound very different. The best gauge of any speaker is to compare it with the competition and you must do so in-person. Listen for clarity and richness, not volume. Allocate at least 50% of your overall sound system budget for speakers. Better speakers should cost $400 to $700 per pair. True audiophiles think nothing of speakers that cost $1,000 per pair. There is no difference between surround- sound speakers and regular stereo.

✔ **TVs**
(Recommended Features)
- none

Price and screen size are the determining factors, since differences in picture quality among the major brands is slight. Viewing performance is influenced more by the signal source (i.e., over-the-air reception, cable, satellite) than by the TV itself. Most extras aren't worth the money, but enhanced audio is a good investment. 27" screens are the standard for the primary TV in most homes, although 30-35" are gaining in popularity. Projection TVs (45"-60") are popular for home theatre set-ups, but they sacrifice brightness and clarity for size.

HOME ELECTRONICS

✔ BUYING TIPS

✔ VCRs
(Recommended Features)

- 2-head machines are adequate. Four or 6-head models have noticeably better slow-motion capabilities, but few people use these features enough to justify the added expense.
- On-screen programming
- Hi-fi sound capability for your primary machine. Mono sound is o.k. for the bedroom or kitchen.
- Forget the hype surrounding high-end machines. Simple is better.

✔ Camcorders

Three formats to choose from, each with pros and cons:

VHS: Large, bulky camera allows you to plug full-size tapes directly into your VCR with no adapter.

VHS-C: Compact mini-cassette plugs into your VCR with adapter housing. Recording times are relatively short (30 minutes) and sound quality is only fair.

8mm: Mini-cassettes can hold two hours of quality video with improved sound quality, but camcorder must be plugged into your TV to view tapes.

Note that all three systems have upgraded versions with superior picture quality (SVHS, SVHS-C and Hi-8). These systems are more expensive than regular versions and require TV sets which are equipped with S video inputs. Unless you plan on a re-make of "Gone with the Wind," buy a standard model with basic features including a 10-12x zoom. Color viewfinders, image stabilizers and larger zoom lenses aren't needed and needlessly increase the price you'll pay.

Cameras

✔ **Point & Shoot
(Recommended Features)**
- 38-70mm or 30-105mm zoom lens
- Auto-focus (avoid "fixed focus" or "focus-free models)

Best camera if you care more about memories than taking professional-quality photographs. Choose from cameras which use standard 35 mm film or newer APS film cartridges. APS cameras are generally smaller and allow users to choose standard, wide angle and panoramic versions of every shot. The advantage of cameras that use the 35mm format is that film is cheaper and pictures cost less to develop.

✔ **Single Lens Reflex [SLR]
(Recommended Features)**
- 35-135mm or 28-200mm zoom lens (pass up typical 50mm lens)
- Auto focus/auto exposure
- LCD panel display

The right choice if you want top-quality photographs and don't mind the extra weight and slightly-longer set-up time. Available in both 35mm and APS film formats.

✔ **Digital
(Recommended Features)**
- 1,152 x 875 pixel resolution or better
- Removable/reusable memory cards
- Optical zoom lens
- Optical and LCD color viewfinders

View pictures immediately, save on development costs, e-mail your results anywhere in the world, print copies in any size format and store your pictures on optional CD-ROM disks. The camera of the future, priced accordingly.

ELECTRONICS

HOME ELECTRONICS WORKSHEET

Step 1

Before you shop, research the equipment and features you are looking for using *Consumer Reports* or *Consumers Digest* recommendations.

Recommended Manufacturer(s)

_____

_____

_____

Recommended Model(s)

_____

_____

_____

Step 2

What are the most important features for the equipment you are purchasing, based on the recommendations in Step 1 as well as the information summarized in this chapter?

Features I Need

_____

_____

_____

Features I Don't Need

_____

_____

_____

Step 3

Go to the nearest discount electronics or camera store in your area (*Circuit City, Best Buys, Wards,* etc.) and research the prices for models which match the criteria you've identified in Steps 1 and 2. Don't purchase the item yet.

Manufacturer

_____

_____

_____

Model No.

_____

_____

_____

Price

_____

_____

_____

HOME ELECTRONICS WORKSHEET

Step 4

Contact several of the discount
sources identified in this chapter.
Do they beat the price(s) from your
local retailer? Don't forget to consider shipping charges. Also,
remember that you probably won't
pay sales tax on an order from an
out-of-state source.

Discount Source	Model	Price (including shipping)
_____	_____	_____
_____	_____	_____
_____	_____	_____

Step 5

If you have extra time, consider doing
a product search on the internet
using a shopping agent such as *C-
Net* (www.shopper.com), *Killer App
Express* (www.killerapp.com) or
Price Scan (www.pricescan.com).

Step 6

If the price from a discount source is
significantly better than your local
retailer, buy from the discount
source. If there is little price advantage, buy locally.

Guide to BUYING COMPUTERS

Recommended Discount Sources

Computers, Peripherals and Software

Computer Discount Warehouse
800-806-4239
www.cdw.com

PC Connection
800-243-8088
www.pcconnection.com

Microwarehouse
800-397-8508
www.warehouse.com

PC Nation
800-969-5255
www.pcnation.com

Universal Computer
800-960-1688
www.ucdweb.com

First Source
800-858-9866
www.firstsource.com

Egghead
(web only)
www.egghead.com

Manufacturer Direct

Dell Computer
800-999-3355
www.dell.com

Gateway
800-846-4208
www.gateway.com

Compaq
800-282-6672
www.compaq.com

Apple
800-795-1000
www.apple.com

Hewlett Packard
800-829-4444
www.hp.com

IBM
800-411-1932
www.ibm.com

Tangent
800-223-6677
www.tangent.com

Micron Electronics
800-423-5891
www.micronpc.com

Quantex
800-346-6685
www.quantex.com

Used Computer Equipment

Boston Computer Exchange
617-625-7722
www.bocoex.com

Computer Renaissance
612-520-8583
www.cr1.com

Web Shopping Agents

Killer App Express
www.killerapp.com

C-Net
www.cnet.com

Price Scan
www.pricescan.com

Product Finder
www.excite.com

Shop the Web
www.amazon.com

Recommended Discount Sources *continued*

Online Equipment Auctions

Bidfind
www.bidfind.com

UBid
www.ubid.com

Web Auction
www.webauction.com

Price Watch
www.pricewatch.com

On Sale
www.onsale.com

E-Bay
www.ebay.com

Haggle Online
www.haggle.com

✓ Buying Tips

In General

✓ Consider the future.

Because computer technology becomes "old" approximately every 18 months, you should anticipate the move to ever faster and more powerful machines by purchasing a system which incorporates the latest developments for a computer of its size and class. Buying last year's model at a discount may not seem like such a good deal three or four years from now.

✓ Don't buy more than you need.

Entry-level PCs for the home can be purchased for $800 or less, while high-performance systems capable of running the most sophisticated business and game software can cost $2,500 to $3,500. You wouldn't buy a tractor if all you needed was a lawn mower, so don't buy the most elaborate computer system if something more basic will do.

This is particularly true if you plan on using your computer almost exclusively for internet access. Several internet service providers, including

CompuServe, have announced plans to offer free computers in return for one or two year service agreement. These computers do not have the speed or the memory of more powerful models, but provide adequate power for most internet applications. If you are considering a computer for all-around use, not just for cruising the net, you will want a system that meets the criteria list on the following pages.

Equipment Ratings

Consumer Reports
www.consumerreports.com

Consumers Digest
www.consumersdigest.com

Compare Net
www.compare.net

HOME ELECTRONICS

✔ BUYING TIPS

✔ Home Computers
(Recommended Features)
- 266 MHz – 450 MHz CPU comparable to Intel Pentium II or
- 166 MHz – 233 MHz CPU comparable to Intel Pentium MMX
- 32 MB – 64 MB of Ram
- 512 K Cache
- 24x – 40x CD-Rom Drive
- 4 MB – 8 MB Video Ram
- 56K bps modem

- 14"- 20" SVGA monitor with 1024 x 1280 resolution
- Hewlett-Packard color Desk Jet or Laser Jet series printer

*Apple computer has returned to favor among many first-time buyers, but you will find PC-based systems to be the better choice for most users. Most software titles are designed for the PC/Windows environment and PCs are used almost exclusively in the workplace. Avoid computers manufactured by **Packard Bell, AST, Acer/Aspire, NEC** and **CTX**. These systems have very poor reliability ratings.*

✔ Laptops
(Recommended Features)
- 233+ MHz CPU
- 32 MB of Ram
- TFT-LCD (thin film transistor/liquid crystal display) active matrix screen
- 56.6K bps modem
- Nickel-metal-hydride or lithium-ion batteries with 2 hr. capacity
- Comfortable, easy-to-use keyboard and pointing device

Notebook computers are nearly double the price of comparably- equipped desktop machines. Make certain you purchase a system which has an easy-to-read screen and a comfortable keypad. Size and weight are important considerations, particularly if you do a lot of traveling.

✔ Scanners
(Recommended Features)
- 300-600 dots per inch (dpi) resolution
- 24 or 34 bit recognition

- Optical Character Resolution (OCR) Software

Scanning technology has improved dramatically, even for the least expensive machines.Choose a flatbed scanner, rather than a sheet-fed or handheld model, for best results.

✔ Upgrades
(Recommended Features)

- **Speed**
  Computers which run on a 386 or 486 processor are probably not worth upgrading. Pentium systems which operate at 120 MHz or less can usually be upgraded by purchasing Pentium MMX micro processors (166-233 MHz) or Pentium II motherboards for less than $400. Quality manufacturers include **Intel, Asus, Amptron, Matsonic, VX Pro, Micronics** and **Tyan**.

- **Memory**
  Easy and cheap to upgrade. Choose 16 or 32 MB upgrades in a type which is compatible with your microprocessor for less than $150.

- **Hard Drives**
  Add a 2-4 GB hard drive for less than $200. Quality manufacturers include Western Digital, Seagate and Fujitsu.

- **Removable Storage**
  Eliminate the need for outdated 1.44 MB floppy disks by installing an Iomega 100 MB zip disk drive or the even better Imation SuperDisk 120 MB system for less than $150.

In many cases, upgrading your existing computer is far cheaper than buying a new one. Most installations can be done at home if you are even remotely handy, but you can also have the job done by a professional for $25 -$50 per part. If you have a Windows 95 or Windows 98 operating system, new components should be recognized by your machine automatically. Always check with vendors to make certain the components you buy are compatible with your existing computer.

HOME ELECTRONICS

BUYING COMPUTERS WORKSHEET

Step 1

Before you shop, research the equipment and features you are looking for in **Consumer Reports** (www.consumereports.com), **Consumers Digest** (www.consumersdigest.com) or one of several computer magazine ratings guides published by **Byte** (www.byte.com), **PC Magazine** (www.zdnet.com) or **Computer Shopper** (www.computershopper.com). Keep in mind that Byte, PC Magazine and Computer Shopper are advertiser supported. If you do not have time to do independent research, rely on the recommendations in this chapter.

Recommended Manufacturer(s)

_____   _____

_____   _____

Recommended Model(s)

_____   _____

_____   _____

Recommended Specifications

_____   _____

_____   _____

Step 2

What are the most important features for the equipment you are purchasing?

Features I Need   *Features I Don't Need*

_____   _____

_____   _____

_____   _____

BUYING COMPUTERS WORKSHEET

Step 3

Do a product search on the internet using a shopping agent such as *C-Net* (www.shopper.com), *Killer App Express* (www.killerapp.com) or *Price Scan* (www.pricescan.com). If you do not have access to the web, go to your nearest discount computer store in your area (i.e. *Comp USA, Computer City, Circuit City*) and check out the prices for models which match the criteria you've identified in Steps 1 and 2.

Item _____

Vendor	Price	Web Address or Phone No.
_____	_____	_____
_____	_____	_____
_____	_____	_____

Step 4

Contact several of the discount sources identified at the beginning of this worksheet. Do any of them beat the results from the previous step? If you are buying a complete computer system, check out the offerings from several mail-order manufactures such as *Dell Computer* (800-999-3355/www.dell.com), *Gateway* (800-846-4208/www.gateway.com), *Tangent* (800-223-6677/www.tangent.com), *Micron Electronics* (800-423-5891/www.micronpc.com) and *Quantex* (800-346-6685/ www.quantex.com) for a system with comparable features.

Discount Source	Price	Web Address Phone Number	Mail-Order Source	Model No.	Features	Price
_____	_____	_____	_____	_____	_____	_____
_____	_____	_____	_____	_____	_____	_____
_____	_____	_____	_____	_____	_____	_____
_____	_____	_____	_____	_____	_____	_____
_____	_____	_____	_____	_____	_____	_____
_____	_____	_____	_____	_____	_____	_____

BUYING COMPUTERS WORKSHEET

Step 5

If you have extra time, check out some of the web auction sites to find out whether there is an active auction for the item you want. Try **Web Auction** (www.webauction.com), **UBid** (www.ubid.com), **Price Watch** (www.pricewatch.com) and **On Sale** (www.onsale.com). You can even be more specific by using **BidFind** (www.vsn.com), a site which allows you to search more than 100 auction sites simultaneously for the item you are trying to locate.

Consider making a bid which is at least. half of the lowest price you identified from any of the sources in previous steps. Remember that if you are a successful bidder, pay by credit card, C.O.D. or by using an internet escrow service. **Escrow** (www.iescrow.com) and **Trade-Direct** (www.trade-direct.com) are neutral third parties that assure both the buyer and seller are protected.

Step 6

Summarize your best options. Don't forget to consider delivery charges as well as any potential savings you may enjoy on sales tax from an out-of-state source.

Source	Price	+	Sales Tax(?)	+	Delivery Charges(?)	=	Total
_____	_____		_____		_____		_____
_____	_____		_____		_____		_____
_____	_____		_____		_____		_____

Guide to
MAJOR
APPLIANCES

Recommended Discount Sources

Best Buy
www.bestbuys.com

Circuit City
www.circuitcity.com

Wards
www.wards.com

Buying Tips

✓ **Avoid the bells and whistles.**

Remember that when it comes to major appliances, the dioffierences between most major models and brands is largely cosmetic. You will pay a premium for extra storage bins in refrigerators, additional cleaning cycles for washers and dryers and pre-programmed cook cycles for microwave ovens—none of which is worth the extra money. Stick with standard models for the best values.

✓ **Remember energy costs.**

Operating costs for refrigerators, washers and dryers, as well as dishwashers must be posted by law on all retail displays for such items. Read them carefully. Energy differences between competing brands of as little as $20 or $30 per year can amount to hundreds of dollars over the usual life of a product. Factor these differences into your price comparisons.

✓ **Shop the clearance sales.**

Because there are really no viable alternatives to your local discount appliance stores, compare prices and try to buy during clearance sales. Do not hesitate to ask the salesman when the next major sale is scheduled.

✔ BUYING TIPS

✔ Washing Machines

- Large-capacity machines help save hot water by reducing the number of loads you do each week.
- Avoid digital displays or other expensive options.

- Recommended price range: $350-375

- Recommended Brands: **Maytag, Hotpoint, GE, Sears, Whirlpool**

✔ Clothes Dryers

- No one cares whether your washer and dryer match. Choose the best deal on a dryer, regardless of its appearance.
- Choose models with automatic drying cycles to reduce energy consumption.
- Select a gas dryer if you have the option. (Basic models cost 70% less to operate than electric models.)
- Avoid digital displays

- Recommended price range: $250-300

- Recommended Brands: **Maytag, Whirlpool, Sears, Hotpoint, GE.**

✔ Refrigerators

- Always read the energy label affixed to the refrigerator door. Add the 10-year operating cost to the price of each model to determine the true cost of ownership.
- Avoid door-mounted cold water and ice dispensers. They add $100s to the price.
- Don't get an ice maker unless you absolutely need one. (Ice makers have a history of break-downs.)
- Choose basic models with a minimum of separate compartments and temperature zones.

- Recommended price range: $450-550

- Recommended brands: *All brands are reliable.*

✔ Dishwashers

- Choose models with fiberglass insulation to reduce noise during operation.
- Buy models than can operate at water temperature of 120 degrees or less.
- Avoid digital displays and machines with multiple wash cycles.

- *Recommended price range: $225-300*

- *Recommended brands:* **GE, Whirlpool, Hotpoint**

✔ Microwave Ovens

- Choose mid-size models (600 watts) for best performance. Compact models are too small and too slow, and large models are overpriced since the extra capacity is usually unnecessary.
- Never buy extras like browning elements, turntables or temperature probes. Use microwaves for thawing and reheating foods, not for everyday cooking.

- *Recommended price: $150-200*

- *Recommended brands: All brands are reliable.*

HOME ELECTRONICS

BUYING MAJOR APPLIANCES WORKSHEET

Step 1

Before you shop, research the equipment and features you are looking for in **Product Review** (www.productreviewnet.com), **Consumer Reports** (www.consumereports. com) or **Consumer's Digest** (www.consumersdigest.com) for recommendations. If you do not have time to do additional research, you should know that **Maytag, Hotpoint, GE, Kenmore, Whirlpool** and **Hotpoint** all have reputations as quaility brands.

Recommended Manufacturer(s)

_____   _____

_____   _____

Recommended Model(s)

_____   _____

_____   _____

Step 2

What are the most important features for the equipment you are purchasing?

_____   _____

_____   _____

Step 3

Visit several discount appliance stores in your area. If you are uncertain where to shop, you might try the Yellow Pages or contact several national discount chain stores on the internet, such as **Circuit City** (www.circuitcity.com), **Wards** (www.wards.com), or **Best Buy** (www.bestbuy.com) to identify the store nearest you.

Step 4   *Pricing Survey*

Conduct a price survey for the model(s) that interest you and choose the best deal.

Washing Machines	A	B	C	D
Store	_____	_____	_____	_____
Manufacturer	_____	_____	_____	_____
Model#	_____	_____	_____	_____
Capacity	_____	_____	_____	_____
Features	_____	_____	_____	_____
Price (w/ delivery)	_____	_____	_____	_____

Clothes Dryers	A	B	C	D
Store	_____	_____	_____	_____
Manufacturer	_____	_____	_____	_____
Model#	_____	_____	_____	_____
Features	_____	_____	_____	_____
Price (w/ delivery)	_____	_____	_____	_____

Refrigerators	A	B	C	D
Store	_____	_____	_____	_____
Manufacturer	_____	_____	_____	_____
Model#	_____	_____	_____	_____
Size (cu. ft.)	_____	_____	_____	_____
Price (w/ delivery)	_____	_____	_____	_____
10-yr. operating cost	_____	_____	_____	_____
Total cost of ownership	_____	_____	_____	_____

(Sales price + 10-yr. operating cost)

Dishwashers	A	B	C	D
Store	_____	_____	_____	_____
Manufacturer	_____	_____	_____	_____
Model#	_____	_____	_____	_____
Features	_____	_____	_____	_____
Price	_____	_____	_____	_____
Installation (optional)	_____	_____	_____	_____

Microwave Ovens	A	B	C	D
Store	_____	_____	_____	_____
Manufacturer	_____	_____	_____	_____
Model#	_____	_____	_____	_____
Price	_____	_____	_____	_____

HOME ELECTRONICS

HERE'S THE PROOF

We've told you the important tips you need to know about buying home electronics, cameras, computers and major appliances. Here are some real-life examples that prove our suggestions can save you *big* money.

Suggestion: Check out the prices of TVs, stereos and other home electronics at recommended discount sources, either by phone or via the internet, before buying from local retailers.

Example: We checked the sale price at a local Circuit City store in Reston, Virginia for the sale price on a JVC 32" color TV (model AV 32950) and then looked up the same item on the web at **Consumer Direct Warehouse** (www.consumer-direct.com). The internet price, *including* delivery, was $100 less than the price at **Circuit City**.

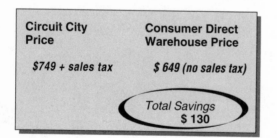

Circuit City Price	Consumer Direct Warehouse Price
$749 + sales tax	$ 649 (no sales tax)

Total Savings
$ 130

Suggestion: Use a web shopping agent to locate the lowest price on computer equipment and home electronics.

Example: We found a **Panasonic** camcorder (model PVL 658) on sale at a local **Wards** appli-ance store for $699. We then used the shopping agent at **C-Net** (www.shopper.com) and found the same item for sale at the **Electronics Zone** (www.800.com) for $574.99 and at **Best Stop Digital** (www.beststopdigital.com) for $560.

Local Sale Price	Web Agent Best Buy
$699	$ 560

Total Savings
$ 139

Suggestion: Try a web auction to find discounted computer equipment at a fraction of the retail price.

Example: We tried the auction at **Mac-Warehouse** (www.macwarehouse.com) which we found through the auction product locator at **Bid Find** (www.bidfind.com). There we were able to find a UMAX S-12 flatbed scanner which lists for $1,050. At the auction close, the winning bid for this unopened system was $200, a savings of more than $800.

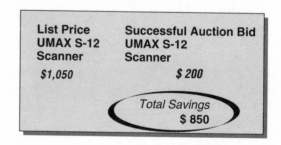

List Price UMAX S-12 Scanner	Successful Auction Bid UMAX S-12 Scanner
$1,050	$ 200

Total Savings
$ 850

HERE'S THE PROOF

Suggestion: Don't buy a refrigerator without considering annual utility costs.

Example: We looked at two competing brands of a 20-cubic-foot, no-frost refrigerator/freezer at **Circuit City**, an appliance discounter in McLean, Virginia. Refrigerator "A", made by **GE**, had an energy guide rating of $77 per year. Refrigerator "B", made by **Whirlpool**, was rated at $90 per year. The $13/year difference may not seem like a lot, but look what happens over 20 years of use and an inflation rate of 4%.

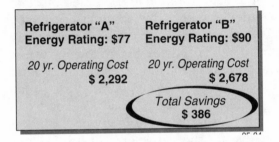

Refrigerator "A" Energy Rating: $77	Refrigerator "B" Energy Rating: $90
20 yr. Operating Cost **$ 2,292**	*20 yr. Operating Cost* **$ 2,678**
	Total Savings **$ 386**

Suggestion: Avoid top-of-the-line appliances priced higher than basic models because of digital displays, fancy control knobs and other "meaningless" features.

Example: Again, we surveyed prices at **Circuit City** in McLean, Virginia, for electric ranges, refrigerators and washing machines. On average, basic models were $80 – $100 cheaper.

Basic Model	Top-of-the-Line
Whirlpool Electric Range *(Regular Controls)* Model No. **WH1 RF 370**	Whirlpool Electric Range *(Digital Controls)* Model No. **WH1 RF 375**
Sales Price **$ 499**	*Sales Price* **$ 579**
Savings **$ 80**	
Whirlpool Refrigerator *(Regular Ice Maker)* Model No. **WHED20GKVX67**	Whirlpool Refrigerator *(In-Door Ice Dispenser)* Model No. **WHED20GKVX75**
Sales Price **$ 789.99**	*Sales Price* **$ 900.97**
Savings **$ 111**	
Kitchen Aid Washer *(3 temp settings/ 4 cycles)* Model No. **AB74892**	Kitchen Aid Washer *(4 temp settings/ 6 cycles)* Model No. **AB85030**
Sales Price **$ 399.97**	*Sales Price* **$ 499.97**
Savings **$ 100**	

HOME ELECTRONICS

Chapter Thirteen

Secrets of the Supermarket

Why is it a big deal if I save a few cents at the supermarket?

Believe it or not, groceries are probably the second largest item in your household budget (after the rent or mortgage). In most families, the annual grocery bill is easily $7,000 to $10,000, which means that over a lifetime the money you spend at the supermarket will top half a million dollars!

Despite the huge stakes involved, most trips to the grocery store are poorly planned and executed. Yet, even modest steps can result in a reduction at the checkout counter of 20 to 40%. Learn these "secrets of the supermarket" and you can add thousands of dollars to your disposable income every year.

What's the "secret"?

The key is to approach every trip to the grocery store strategically. Most of us do very little preparation before we shop and once in the store we fail to pay close attention. We shop with our eyes instead of our brains. We choose with our emotions. And because we lack a discipline and a strategy, we are easy prey for those who do the big food companies and grocery chains. They have designed everything in the store, from the height of a shelf to the color of a box of detergent, to make you buy. The "secret" is learning how to out-think and out-smart the food companies at their own game.

Step one is to always make a list of what you need. Not a half-crumpled piece of notepad with a few essentials scribbled on it. A real list that covers everything you will need for the following week. The reason for the list is two-fold. First you don't want to forget anything since you'll be forced to make a second trip during the week. Remember the more trips to the supermarket, the more you'll spend. The second reason for a thorough list is to avoid temptation. Every time you shop you are exposed to impulse items that will inflate your grocery bill, like hot fresh bread from the bakery, a new entrée in the frozen food section, or a prepared item in the deli case. If you don't go to the store as often, you cut down the opportunities to overspend. And if you're using a list, and you stay focused on it, you're concentration is less likely to wander to things you don't need. In short, a list helps you to resist the temptation to shop impulsively. Purchases based on your whims and emotions, not your needs, are the number-one reason for inflated grocery bills. But there are other "do's and don't's" as well.

Ten Commandments of Supermarket Shopping

1. Never shop on an empty stomach.

You buy more impulsively when you're hungry. Not only will you load up on items to satisfy your immediate cravings, but you are more likely be more influenced by the store's marketing ploys.

2. Avoid shopping with children whenever possible.

It's nearly impossible to keep focused when you are chasing after the little ones. Stores are designed to get people excited about buying. The displays. Adults can keep their emotions under control, at least consciously, but kids are totally vulnerable. The stores know this, which is why the displays for items like Cap'n Crunch cereal are strategically placed at a 7-year-old's eye level. Incidentally, not only is it better to shop without your kids, it is also preferable to leave your spouse home as well. When two adults shop together, one winds up playing the "child" role and the other becomes the "parent."

3. Never use coupons except for items you would normally buy without them.

Buying something you wouldn't otherwise choose, just because you can save 35 cents, isn't a bargain. Coupons are typically offered on highly-processed, over-packaged items that are usually the worst values in the supermarket. While there are always exceptions, people using coupons tend to make unwise choices about their product selections. For example, in many cases even with the coupon, the discounted item is still not as good a deal as a generic brand or substitute. If you do decide to clip and save — and about 80% of households use coupons to some degree — make sure you limit their use to items already on your shopping list.

4. Buy extra quantities when prices are good.

The old saying – get while the getting is good – could not be more appropriate when it comes to grocery shopping. The time to buy chicken breasts or cereal or a hundred other items is when those items are on sale. Buy extra quantities — freeze or store the rest. Many people use this technique to a limited degree. They might buy one extra package of chicken, for example, on sale. That's a start, but our strategy is to buy as much of a sale item as you can comfortably store and consume, during its shelf life. In other words, when chicken is on sale, don't just buy one extra package, buy five or six! You can usually store frozen meats for up to two months. Most fruits and vegetables will last at least two or three weeks in the refrigerator, while canned goods can be safely consumed within two years.

5. Always check the unit prices of every item you buy.

Comparing unit prices – the cost of a product expressed by unit of measure (per ounce, per pound, per quart, etc.), is the only reliable way to compare the relative value of different brands and package sizes. Not surprisingly, supermarkets try to de-emphasize unit prices by posting them in microscopic type next to the shelf price.

Ten Commandments of Supermarket Shopping

6. Learn the pricing fluctuations of the items you buy most.

There is usually a predictable ebb and flow to the prices of most items in the supermarket. Fresh meats and vegetables follow the simple rules of supply and demand. When products are plentiful and in-season, they are less expensive. When supplies get tight, prices go up. Packaged foods follow more complex pricing patterns dictated by product manufacturers and a variety of factors. The point is that if you can learn to recognize price changes, you will know immediately when you should be stocking up with extra quantities. We'll show you how to maintain a price monitor to help you with this process in our step-by-step instructions at the end of this chapter.

7. Buy the best, but only in season.

Even though it may seem obvious, you should be buying more of certain meats, fruits and vegetables when they are in peak season since prices are at their lowest. Most shoppers practice this rule to a limited degree, but they don't take it far enough. The trick is to keep a ready supply of ziplock bags and freeze as much of an item as you can. You can easily store frozen berries, peaches, broccoli, Brussels sprouts, green beans and peas, not to mention steak and poultry, for several months. The flip side of this rule is to avoid certain items when they are out of season. You may be able to find watermelon in January at some outrageous price, but putting it in your cart is not a wise shopping decision.

8. Stay away from in-store delis and bakeries.

In-store prepared foods and baked goods are at the heart of a supermarket's strategy to lure you into making impulse buys. These areas of the store also return the biggest profits. The most outrageous example is the salad bar. There you can find shredded fresh carrots selling for $2.99 a pound – just a few steps away from the regular produce aisle, whole carrots are selling for 35 cents a pound. Get the picture?

9. Remember "bigger" doesn't always mean "cheaper."

The average shopper always assumes that the larger version of their favorite product is a better buy. Not necessarily. In many cases, good things come in the smaller package. Find out for sure which size is the better deal by always checking the unit price.

10. Don't assume that price scanning is accurate.

Tests by a leading university consistently show that most supermarket scanning systems are in error as much as 10% of the time, costing consumers an estimated $1 billion per year in inflated charges. Most shoppers rarely pay much attention as their groceries are scanned. Those that do canoften save themselves from being overcharged. The easiest way to keep track is by writing down shelf prices on your shopping list as you put an item in your shopping cart.

Can you use the internet to improve your results at the supermarket?

As far-fetched as it sounds, you can order your groceries on the internet at **NetGrocer** (www.netgrocer.com) and they will gladly send your delivery to your home via Federal Express. Selection is rather limited and does not include fresh meats, vegetables or anything else that requires refrigeration. We do not expect them to be in business for very long. If you want a practical idea on how you can use the web to lower your food bill, log on to **ValuPage** at www.valupage.com. There you can download coupons for free which are good at your local supermarket. Most of the discounts are in denominations of 50 cents to $1.00. Instead of receiving an immediate credit on your grocery bill, you're issued "web bucks" which are printed with your receipt. Web bucks can then be used for a credit on any item during your next trip to that supermarket. If you plan on taking advantage of this service, don't forget our general advice on coupons. Use them only for items you would have otherwise purchased without the discount.

Are there shopping hints for specific items?

There are specific things you should know for just about every category in the store. Here's a brief overview:

✔ BUYING TIPS

Apples
- Apples are seasonal fruit (Fall), even though you can find them in the store year-round because they can be stored for long periods. In Spring or Summer, choose alternative fruits which are cheaper and fresher.

Aspirin
- Buy generic aspirin, not name brands (i.e. **Bayer, Anacin, Excedrin**). Name brands are no more effective according to the U.S. Food & Drug Administration (FDA), yet cost 3 to 5 times more for an equivalent amount.
- Don't pay more for name-brand aspirin substitutes (**Tylenol, Advil,** etc.) Choose generic brands of the same compounds (acetaminophen or ibuprofen).

Baby Food
- Make your own version of baby foods by steaming fresh fruits, vegetables and meats, then processing in a blender or food processor with a little water. Freeze in ice cube trays, then transfer to plastic bags and thaw as needed.
- Save money by diluting regular juices with water instead of buying juices bottled for baby.
- Choose larger jars and use over several days rather than buying single servings (larger jars have lower unit prices).

Bacon
- Buy less-expensive brands but check individual packages for fat content by examining the viewing window on reverse side of label. Experts can detect little difference in taste or quality among brands.

G R O C E R I E S

✔ BUYING TIPS

Beans

- Dry beans are considerably less expensive than canned. Make a large pot and freeze leftovers to save 300% or more.

Beef, Pork and Lamb

- Learn the difference between various beef cuts. Better cuts are often only pennies more per pound, but noticeably superior in tenderness.

- Save $1-2 dollars per pound by cutting large beef cuts into premium steaks or chops at home. Examples:
  Rib Roast into Rib Steaks
  Porterhouse into Filet Mignon
  Pork Loin into Loin Chops
  Rack of Lamb into Lamb Chops

- Avoid store-marinated meats, which often sell for up to double the price of regular cuts.

- Choose lean ground beef (10-15% fat) instead of regular hamburger. Even though lean hamburger is more expensive per pound, it shrinks less, so you get more servings. It is also healthier.

- Follow this guide for tender steaks and roasts.

	Standing Roast	Large Steaks	Small Steaks	Stews & Pot Roasts
More Tender	Tenderloin	Porterhouse	Filet Mignon	Chuck Roast (Shldr.)
	Strip Loin	Rib	T-Bone	Chuck Roast (Blade)
	Rib Roast	Sirloin	Strip Loin	Bottom Round
	Sirloin Roast	Top Round	Delmonico	Rump Roast
	Round Roast	Sirloin Tip	Rib Eye	Brisket
	Chuck Roast	Chuck (Shldr.)		Flank
Less Tender	Eye Roast	Flank		Short Ribs

Berries

- Buy strawberries, blueberries and blackberries at the height of their season when prices are lowest. Wash, dry and lightly sugar them to taste. Then freeze in bags for use later in the year.

Broccoli

- Don't pay for fibrous stalks you won't use. Break off lower stalks before putting broccoli in your grocery cart. Never buy frozen broccoli before comparing unit price (price per pound) to fresh broccoli in the produce section.

Butter

- Never buy whipped butter. Whipping increases volume by adding air, meaning you get less dairy product for your money.

Cabbage

- Consider using cabbage as an alternative when other fresh produce (broccoli, green beans, zuchini, etc.) is expensive. Cabbage is nutritious, versatile and very cheap. Stir-fry with oil and garlic, make slaw with sugar, vinegar and mayonaise, or boil.

✔ BUYING TIPS

Cake Mixes
- Use mixes rather than buying cakes and cookies from the bakery section. Mixes cost 3 or 4 times more than combining the dry ingredients yourself, but are still a bargain compared to having someone else bake for you.

Candy
- Don't be fooled by bite-sized packaging of candy bars. Although it may look like you get a lot for your money, the unit price (per pound) for mini-candy is considerably higher than the price of regular-size bars.

Canned Fruits & Vegetables
- Buy generic canned goods. While national brands may be more uniform in size, shape and color, they taste the same and do not merit higher prices.

Carrots
- Like cabbage, an inexpensive, highly-versatile vegetable. As a side dish, use as an alternative to higher-priced vegetables. When lettuce is over-priced, use grated carrots or carrot slices as an alternative salad.

Cereals
- Never buy vitamin fortified cereals (*Total, Product 19,* etc.) They are excessively priced, and the vitamin supplements are completely unnecessary.

- Add your own raisins or nuts to plain bran flakes. Manufacturers charge more when they add these ingredients.

- Buy generics or store brands — they are considerably less expensive than national brands and often made by the same manufacturers.

- Add your own sugar. Pre-sweetened cereals contain pennies of added sugar, but cost at least $1 more than unsweetened versions. (Examples: corn flakes vs. frosted flakes, shredded wheat vs. frosted shredded wheat).

- Buy oatmeal in bulk food section, rather than pre-packaged to save up to 50% per pound.

Cucumbers
- Use cucumbers, like carrots, as a salad alternative when lettuce is over-priced.

Cheese
- Buy cheese in blocks. Slicing, grating, shredding and extra packaging add to costs and reduce freshness.

Chicken
- Never waste chicken bones and skin. Simmer for two hours in several quarts of water to make stock, which can be used as a base for almost any kind of soup.

- Don't reject boneless, skinless chicken breasts as too expensive without considering the yield of regular breasts you must de-bone yourself. One pound of regular breasts yields approximately 1/2 pound of boneless, skinless meat. If boneless breasts are less than double the price per pound of regular chicken, the boneless is more economical.

- Don't be fooled by brand-name chicken marketing claims. Branded chicken costs more per pound, yet there are few if any differences in quality that would justify the higher price.

✔ BUYING TIPS

Coffee & Tea
- Splurge on coffee and tea without guilt, since the cost per serving is only pennies, regardless of the brand you choose.

- Choose whole beans, instead of pre-ground, to preserve flavor and freshness longer.

Cold Remedies
- Cold remedies do not cure a cold or shorten its duration.

- Multi-symptom products are generally higher-priced and in some cases introduce drugs into your body that you don't need. Treat only symptoms you have:

  Aches, Pain & Fever — Aspirin
  Nasal Congestion   — Decongestant Nasal Spray
  Dry Cough — Cough Suppressant

- Avoid night-time cold remedies. In most cases, alchohol is a primary ingredient, used to temporarily mask symptoms and induce sleep. You can achieve the same results with your favorite cocktail.

- Buy generic aspirin and aspirin substitutes. Brand aspirin (**Bayer, Anacin, Excedrin**, etc.) are no more effective according to the Food & Drug Adminstration (FDA), yet cost 3-5 times more.

- Don't pay more for an aspirin substitute (i.e., acetaminophen or ibuprofen) unless you need it for medical reasons. If you do need a substitute, choose generic versions rather than brand products (**Tylenol, Advil,** etc.) for the same reasons as listed above (see asprin)

Cookies & Crackers
- Watch unit prices! Brand name versions of all-time favorites (i.e., **Oreos**) cost almost double the cost per pound of generics.

- Avoid novelty cookies — (i.e., candy-coated chocolate chip, mini-sized Oreos, fat-free Fig Newtons) which cost considerably more per pound than conventional versions of the same products.

Coupons
- Use coupons only when the discounted price of a name-brand product is cheaper than the non-discounted price of a generic alternative.

- Never use coupons for products that you would not otherwise buy without a coupon. Remember that coupons are intended to encourage impulse buys — the No. 1 enemy of the frugal shopper.

Diapers
- Try to avoid the supermarket for diapers. You can generally find much better prices at discount drug and merchandise stores where you can buy in bulk.

✔ BUYING TIPS

Dishwashing Liquid
- Name brands are a better buy than generics because they are more concentrated and cost less per use. Buy them with coupons or when they are sale-priced.

Eggs
- Compare prices of small, medium, large and jumbo eggs by weight. Generally, jumbo eggs are a better buy than large eggs.

- Forget brown eggs — they are identical to white eggs in taste but are often priced higher.

- Grade AA, Grade A and Grade B eggs differ in size and appearance, but the quality differences are unnoticeable to most consumers. Grade AA eggs have firm, high yolks and thick whites. Lesser grades look less perfect but taste the same.

Egg Substitutes
- Don't pay a premium for egg substitutes (*Egg Beaters*) which are 99% egg whites. If you want a cholesterol-free egg product, separate the whites from the yolks using fresh eggs and save 75%.

Fabric Softeners
- Believe it or not, dryer sheets are less expensive than liquids and equally effective!

Food Wraps
- Watch unit prices carefully. Boxes of plastic wrap and aluminum foil may look comparable but contain vastly different quantities. Unit prices are your easiest comparison for value.

- Choose larger rolls (200-300 feet). They are cheaper per foot than smaller sizes (50-75 feet).

Frozen Entrees
- Avoid frozen entrees in favor of freezing home-cooked meals you make in double or triple batches.

- Packaging of frozen foods is notoriously deceptive. Next time you are thinking about buying a frozen entree, ask yourself whether the last one looked or tasted anything close to what came out of the microwave?

- Don't be fooled by the relatively inexpensive cost per package. Prices are low because the quantities of expensive ingredients (chicken, beef, etc.) are so meager.

Frozen Vegetables
- Some frozen vegetables compare favorably in price to fresh produce during certain times of the year. Always compare unit prices between fresh and frozen before deciding which to buy.

- Buy plain frozen vegetables. Avoid medleys with butter or cheese sauces. Manufactur- ers aggressively inflate prices when they add a few ingredients which turn a "vegetable" into a "side dish". Don't be fooled. You can do the same thing with a teaspoon of butter, a dash of cream, or a cheese grater and save more than 50%.

Hot Dogs
- Brand-name hot dogs are more than double the price of generics or store brands. Buy generic all-beef or chicken frankfurters and enjoy comparable quality for a lot less money.

✔ BUYING TIPS

Household Cleaners

- Use generic amonia and bleach instead of fancy kitchen and bath cleaners which rely on the same ingredients, but add colors and fragrance to justify a higher price.

  For example: You can make one quart of window cleaner using 10 cents worth of amonia. A comparable amount of Windex will cost approximately $3.50 per quart. Other products which can be replaced by amonia or bleach:

  > *Top Job*
  > *Lysol Kitchen and Bath Cleaner*
  > *Ajax Liquid*
  > *Tylex*
  > *Tidy Bowl*

- Consult the back of amonia and bleach containers for instructions on proper dilutions for various household chores.

Ice Cream

- Choose bulk ice cream in pints, quarts or half gallons, rather than novelty items (bars, sundaes, etc.). Most ice cream novelties sell at huge premiums to regular frozen desserts.

- The major difference between cheaper and more expensive brands of ice cream is density and quality of ingredients. Cheaper ice creams usually contain more air. Gourmet brands have less air, so you are likely to be satisfied with a smaller serving.

Juices

- Always buy orange, grapefruit or apple juice in frozen concentrate. Adding your own water saves you and the manufacturer money. Juice in cartons or glass containers are up to twice as expensive, and the quality is generally no better.

- Buy the cheapest brands. Experts have a hard time distinguishing between taste and quality of competing brands even though there are huge price variations.

- Know the difference between a fruit juice and a fruit drink. Fruit drinks contain mostly water, sugar and natural or artificial flavorings. Some may contain a small amount of fruit juice (10%) but not enough to make a major nutritional difference. If you are buying fruit drinks, choose powdered mixes like Kool-Aid, rather than pre-packaged. As with juice concentrates, why pay for water when you can add your own?

Laundry Detergents

- Almost any liquid or powder will do a good job on averageloads. Do not pay for premium brands.

- Forget special detergents for hand washables (i.e., **Woolite**). A substitute which works just as well is regular dishwashing liquid.

- In new highly-concentrated forms, liquid detergents are nearly as economical as powders. To judge the better buy, compare cost per load rather than unit price.

$$\frac{\text{Product Cost}}{\text{Loads per Package}} = \text{Cost per Load}$$

✔ BUYING TIPS

Lettuce
- Lettuce prices vary greatly depending on changing weather and crop yields. Avoid lettuce when prices are at their highest, substituting carrots, cabbage or cucumber as salad alternatives.
- Store lettuce wrapped in a paper towel, surrounded by a plastic bag to increase shelf life and preserve freshness.

Luncheon Meats
- Compare unit prices of pre-packaged luncheon meats to the deli items in your local super market. In many cases, pre-sliced and pre-packaged lunch meats are more expensive.

Onions
- Never assume that 5 lb. or 10 lb. bags of onions are cheaper than loose onions. They may be cheaper, but not always.

Oranges
- Oranges are priced according to size and uniformity of shapeand color. Do not assume that larger fruit is necessarily better tasting or a better value. Smaller oranges are usually a better deal.

Pancake Syrup
- Choose Karo pancake syrup as a less-expensive alternative to pricier brands such as *Aunt Jemima* or *Mrs. Butterworth*.
- If you want real maple syrup, do not buy Log Cabin brand, which is 10 % maple syrup and 90% corn sweetners. Carefully read labels and choose only 100% Grade A maple syrup.

Paper Towels
- Expensive brands are thicker and more absorbent than necessary for most jobs. It is more cost-effective to buy a less expensive brand and use more on the few occasions when you need to clean a major spill.
- As an even better alternative, use re-useable dish towels instead of paper.

Pasta
- Dry pasta tastes as good or better than fresh pasta and costs one-third less per serving.
- Buy the least-expensive brands — experts find little difference in taste or quality between different brands of pasta.
- Avoid noodles & sauce mixes which are 5-7 times more expensive than you can make yourself in a comparable amount of time.

Pet Food
- Dry cat food and dog food is better for your pet and less expensive.
- Buy larger bags, since pet food has a very long shelf life and is far cheaper in bulk-size bags.

G
R
O
C
E
R
I
E
S

✔ BUYING TIPS

Popcorn

- Buy generic popping kernels — not "gourmet" brands. There is little if any difference in quality, even though gourmet varieties are three or four times as expensive.

- Pop your own. Microwave popcorn is 10 times more expensive than corn you pop yourself.

- Cut down on fat and calories by using less oil or an air popper — not by purchasing "lite" versions of microwavepopcorn.

Potatoes

- As with onions, carefully compare unit prices of bagged vs. loose potatoes. Bagged potatoes are usually, but not always, cheaper.

Rice

- Buy the cheapest brands — rice is generic.

- To eliminate stickiness, add rice to boiling water, remove from heat, let stand for one minute, drain & rinse, then prepare as directed. Do not buy **Uncle Ben's Converted Rice** which is up to 3 times more expensive per serving.

- Never buy **Minute Rice**. Regular rice takes an extra ten minutes to prepare, but is one-fourth the price.

Salad Bars

- Before you buy from the salad bar, compare the price per pound to the cost of the same items in the produce section. Salad bars can be up to 10 times more expensive than if you purchased the items separately.

Salad Dressings

- Price is not always a good indicator of price or quality. Some of the best-rated dressings are not the most expensive.

- It is much cheaper to make your own dressings using oil and vinegar. Make a large batch and store in glass jars.

- Buy generic brands of mayonaise. National brands are made from identical ingredients but are often priced 50% higher.

Shampoo

- Save money on shampoos and other personal care products by shopping for them at discount drug stores — not supermarkets.

- Stop using expensive brands. Experts find little if any difference in performance among more than 60 brands tested, yet prices ranged from 2 cents to 17 cents per use.

- The biggest difference between brands (besides price) is color and fragrance, neither of which does anything for your hair.

- Conditioners are helpful, but like shampoos, there is little difference in performance between different brands. Focus on the less-expensive brands.

Shaving Cream

- Buy the cheapest brands — all shaving creams are rated similarly. None protect you any better against nicks and cuts.

✔ BUYING TIPS

Skin Lotions
- The leading ingredient in almost all skin creams is mineral oil or glycerin, yet prices range from $2.50 per pint to more than $7. The cheapest brands work just as well according to leading dermatologists.

Soup
- Other than for occasional convenience, there is no excuse for buying soup in a can. You can make your own soup for pennies which is vastly superior in flavor and quality.

Spices
- To buy spices at reasonable prices, avoid the supermarket. Shop at ethnic markets where spices are sold in bulk — without the fancy glass jars.
- Never buy spice blends — they are mostly salt, yet manufacturers charge premium prices.
- Avoid dehyrdated onions, garlic, parsley, and green pepper. On a unit-price basis, they cost anywhere from $30 to $150 per pound! The real thing is much cheaper and better tasting.

Toilet Paper
- Check unit prices. All rolls may look the same but some contain far fewer sheets.
- Avoid national brands. They are more than double the price, and most people cannot detect much difference in quality.

Toothpaste
- Buy big! Large tubes cost much less than smaller quantities.
- Forget pumps. They cost 30-40% more than tubes.

Trash Bags
- Check unit prices. Packages may look the same, but some contain far fewer bags per box.
- Buy cheap trash bags — remember that they're for garbage! If you occasionally need a stronger bag, use two.

Yogurt
- Add fruit or preserves to plain or vanilla yogurt instead of buying fruit-flavored yogurts in individual serving sizes. 32-ounce containers of plain yogurt sell for half the priceof 8-ounce yogurt cups with fruit already added.

How can I ever hope to learn all the information you just summarized?

You must remember that supermarket shopping is a process, not a pop quiz. Try to incorporate as many hints as possible each time you shop, but don't be surprised if it takes several months of practice before it becomes second nature. To help you along, we've prepared checklists which you should refer to each time you set out for the supermarket, and again before you put any item in your grocery cart. If you refer to the checklists regularly, you should have no problem reducing your grocery bill by 20-40%.

✔ SHOPPER'S CHECKLIST

AT-HOME CHECKLIST
Ask the following questions before YOU leave your house.

_____ Is my shopping list complete?

_____ Am I shopping alone (no kids) to minimize distractions?

_____ Am I shopping on a full stomach to discourage impulse buys?

_____ Does my list include enough items so I don't need a return trip to the store for at least one week?

IN-STORE CHECKLIST
Ask the following questions before YOU place any item in your cart

_____ Is this item on my shopping list?

_____ Have I checked the price monitor to see if the price is a good or bad buy?

_____ Have I chosen the brand with the lowest unit price for the quantity I need?

_____ Have I considered the lower-priced generic?

_____ Can I make this product better or cheaper myself in approximately the same amount of time?

_____ Have I purrchased extra quantities if this is an exceptional buy?

HERE'S THE PROOF

We went shopping at a local grocery store in Washington, D.C. area to prove how much you can save on a typical grocery bill following the advice in this chapter. The shopping list includes 29 standard items commonly found in most pantries. We used two grocery carts, selecting items off our list two ways.

For Cart A, we shopped without paying much attention to price or detail. When there was a brand name, we bought it, and we generally chose convenience over value.

For Cart B, we rigorously followed the lessons of the Supermarket Savings System. We chose generics where possible, always looked at the unit price and concentrated on finding the best deals.

The result? We filled grocery Cart B with all the items on our shopping list for nearly half the money we spent for Cart A—a *$48.00 savings!*

HERE'S THE PROOF

Without the Supermarket Savings System		With the Supermarket Savings System		Comments
Del Monte Canned Pears 32 oz.	*1.78*	Canned Pears Generic 32 oz.	*1.26*	*Same quality, 30% cheaper*
Fresh Fruit Strawberries 16oz.	*1.69*	Fresh Fruit Bananas 16oz.	*.20*	*Save by avoiding out-of-season produce*
Lettuce Iceburg	*.99*	Lettuce Romaine	*.59*	*Take advantage of sale-priced items*
Green Giant Spinach Frozen 16oz.	*1.19*	Spinach Fresh 16 oz.	*.69*	*In this case fresh is the better buy.*
Fresh Broccoli 16oz.	*.99*	Fresh Cabbage16oz.	*.30*	*Cabbage is the low-cost, in-season choice in this case.*
Del Monte Green Beans 16oz. can	*.62*	Generic Green Beans 16oz. can	*.51*	*Same quality 18% cheaper*
Frozen Shredded Potatoes	*2.12*	Fresh Potatoes you shred	*.50*	*Same cooking time. You spend 2 minutes to shred potatoes.*
Kraft Mayonnaise 16oz.	*2.25*	Mayonnaise Generic16oz.	*1.59*	*Experts detect no difference in quality.*
Contadina Fresh Fettuccine16oz.	*3.36*	Dry Fettuccine 16oz.	*1.72*	*Fresh is trendy but dry pasta tastes the same when cooked.*
Oscar Mayer Bacon 16oz.	*3.29*	Generic Bacon 16oz.	*1.39*	*Experts say all bacon is similar.*
3 12oz. Rib Steaks	*14.80*	1 Rib Roast cut into 3 12oz. steaks	*12.78*	*Same cut of meat but you make three slices.*
1 dozen jumbo Eggs	*1.08*	1 dozen medium Eggs	*.70*	*Medium eggs are almost as big but cost 36% less.*
6 Hard Rolls	*1.29*	6 Hard Rolls 1-day-old on sale	*.86*	*You probably will not notice a difference in the day-old bread.*
Orville Redenbacher Microwave Popcorn 4 boxes at 1.88/box 12 servings	*7.52*	**Orville Redenbacher Popcorn** 32oz. jar 53 servings	*2.60*	*To get the comparable yield of one 30oz. jar of popcorn kernels you would have to buy $3 of microwave popcorn.*
Tropicana Orange Juice half gallon	*3.59*	Generic concentrate half gallon	*1.15*	*The only difference with frozen concentrate is that you add the water yourself.*

Without the Supermarket Savings System		With the Supermarket Savings System		Comments
Mazola Corn Oil 16 oz.	1.33	Generic Corn Oil 16 oz.	.74	Price is the only difference.
Uncle Ben's 1lb. box	1.29	Bulk Generic Rice 1lb.	.34	Price is the only difference.
Chicken Legs regular pack 1lb.	1.49	Chicken Legs Jumbo pack 1lb.	.79	Buy in bulk freeze for future meals
Whipped Cream 7oz. can	1.68	Whipped Cream 7 oz. carton	.77	Use your mixer and save 118%
Ground Chuck Patties 2lbs.	4.38	Ground Chuck 2lbs.	3.32	Why pay more for 15 seconds of labor?
Hunt's Tomato Sauce 15oz. can	.73	Generic Tomato Sauce 15oz. can	.47	Price is the only difference.
Oscar Mayer Bologna 16oz. package	3.12	Generic Bologna 16oz. package	2.39	No perceptible difference in taste or quality.
Stovetop Stuffing Mix 16oz. package	3.73	Generic Stuffing Mix 16oz. package	1.78	Add your own spices and save $1.95..
Kraft Shredded Cheddar Cheese 16oz. package	4.30	Generic 16oz. Cheddar Block	3.49	Grate your own and save 19%.
Bayer Asprin 200 ct.	8.58	Generic Asprin 200 ct.	2.40	Same ingredient.
Tilex Bathroom Cleaner 1 quart	4.23	**Chlorox** Bleach 1 quart	.70	Same active ingredient.
Tide Laundry Detergent 16oz. liquid	2.22	**Dash** 16oz. liquid	1.33	Lesser-known brands have acceptable cleaning power for a lower price.
Bounty Paper Towels 100ct.	1.60	Generic100ct.	.84	Why pay more if you throw them away?
Healthy Choice Turkey Dinner 60z. frozen entreé 2 servings	6.44	Whole Turkey Breast comparable servings -make yourself	.74	You pay a huge premium for convenience.
Top Job with Ammonia Kitchen Cleaner 16oz.	3.07	Lemon-scented Ammonia 16oz.	.75	Same cleaning power without the fancy fragrance.
Quaker Oatmeal 16oz.	1.47	Generic bulk 16oz.	.59	
Kellogg's Frosted Flakes15oz.	2.99	Generic Corn Flakes 15oz. add own sugar	1.39	Adding your own sugar costs less than 15 cents.
TOTAL	**$98.50**	**TOTAL**	**$50.36**	**TOTAL SAVINGS** $48.14

GROCERIES

Conclusion

If you have read all of the information in this book from cover to cover, you should have no doubt that you can dramatically reduce the prices you pay for virtually every product and service imaginable.

It may be by using a little-known discount source or locating a particular internet site. It could be by knowing the right questions to ask a salesman or using negotiating techniques that have been proven to work. It may be as easy as saying "no" to an extended warranty or turning thumbs down on upscale versions of basic products.

The answers to your questions and step-by-step instructions will be right here waiting for you, whenever you need them.

But will you use them?

In the weeks and months ahead, you will be fighting some real and very familiar temptations. Shopping is in large measure an emotional activity. We are usually our most impatient when we want or need something. The first tendency is to jump in the car, rush to the nearest store and seek instant gratification, even when we know better.

So while you may know a better way after reading these pages, you may be surprised at how easy it will be to fall back on familiar habits. When the moment comes to buy, the tendency is

to forget lessons learned and grab what you crave. Immediately.

How do you stay on track?

You start by recognizing that you will have a tendency to be impatient at the very moment you should be cool. For the next few months, plan on returning again and again to the relevant chapters in the book. You may think you've mastered the information after a single read, but resist the temptation to "wing it." Check yourself before you reach for your wallet. Force yourself to do exactly what the step-by-step instructions ask you to do, even when you think you already know the answers. Just like in the gym, proper technique is the key to superior results. You are learning a process. One experience will reinforce the next.

One way to stay motivated is by keeping track of your results. Life is a game of numbers. It's why golfers maintain their handicaps and baseball players are constantly checking their batting averages. When you keep track of the money you save, you have a way to measure results.

After all these years, I still like to track my money-saving skills. Last week, for example, I ripped up a sales order with an interior decorator after I did some checking and found that I could buy the same window blinds over the internet for $2,400 less than her price quote.

The entry was immediately noted in my savings diary, along with hundreds of other notations I have made throughout the year.

A few more cases in point:

Ordering a glass of ice water with a wedge of lemon instead of iced tea saves me approximately $200 per year on lunch expenses;

Raising the deductibles on my auto and homeowners insurance netted me nearly $750;

I saved nearly $400 on a recent vacation to Sarasota, Florida because I used a discount card from a national travel club; and

Installing a timer on my water heater has already cut my electric bill $110 in less than six months.

So far this year (it is July), the total in my savings diary is more than $9,500. It's now like a game to me. I'm motivated to save, because I like to see the total in my diary grow. It's become a challenge, turning the hunt for bargains into something of an adventure. You will find that keeping a savings diary will be a powerful motivator for you, as well.

There's really not much more to it.

Refer back to the book often.

Keep in mind you are learning a process which is mastered over time with lots of practice.

Recognize you own impatience when you shop.

Keep score to stay motivated.

And have fun.

Now go out there and shrink the bills!

Index

Index

Index

Special Offer

Secrets of the Supermarket Revealed!

Did you know the layout of a grocery store is designed like a Las Vegas casino so you will spend more money?

Or that many families could fund their *entire* retirement if only they knew how to buy their groceries smarter and cheaper?

It's true! Americans waste more money at the supermarket than just about anywhere else.

Honey, I've Shrunk the Bills explains many of the techniques you can use to reduce your grocery bills substantially. But there simply wasn't room for all the money-saving tips. After all, the average supermarket stocks more than 10,000 items!

That's why Jack Weber designed a separate program to take you aisle-by-aisle and item-by-item through the entire grocery store called *Secrets of the Supermarket.*

You'll receive two 60-minute cassette tapes plus a workbook that reveal little-known facts that can help you save $2,000 or more every year on everything from aspirin to zucchini.

Learn how to make your own cleaning solutions for just pennies a bottle! Discover how to turn a rib roast into a rib steak with just one pass of a knife and save $2 per pound! Find out how to freeze fruits and vegetables at their peak of flavor (and lowest price of the season) for year-round savings.

Once you listen to the tapes, you will be amazed at how much you can save.

To order *Secrets of the Supermarket,* send $14.99 to:

Secrets of the Supermarket
Special Offer
47778 Brawner Place
Sterling, VA 20165

To charge your order, please call 703-406-7678.